KV-637-855

Political Altruism?

Solidarity Movements in International Perspective

Edited by Marco Giugni and Florence Passy

ROWMAN & LITTLEFIELD PUBLISHERS, INC.
Lanham • Boulder • New York • Oxford

ROWMAN & LITTLEFIELD PUBLISHERS, INC.

Published in the United States of America
by Rowman & Littlefield Publishers, Inc.
4720 Boston Way, Lanham, Maryland 20706
http://www.rowmanlittlefield.com

12 Hid's Copse Road, Cumnor Hill, Oxford OX2 9JJ, England

Copyright © 2001 by Rowman & Littlefield Publishers, Inc.

All rights reserved. No part of this publication may be reproduced, stored in a retrieval
system, or transmitted in any form or by any means, electronic, mechanical,
photocopying, recording, or otherwise, without the prior permission of the publisher.

British Library Cataloguing in Publication Information Available

Library of Congress Cataloging-in-Publication Data

Political altruism? : the solidarity movement in international perspective / edited by
Marco Giugni and Florence Passy.
    p. cm.
    Includes bibliographical references and index.
    ISBN 0-8476-9880-7 (alk. paper) — ISBN 0-8476-9881-5 (pbk. : alk. paper)
    1. Social Movements. 2. Solidarity 3. Altruism. I. Giugni, Marco. II. Passy,
Florence.

HN17.5 .P627 2001
303.48'4—dc21
                                                                    00-055294
Printed in the United States of America

⊖™ The paper used in this publication meets the minimum requirements of American
National Standard for Information Sciences—Permanence of Paper for Printed Library
Materials, ANSI/NISO Z39.48-1992.

QM LIBRARY
(MILE END)

Contents

Part III Transnational Dynamics

Preface

This book's main title ends with a question mark. This is a deliberate choice. It represents the exigency not to determine *ex ante* something which must at best be assessed at the end, once we have gone through theoretical ideas and empirical analyses that put us in a more comfortable position to draw some conclusions. Political altruism and solidarity are analytical categories that capture both social reality and human desires. Our task as social scientists is to put our desires aside and thus avoid proceeding from a normative point of view in favor of a sane skepticism which must inform scientific analysis. This is the spirit that has guided our inquiry into the world of altruistic and solidary behaviors.

The concrete object of the discussions offered in this book is represented by the solidarity movement as a form of collective action and civic participation. In spite of being one of the most substantial and active areas of participation, it has largely been neglected in previous work on social movements. With this book we hope to shed some light on this movement and, above all, to encourage further work in this field. In order to do so, we have asked leading scholars of social movements and contentious politics to address certain aspects of solidary action, both from a theoretical and from an empirical point of view. They all deserve our gratitude for having accepted our invitation and put their intellectual skills to the benefit of this enterprise.

The volume divides into three parts. The two chapters in part I introduce us to the subject matter by stressing its relevant theoretical aspects. Florence Passy's (chapter 1) is the actual introduction to the book insofar as she addresses definitional issues, retraces the historical development of the solidarity movement, shows its various areas and levels of intervention, provides a brief overview of its mobilization in the European context, and finally opens up the discussions to follow in the other chapters by pointing to certain paradoxes and theoretical challenges related to the concept of political altruism. Charles Tilly (chapter 2) locates altruistic behavior in a larger context and discusses in particular altruism (i.e., a situation in which an actor sustains harm while another actor gains benefits) and destruction (i.e., an actor sustains harm while another actor likewise sustains harm). His effort is aimed at identifying mechanisms that set altruism or destruction in operation and therefore help us to explain these forms of collective action.

The five chapters in part II address national dynamics of political altruism. Each focuses on a given country. Olivier Fillieule (chapter 3), drawing on the case of France, points out certain methodological aspects of the study of the solidarity movement. Specifically, he warns us of the danger of reification; he stresses the importance of a micro-sociological analysis which stresses individual reasons and motivations; and finally suggests explaining the latter in the encounter of social and associational contexts with individual histories and biographies. The contribution by Costanzo Ranci (chapter 4) has a special status in the volume insofar as it focuses on nonprofit organizations, whose actions aim above all to provide services and protect disadvantaged social groups rather than to perform political actions. Thus he deals with what we may call *social* altruism rather than *political* altruism. In doing so, he looks at the determinants of voluntary action and unveils some of the changes it has undergone, with special attention to Italy. Florence Passy and Marco Giugni (chapter 5) introduce a comparative component in the analysis by drawing a parallel between the solidarity and ecology movements in Switzerland. They show that participation in these two movements follows similar processes and that, therefore, the solidarity movement must not be considered as a phenomenon *sui generis*, but is simply a variant of contentious politics. The last two chapters in this part of the book shift the level of analysis from individual participation and organizational dynamics to mobilization in a whole political issue field. Ruud Koopmans (chapter 6) examines antiracist mobilization in Germany. He argues that antiracist and solidarity actions are successful to the extent that the movement's organizers are able to activate preexisting solidarities, identities, social networks, values, and norms. In other words, social movements must succeed in drawing already mobilized groups into their camp. Paul Statham (chapter 7) adopts a similar methodological approach based on the analysis of public claims to show the impact of political opportunities, both institutional and discursive, on claim-making of antiracist and pro-migrant movements in Britain. He points in particular to the role of state policies in the field of immigration and ethnic relations.

The solidarity movement has an international and transnational scope. Therefore the four chapters in part III all address these aspects of political altruism. Sarah Soule (chapter 8) draws from work by social psychologists and psychologists to show the processes of imitation and diffusion of altruistic behaviors. She focuses on the modeling of altruism and the observation of wrongdoing, two situational factors that were stressed by the research traditions on which she draws. She discusses these factors in the case of the student divestment movement in the United States. Christian Lahusen (chapter 9) addresses a particular form of international solidarity: certain mega-events of the so-called rock-for-a-cause era of the 1980s and 1990s, the most famous being perhaps the Live-Aid concert tours of 1985. He argues that the transnational audiences and cultures created by these events increase the scope and outcome of political mobilization. These events, however, are an "embattled terrain," as the transnationalization of mobilizing structures depends on the ability to combine international solidarity with a concern for social and political rights. With the contribution by Ivana Eterovic and Jackie Smith (chapter 10) we see altruism operating at the world scale, as they discuss the ways in which changes in the global system have affected the possibilities for transnational mobilization. They do so by looking at the transnational social movement organization EarthAction in an attempt to examine how it was able to overcome national differences to promote transnational solidarity. They suggest that a new form of political action and identity is emerging, and point to the presence of a new transnationalism, more reciprocal and more appreciative of global interdependence than earlier forms of altruistic activism known as "third world solidarity." Simone Baglioni (chapter 11) addresses similar issues. After having briefly retraced the historical evolution of solidarity movement organizations, he examines their role in situations of serious conflict such as civil wars. Based on an analysis of the involvement of these organizations in the war in former Yugoslavia, which he considers as a paradigmatic case, he argues that solidarity movement organizations contribute, not only to the physical survival of populations involved in a conflict, but also to the formation of collective identities and the creation of an active global consciousness.

Finally, in the conclusion, Marco Giugni (chapter 12) pulls together the main themes and arguments of the book by bringing to the fore a number of conceptual distinctions that underlie the analyses of the preceding chapters. In the end, we hope this book will shed light on a social movement that has largely been understudied and stimulate a reflection on political altruism. We will leave it to the reader to judge whether the question mark in the title must be dropped or retained.

Part I

Introduction

1

Political Altruism and the Solidarity Movement

An Introduction

Florence Passy

> Altruism is not . . . an agreeable ornament to social life, but it will forever be its
> fundamental basis. How can we really dispense with it?
> —Emile Durkheim

Eva is dressing to get out in this windy winter night. Like every Wednesday, she is meeting with the other committee members of the Elisa Network. This meeting promises to go on for a long time. They must decide if they have enough resources to join other organizations that help refugees and asylum seekers in order to organize a common campaign against the new law on the status of refugees adopted by the Swiss government. They must discuss several difficult cases of deportation of asylum seekers, and one of these cases is under Eva's responsibility. Finally, they must elect a new directing committee of the organization for the coming year. Eva is worried. She has spent the whole week running from one government office to another, meeting many people to get advice, spending hours with the organization's lawyer in order to find a solution for Azis, a young Algerian who asked for political asylum in Switzerland. The federal office in charge of asylum has just denied giving him refugee status. Algeria is not deemed to be a dangerous country that violates human rights. Therefore, Azis cannot prove that he was a victim of violent aggression in his country, where a civil war has already killed thousands of people. Azis is not a journalist, nor a member of a human rights organization; he is simply a bricklayer who, one day, voiced too loudly his opinion about his country, about violence, about repression. After numerous anonymous threats and a physical attack on his way home from work, he decided to run away and look for asylum in a European country. Once he arrived in Switzerland, one of his compatriots gave him the address of the Elisa Network in case he had troubles with the Swiss administration—which happened. Eva, a thirty-year-old high school teacher, is his only legal support. She is used to this type of situation. Since she decided to join the Elisa Network ten years ago, she has seen hundreds of such situations.

Eva is not the only one who is deeply involved in this political struggle; hundreds of activists are engaged in defending the interests, rights, and identities of refugees, asylum seekers, and immigrant workers all over Europe. One of Germany's largest protest marches after the country's reunification in 1989 addressed this issue. In the late 1980s, Germany witnessed a worrisome wave of violent attacks against foreigners, with refugee centers burned out, Turkish and Afghan shops destroyed, and immigrants physically threatened. Hoyerswerda and Rostock were on the front page of newspapers, but many other German cities faced the same rise of racist attacks. In fall of 1992, 300,000 people went into the streets of Berlin to protest the rise of racism in the country. Some of them were similar to Eva; others were certainly less involved than she. But all shared the same outrage for what was going on.

Switzerland is not the only place in the world to host immigrants, of course, although with nearly one-fifth of the population being made up of foreigners, Switzerland has one of the world's highest shares of non-national citizens. Other countries are in a similar situation: France, for example, with the fight for the regularization of the *sans-papiers*; Italy, with the influx of illegal immigrants from Albania, Kosovo, and Turkey, who join the Italian coast through the Adriatic Sea along with those entering from the southern coast of the Mediterranean coming from Algeria and Tunisia; Austria, with particularly high levels of anti-immigrant sentiment; Belgium, England, the Netherlands, Sweden, Spain—in short, virtually all European countries are faced with the "hot" issue of migration. While governments generally try to implement increasingly restrictive immigration laws, many European citizens feel threatened by these newcomers and are participating in a new wave of racism and xenophobia. Many other Europeans like Eva organize campaigns against such restrictions, fighting discrimination against immigrants in their host society, offering them legal as well as material support, and mobilizing to claim political, social, and cultural rights for foreigners.

Not all these people are politically engaged to defend the interests, rights, and identities of immigrants. Some are involved in human rights organizations that seek state protection for people whose fundamental rights are violated, while others are working on behalf of the populations of the so-called Third World, asking for education, health care, and more generally, a better human development of these populations. We all still have in mind the more than a decade-long international campaign against apartheid in South Africa; the large mobilizations in support of new political regimes in Central America; the support given by many people and organizations to the Mothers of the Plaza de Mayo in Argentina, who were—and still are—looking for their daughters and sons who disappeared during the military regime; the public campaigns aimed to raise money for the victims of famines in sub-Saharan Africa; the wave of protest in many Western countries against the repression by the Chinese authorities of the student movement on Tienanmen Square; or the international campaign promoted by Third World organizations to stop the production of landmines. These are all well-known cases, but thousands of similar actions have been carried out all over Europe and North America.

Altruism takes on a political and collective form with the emergence of the *solidarity movement*. Individuals who are involved in this movement defend the interests, rights, and identities of others. We have given above some examples of those aided: asylum seekers, political refugees, immigrant workers, peoples whose human rights are being infringed, victims of racist acts or sentiments, and populations of Third World countries. The acts of political mobilization by those in the movement do not serve their own interests. These individuals do not stand to benefit directly from their participation in contentious collective action. These militants have been defined by McCarthy and Zald (1977) as "conscience constituents." In contrast, participants in labor, civil rights, gay, women's, ecology, and antinuclear movements—only to mention a few examples—obtain from their actions new collective goods or at least prevent new "collective bads," to the extent, of course, that mobilization is successful. Unlike these individuals, when Eva joins the Elisa Network committee on Wednesday, when she takes part in public demonstrations to protest restrictive immigration measures, when she collects money for a new campaign denouncing police violence against asylum seekers who are registering at the country's borders, she does not benefit from the substantial outcomes of her actions. In this sense, the solidarity movement may be seen as an instance of *political altruism*. But is it really so? Is this movement a genuine political expression of altruism? And, as a corollary, does the solidarity movement, which is potentially distinct from other types of contentious collective action, follow its own specific logic of mobilization? If this is the case, how is the solidarity movement distinct from other movements whose members received directly the benefits of their involvement? These are the central questions that lie at the heart of this book and that pervade all the following chapters.

Political Altruism: A Definition

Before we discuss these questions in more detail, it is worthwhile to better define the notion of political altruism. In fact, there hardly is a consensual definition of altruism. Authors from different fields define it differently. Nevertheless, definitions given by psychologists—which are as numerous as the authors who have written on this topic—emphasize two peculiarities of altruism that are relevant for our purpose: its intentional-oriented character and the actors' costs/benefits balance (Piliavin and Charng 1990). While the latter characteristic has gained a large consensus in the literature, the former characteristic has been emphasized by motivational approaches. Contrary to behaviorist approaches, which define altruism as "social behavior carried out to achieve positive outcomes for another rather than for the self" (Rushton 1980, 8)—that is, they stress what individuals do regardless of their motivations—motivational approaches define altruism as "a motivational state with the ultimate goal of increasing another's welfare" (Baston and Shaw 1991, 108). This perspective brings important elements to the definition of altruism by viewing it as a rational behavior. Thus altruism becomes a motivated individual act which stems from intentions. In this tradition, Bar-Tal (1985-86) provides a definition of altruism based on five characteristics of this human behavior: "altruistic behavior (a) must benefit to other persons, (b) must be performed voluntarily, (c) must be performed intentionally, (d) the benefit must be the goal by itself, and (e) must be performed without expecting any external reward" (5). The acts of Eva may be described, at first glance, as altruistic. She is acting on behalf of other people; her actions are not performed under constraints; she is doing it voluntarily; she is well aware of the meaning of what she is doing; her actions are rational and have a clear aim; and finally, she is not expecting any material rewards from her engagement. In brief, Eva's behavior on behalf of asylum seekers and political refugees has two characteristics: it is performed intentionally, and entails costs for herself and benefits for others. From the *individual* point of view, Eva's acts have a clear altruistic aim. From the *collective* point of view, her actions, together with those of hundreds of other people mobilizing for the same political goals—i.e., claiming rights for immigrants, for Third World populations, for people whose fundamental rights have been infringed—can be seen as *political altruism*. More precisely, political altruism we define as all actions (a) performed collectively, (b) that have a political aim and (c) an altruistic orientation as defined by Bar-Tal above. Thus, political altruism is a form of behavior based on acts performed by a group or/and on behalf of a group, and not aimed to meet individual interests; it is directed at a political goal of social change or the redefinition of power relations; and individuals involved in this type of social change do not stand to benefit directly from the success deriving from the accomplishment of those goals. Following this definition, the actions performed by the solidarity movement can be charac- terized as political altruism. Participants in the solidarity movement act col- lectively with a clear political aim, and their actions are pursued to the benefit of other people.

Is the contemporary solidarity movement the only example of political altruism within the Western world? Certainly not. In late nineteenth-century England, for example, there were strikes in support of African slaves working in the cotton fields in the American South. African slaves were fighting for freedom, facing a hostile social and economic order that seemed to be fixed forever. They engaged in a long and costly struggle to abolish slavery in the "country of freedom." They received political support from northern enlight- ened political elites, who understood that the slavery system was no longer humanly and economically viable, but also from English textile workers. Despite their hard living conditions, the latter went on strike to support the struggle of thousands of slaves in the United States. Another relevant example of political altruism took place during the Spanish civil war. Socialist activists from all over Europe enlisted in militias to fight against Franco's regime and in favor of socialism and freedom in this southern corner of Europe. Most of them were enrolled in their homeland by their comrades, as they used to call them, and traveled to Spain by bus, train, or foot to bolster their Spanish com- rades, an extremely risky enterprise in which many lost their lives.

Less risky and more recent instances of altruism can be observed in what Wuthnow (1991) calls "acts of compassion." According to this author, 45 percent of the adult population in the United States and almost as many in Europe are engaged in voluntary associations to help other people: drug ad- dicts, battered women, handicapped persons, elderly, ill people, homeless, unemployed, and others.[1] The voluntary sector—i.e., the third sector, located between the market and the state, and made up of nonprofit associations—in Europe and North America is as varied as human troubles. Is supplying as- sistance to the disadvantaged a form of political altruism? This is less clear. Political altruism, as we define it, has three main features: actions pursued collectively, with a clear political goal of social change, and whose outcomes are to benefit others. The nonprofit sector displays the first and the last fea- ture. Assistance to the disadvantaged is organized collectively, usually within formal organizations whose actions should benefit third parties. However, to have an explicit political aim is a necessary condition for characterizing col- lective action as political altruism. This does not mean that volunteering is an aimless enterprise, only that it generally does not have a political aim. Nor does it mean that the voluntary sector does not fulfill a political role in the modern society. As Tocqueville (1956) pointed out many years ago, voluntary associations are a key feature of a strong democracy.[2] Yet, they usually do not engage in political claim-making, nor in social change.[3] Nonprofit organiza- tions provide social help to the disadvantaged, to the "underclass," a task that is not—or not sufficiently—fulfilled by the state, but they are not striving collectively for political changes and are not endorsing a political issue. In other words, they are not involved in a political conflict.

In his groundbreaking book on parties, Rokkan (1970) has shown how these political organizations have built upon preexisting cultural and social cleavages.[4] Once these cultural and social dividing lines are politically framed by collective actors such as parties, interest groups, and social movements, they become political cleavages (Bartolini and Mair 1990). Rokkan stresses five cleavages around which European political parties are structured. These cleavages provide collective actors with social and cultural resources upon which they anchor their claims. Political cleavages are distinct from one another; they have their own coherence and homogeneity (thus providing political actors who are mobilizing around these conflicting lines with a coherent ideological framework); and they are usually supported by specific social categories. The nonprofit sector does not have such underlying political cleavages. On the contrary, it is very heterogeneous and mobilizes a variety of social strata with no coherent ideological framework. Actions coming out of the voluntary sector are not built upon a political cleavage; they are "acts of compassion" which, most of the time, are a palliative to the lack of state intervention.

By contrast, actions carried out by the solidarity movement can be characterized as political altruism: collective actions performed on behalf of other people and built upon a specific political cleavage. Next we turn to the principal features of the solidarity movement. A brief look at its historical, cultural, social, and political anchoring will allow us to unveil its peculiarities. At the same time, this will also highlight the political cleavage upon which its mobilization is based.

From the Old to the New Solidarity Movement: Cultural Resources and Political Cleavages

The solidarity movement builds upon specific cultural and symbolic resources. Human rights violations form the main grievance that underlies its mobilization. As we know from the literature on social movements, grievances and structural social conflicts are a necessary but not sufficient condition for the emergence of contentious collective action. Resources are also needed.[5] Three sets of cultural and symbolic resources—three "master frames" (Snow and Benford 1992)—were available to help the political framing of the human rights grievance: the Christian cosmology, the humanist component of the Enlightenment, and the socialist tradition. The Christian world provides the movement with the idea of helping your neighbor, giving her/him love, assistance, protection, and care. From the humanist component of the Enlightenment, the solidarity movement draws a coherent discourse on the respect for human rights and individual freedom. Finally, the early socialist movement put forth the ideal of a more just and egalitarian society.

These three cultural traditions provide the solidarity movement with crucial symbolic resources, but also with social, material, and human resources. The first organizations to mobilize in the name of human rights emerged within these three social networks, drawing from them material and human support. The first protests held to defend human rights came from religious organizations which pulled together Christians who were motivated by the idea of giving assistance to suffering men and women; by humanist clubs which mobilized intellectuals and libertarians who were nourished by the philosophy of the Enlightenment; and by socialist forums which gathered workers as well as several intellectuals who wanted to work politically for a new egalitarian society.

Thus, like the ecology, peace, and feminist movements, precursors of the contemporary movement are to be found in the late nineteenth century. One of the first organizations to act for the respect of human rights and against racism mobilized in France over the "Dreyfus Affair" in 1898. In that year a young Jewish officer was excluded from the army, officially because he was a traitor, but in fact because he was Jewish. The Ligue des droits de l'Homme was created to support Dreyfus and still exists today. More or less at the same time, in England humanist clubs opposed British colonialism and slavery. In the 1920s, a league against colonial oppression, whose first president was Albert Einstein, was set up in several European countries to criticize colonialism and bring to the fore its abuses.

The two world wars generated other types of human rights organizations. Several organizations were created with the mission of visiting war prisoners, giving them assistance and watching over prison conditions. Other organizations offered relief to war deportees, political refugees, immigrants, families in distress, and others. During that period, all these organizations which acted in favor of people whose human rights—broadly defined—were infringed, drew their resources from the three traditions discussed above and worked most of the time separately. They did not form a unified movement. They looked more like voluntary associations than social movement organizations. Their principal aim was to provide relief to the disadvantaged living in the colonies, to refugees, to immigrants, to war survivors and their families, to the victims of racist acts, as well as to others whose human rights were being violated. They offered relief to other people collectively, but not on the basis of a political conflict. They provided assistance, but in the absence of sustained political claim-making addressed to power holders. At that time, solidarity organizations resembled today's organizations of the third sector.

One had to wait until the late 1960s (in North America) and the 1970s (in Europe) for the emergence of a movement that articulated the human rights issue both politically and within a coherent framework. At that time, the organizations of the solidarity movement, like the early peace, ecology, and feminist groups, underwent a deep transformation, following a not less radical transformation of society. After World War II, Western society went through a long process of change that generated new cultural and social conflicts. The increasingly complex and highly differentiated post-industrial society (Bell 1973; Luhmann 1982) gave birth to new social strains upon which new collective actors based their political claims (Brand 1982; Melucci 1989, 1996; Raschke 1985; Touraine 1978, 1984). According to Kriesi (1989, 1993), contemporary society entails two contradictions which were politicized by the new social movements: control and risks. On the one hand, in contemporary society the public sphere increasingly penetrates the private sphere (Habermas 1984). For example, education and health care, which in previous centuries were left to individuals and families, are now managed and controlled by the state by means of welfare-state policies. Moreover, this highly technocratic society develops more and more sophisticated means of control, supported by the development of computer engineering. The control by the state, as well as by private companies, over the life of individuals has never been as strong as today. On the other hand, the contemporary society becomes a risk society (Beck 1986). New technological advances have produced new risks unknown before. We now have the capability to destroy the planet and humankind by means of nuclear technology (Melucci 1996). Reacting to the increasing control exerted by the state over individual autonomy and pushed by the new technological risks, the new social movements became crucial collective actors on the Western political scene.

The solidarity movement participated fully in this renewal of the social movement sector. As a consequence, the organizations that have emerged since then are quite distinct from the old solidarity associations of the late nineteenth century. First of all, these organizations have a genuine political orientation. Behind their demands—for the respect of human rights, against racism, for helping the Third World, in defense of immigrant workers and political refugees—there is a quest for individual emancipation and a deep democratization both of Western and non-Western society. Second, as a consequence of their mobilization around the new cleavage produced by the contradictions of the contemporary society—that is, as a result of the politicization of their acts—the action repertoire of the solidarity movement has changed (Passy 1998). The old repertoire was dominated by acts of assistance and relief. The movement organizations gave the disadvantaged material and moral assistance, providing them with food, clothes, legal advice, and so forth. While most of the organizations of the new solidarity movement still provide this kind of assistance, now their actions also include political claim-making addressed to power holders. In other words, their traditional assistance-oriented praxis is now paralleled by a political praxis based on the same political cleavage in which the other new social movements are anchored. Third, the political potential of the solidarity movement has been transformed as well. While the old solidarity movement mobilized intellectual, libertarian, and humanist elites, Christians, and workers nourished in the socialist tradition, the new movement has its social roots in the new middle class—more specifically, in one particular segment of the new middle class: the social-cultural specialists (Kriesi 1989).[6] Fourth, a decentralized and more democratic organizational structure has replaced a hierarchical and centralized structure. Finally, the various organizations of the solidarity movement are linked to each other independently of the issues they address. The new movement has a unity and a political coherence that it lacked before, as it mobilizes around the new lines of conflict in contemporary society and rides the political cleavage generated by post-industrial society. In this sense, it has become a genuine social movement. In addition, the solidarity movement has intensified its links to the other new social movements, which now become interconnected. They are all anchored in the same cleavage. This gives them unity and political coherence as a specific movement family.

To summarize, it is in the 1960s and 1970s (depending on the country) that the solidarity movement as we know it today emerged in the public sphere. While the sources of the struggle for human rights, like those pertaining to ecology, peace, and women's movements, date back to the nineteenth century, its anchoring in a political cleavage is more recent. The new lines of conflict, which stem from the transformation of contemporary society, have given birth to a new political actor.

A Multi-Level Movement:
Areas and Levels of Intervention

In addition to drawing its resources from three distinct cultural cosmologies and mobilizing around a specific political cleavage, two other features of the solidarity movement must be stressed: it is active in different areas and on different levels. The old movement comprised only human rights organizations active on the various forefronts of human rights violations: slavery, colonial oppression, immigration, mass deportations, and so forth. The new movement, after its transformation in the 1960s and 1970s, underwent a process of differentiation. Its organizations now specialize in specific domains and are spread over four branches, that is, four *areas of intervention*: human rights, development aid, immigration/asylum, and antiracism.

A first specialization occurred in the 1960s and 1970s, when development aid organizations (for Third World countries) emerged. Within this branch, we find committees looking at particular countries (antiapartheid committees, Nicaragua committees, Eritrea committees, etc.) as well as organizations working more broadly on development aid issues (Terre des Hommes, Caritas, etc.). While the former support specific political regimes and provide these populations with material help, the latter are involved in a more general fashion in the field of development aid. Approximately during the 1980s in Europe, and earlier in North America, the increasing salience of immigration and political asylum issues brought to the fore a third branch of the solidarity movement, mobilizing massively on behalf of immigrants, asylum seekers, and political refugees. The whole twentieth century witnessed important waves of migrations, generally as a consequence of wars. Yet, for a long time, this issue was not framed politically. Human rights organizations intervened to help migrants with material assistance, but did not politically articulate the issue—until the 1980s. Several human rights organizations remain active in this field (e.g., Amnesty International and the Ligue des droits de l'Homme), but they are not the leading actors. About the same time in certain countries and later in others, a further differentiation occurred within the movement with the emergence of a fourth branch: antiracism. This branch is intimately linked to the immigration/asylum area of intervention. It mobilizes to combat racist attacks against foreigners and the rise of the extreme right. The development of this branch of the solidarity movement is specific to Europe, with no counterpart in North America.

Beside its four branches, the contemporary solidarity movement also has different *levels of intervention*. Generally, social movement organizations are active at the local and/or national level. The prevailing level of intervention is to some extent determined by the structure of the state (Kriesi et al. 1995). For example, in France, a highly centralized state, social movements target mostly the national government. In contrast, in federal countries like Germany, Switzerland, and the United States, they often address local authorities. The solidarity movement is no exception to this rule, but here we can identify a fourth level: the international level. The solidarity movement is transnational in scope. Many organizations in the movement are present in various countries, that is, they are transnational social movement organizations (Smith, Chatfield, and Pagnucco 1997). Amnesty International, Terre des Hommes, the Ligue des droits de l'Homme, and the Ligue contre le racisme et l'antisémitisme are only some examples. The fact that the movement often mobilizes on behalf of populations in other countries has facilitated its expansion to the international arena. In addition, such expansion has been pushed further by the existence of supranational political structures, such as the United Nations, which provide the movement with opportunities for acting at that level.

As Tilly (1986a) has shown convincingly, contentious politics parallels transformations in the sources and distribution of power. The modern social movement emerged in the nineteenth century following a long period of construction of the national state. Since World War II, new power centers have been created at the supranational level (e.g., the United Nations and the European Community) although they have not replaced the national ones.[7] In other words, we are not witnessing a shift from the national to transnational level comparable to that which brought the main focus of contentious politics from the local to the national level. Nevertheless, supranational structures offer social movements new political opportunities to address their claims (Passy 1999). In spite of its weakness, the United Nations is a particularly relevant political power center. With the creation of the Human Rights Commission and the possibility for social movement organizations to be granted consultative status—formal acceptance within this supranational political structure—the United Nations offers the solidarity movement real opportunities to address its claims, especially for its human rights and development aid branches, less for its immigration/asylum and antiracism branches. Because immigration policy is still a prerogative of national states and most racist attacks target immigrants in given countries, the two latter branches of the movement continue to focus on the national level. However, it is likely that, if the development of the European Community continues and this power center will be able to frame a coherent and effective immigration policy for its member states (as recent developments would suggest), protests regarding these issues could also shift to the transnational level (Soysal 1994), leading, at least in part, to a Europeanization of social movements (Imig and Tarrow 1999).

Thus, the contemporary solidarity movement is involved in a multi-level game (Marks and McAdam 1996). It mostly targets national authorities, as well as local authorities (particularly in decentralized countries), but it also seizes the political opportunities provided by the United Nations. In doing so, it is comparable to the ecology movement, whose claim-making is also embedded in a multi-level game which comprises the local, national, and—in particular since the 1992 Rio environmental summit—transnational levels.

Patterns of Mobilization: A Brief Overview

Western society values individual freedom, personal success, and self-interest so highly that political altruism should be a marginal form of collective action. Yet, the mobilization by the solidarity movement attests to the opposite. To give a brief overview its mobilization, I draw from the comparative study by Kriesi and others (1995) on new social movements in four European countries: France, Germany, the Netherlands, and Switzerland.[8] But, as we turn to the patterns of mobilization of the solidarity movement, we must raise two theoretical points that have been raised by the political process approach to the study of social movements. Contentious collective action varies in its extent and forms according to the political context and to the salience of political cleavages. More specifically, Kriesi and his colleagues stress the formal structure of the state (i.e., the degree of functional separation of powers, the degree of territorial centralization of the state, the coherence of the public administration, and the presence of direct democratic procedures) and the informal strategies of the authorities towards social movements (i.e., inclusive and facilitating strategies or exclusive and repressive strategies). The latter display more or less disruptive forms of action. For example, there is a striking difference between France and Switzerland as to the movements' action repertoires: in highly centralized France they tend to be more disruptive than in extremely fragmented Switzerland (Giugni and Passy 1993).

In addition to this combination of formal and informal political opportunities, Kriesi and colleagues stress the impact of the configuration of power and the structure of alliances to explain the development of protest over time. In this respect, they argue that the presence of a socialist party—the main ally of the new social movements—in the government lead to the demobilization of these movements. In contrast, when the socialists are in opposition they are facilitated by a powerful ally, particularly so if the socialists are engaged in a struggle for the hegemony within the Left against an important Communist party and use the movements in this struggle.

Finally, Kriesi and his co-authors point to the salience of political cleavages to account for the relative strength of new social movements. They maintain that the new social movements—which mobilized on a new cleavage, as we have seen—are stronger where the traditional cleavages (the class, religious, center/periphery, and urban/rural cleavages) have been pacified. In contrast, in countries where these cleavages still mobilize important social and political forces, the opportunities available for the mobilization of new collective actors are limited. Of the four countries included in the study, only France still has largely salient traditional cleavages, in particular the class and center/periphery cleavages. This, to a large extent, explains the weakness of new social movements in that country.

The emergence and development of the solidarity movement in Europe is much influenced by all these aspects of the political opportunity structure. To begin with, as table 1.1 shows, not only is the whole new social movement family the main force of contention (at least during the 1975-89 period examined by Kriesi et al.), except in France, where traditional cleavages are still dominant. Furthermore, the solidarity movement displays high levels of mobilization in Germany and Switzerland, and the highest overall in the Netherlands. Confirming the cleavages salience hypothesis, France is once again an exception, for the solidarity movement has only weakly mobilized during the period under study. Thus, contrary to expectations that may be drawn from the individualistic orientation of contemporary society, political altruism is far from being a marginal form of contentious collective action. But how did the solidarity movement develop over time in these four European countries?

TABLE 1.1
Distribution of Unconventional Protest Events by Movement
in Four Countries, 1975-1989

	France	Germany	Netherlands	Switzerland
Solidarity movement	9.2	15.0	17.7	16.0
Antinuclear movement (both energy and weapons)	13.2	24.4	16.9	7.9
Ecology movement	4.4	11.3	8.0	10.6
Peace movement	4.0	7.1	5.1	5.3
Squatters' and other countercultural movements	3.0	13.4	14.1	18.4
Women's movement	1.5	1.7	1.6	2.1
Gay rights movement	0.8	0.3	2.0	0.7
Total new social movements	**36.1**	**73.2**	**65.4**	**61.0**
Total other movements	**63.9**	**26.8**	**34.6**	**39.0**
Total	100%	100%	100%	100%
N	2132	2343	1319	1215

Source: Kriesi et al. (1995, 20)

While the pacification of traditional cleavages is a key factor in understanding its relative strength, the configuration of power allows us to account for fluctuations in the level of mobilization. Figure 1.1 shows the number of protest events produced yearly by the solidarity movement between 1975 and 1989. Two findings are worth mentioning. First, perhaps with the exception of France, the general trend shows a growth in the four countries, for the number of events has increased during the period under study. Second, the movement displays important ebbs and flows which differ from one country to the other. The contrasting development of mobilization is particularly striking if we compare the German and French movements; while the former displays an upsurge of activity after 1980, the latter has experienced a sharp decline that lasted until 1984.

The fluctuations in the level of mobilization of the solidarity movement can be explained by the fortunes of the socialist parties. In Germany, we observe an abrupt increase in mobilization starting in 1980, leading to a peak in 1983. Here the movement became part of a larger cycle of protest that involved other movements as well, above all the peace movement. The nuclear weapons issue was at the heart of this protest cycle. At the same time, this strong mobilization was facilitated by the exit of the social-democratic party from the government in 1982. Being in the opposition, the latter could serve as a powerful ally for all new social movements. Previously, it was very difficult for the social-democrats to support the movements, which therefore were lacking a crucial political ally. Thus, the presence of the social-democrats in the opposition facilitated the German solidarity movement in the 1980s. A

Florence Passy

FIGURE 1.1
Number of Unconventional Protest Events of the Solidarity Movement
in Four Countries, 1975-1989

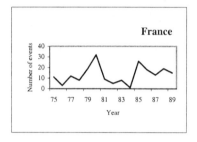

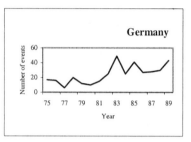

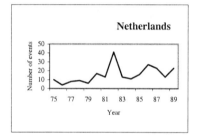

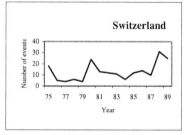

Source: Calculations based on data by Kriesi et al. (1995)

similar trajectory was followed by its Dutch counterpart. As in Germany, in
the Netherlands the solidarity movement was caught in the protest wave
against application of the "double-track" decision by NATO to deploy nuclear missiles in Europe while continuing negotiations for a scaling down of
the atomic arsenal. The peak of the movement's mobilization was reached in
1982. At the same time, the center-left coalition stepped down from governmental power, and this bolstered the actions of the whole new social movement family. In contrast, the French solidarity movement declined precisely
when in the other countries mobilization reached its peak. When President
Mitterrand seized power in 1981, the movement lost its principal ally, the
Socialist party. Moreover, like the other new social movements, the actors
participating in the solidarity movement hoped that the socialists would promote important reforms that would take into account their claims. This dis-
couraged them from mobilizing. However, the movement was revived in
1985, even though the socialists were still in power. In fact, for reasons to
which we shall return below, the French Left largely facilitated the movement's antiracist branch. In Switzerland, the development of the solidarity
movement cannot be explained by a change in the composition of the national

government, as it has remained unchanged since 1959. In a highly decentralized political system such as Switzerland's, the local or regional configuration of power may be more important to fluctuations in the mobilization by social movement than the national one. Much of the fluctuation in the development of the Swiss solidarity movement is due to the issue of political asylum. As in Switzerland asylum policy is implemented by the local powers, the ebbs and flows we observe in Switzerland might largely be explained by changes at the local level.

To summarize, the solidarity movement is an important extra-parliamentary political actor in several European countries. However, as table 1.2 illustrates, the activity of the movements' four areas of intervention is unequal. Generally speaking, antiracism and development aid are the most active branches. Antiracism is particularly strong in France and Germany. More than half of the mobilization of the whole movement in these two countries occurs in this area, whereas in the Netherlands and Switzerland development aid is the most frequently raised issue. How can we explain these differences, which seem to separate the two large countries from the two smaller ones? Since the beginning of the 1980s, France and Germany have witnessed a revival of extreme-right activism which has fostered politicization of the immigration issue. In France, the Front National has framed its discourse around this issue. The German extreme right, mostly organized as an extra-parliamentary actor, did the same. In these two countries, immigration politics was marked by worrisome waves of racist attacks against asylum seekers and immigrant workers. This offered the solidarity movement an opportunity to mobilize, and hence provoked strong countermobilization organized mainly by leftist parties and by the movement. In addition, in France the Socialist party continued to support the antiracism branch of the movement even while in government. The socialists used antiracist groups—particularly, SOS-Racisme—to destabilize the right-wing parties and counteract the spectacular rise of the Front National (Duyvendak 1995). While their support was guided by strategic reasons, it provided these organizations useful political opportunities.

The extreme right was also active in the Netherlands and Switzerland, but to a lesser extent, which might explain the weaker antiracist mobilization. In these two countries, the solidarity movement mobilized mainly on development aid issues. Why is it so? A possible explanation lies in the impact of institutional facilitation. In the Netherlands and Switzerland the prevailing strategies of the authorities towards social movements are inclusive, hence facilitating their mobilization. However, even states that follow inclusive prevailing strategies do so only—or at least mostly—toward the movements' moderate sectors. In the case of the solidarity movement, the development aid branch and the human rights branch comprise the most moderate sector. In Switzerland, its moderation has even contributed to the elaboration of strategies of cooperation between the movement and the state (Giugni and Passy

TABLE 1.2
Distribution of Unconventional Protest Events of the Four Branches
of the Solidarity Movement in Four Countries, 1975-1989

	France	Germany	Netherlands	Switzerland
Human rights	9.1	10.1	15.3	17.0
Development aid	13.7	28.7	47.0	50.0
Immigration/asylum	16.4	11.9	13.7	29.7
Antiracism	60.7	49.2	24.0	3.4
Total	100%	100%	100%	100%
N	219	494	313	296

Source: Calculations based on data by Kriesi et al. (1995)

1998). Thus, the facilitating strategies of the authorities in the Netherlands
and Switzerland towards the moderate development aid organizations led this
branch of the movement to a high level of mobilization.

Finally, we observe the relatively weak mobilization of the human rights
branch, the movement's oldest area of intervention. This is partly due to the
fact that its claims are spread over the other branches. But, above all, human
rights organizations, as mentioned above, find important political opportunities at the international level. While, overall, this is certainly the less active
branch of the movement, it is also probably less active at the national level
than at the international one.

Political Altruism:
Paradoxes and Theoretical Challenges

As we have seen, the solidarity movement displays certain features: it is (apparently) altruistic-oriented; it mobilizes based upon a specific political
cleavage; it is embedded in a specific social environment that gives it cultural
and symbolic resources; it operates in different areas of intervention; and acts
at different levels of intervention (especially at the international level).
Among all these characteristics, the altruistic orientation is, at least at first
glance, the one that sets it decidedly apart from other movements. But this
feature raises two paradoxes: the first could be defined as a cultural paradox,
while the second is of a theoretical nature. These paradoxes are worth briefly
discussing here.

The first paradox was hinted at in the discussion above. The solidarity
movement has emerged in Western society, which puts individualism, individual freedom, self-interest, and personal success high in the hierarchy of
social values. In this society, however, thousands of people join the solidarity
movement with the aim of providing other persons with material and moral

support. How can we make sense of such altruistic political behavior in a society that is mainly concerned with enhancing the value of the self? This paradox has been framed by Wuthnow (1991) in his study of the voluntary sector in the United States. He faces exactly the same dilemma raised by the solidarity movement: while the dominant myths of the American society value individualism, more than half of the adult population volunteers on a regular basis, that is, they act on behalf of other people. Wuthnow shows that, in the end, this paradox does not exist, for "acts of compassion" are in fact a channel of self-expression. They help people to "feel better" and are a way to convey caring feelings. Volunteering is, according to Wuthnow, a way to express one's own individuality. If this conclusion proves correct, it should have two main implications. First, "acts of compassion" are not inconsistent with Western society's dominant value of individualism. Second, we can wonder about the altruistic bases of the kind of behavior studied by Wuthnow. According to Bar-Tal's (1985-86) definition, one of the four characteristics of altruism is to perform a deed without expecting any reward. "Feeling better" would be one such reward. Therefore, those who perform "acts of compassion" do get rewards. Here we could start a broader discussion about internal and external rewards, but this would take us too far from the present purpose. Suffice it to say that Bar-Tal speaks of external rewards, while those received by the people interviewed by Wuthnow are internal ones. Their rewards do not come from the individuals' external environment, but rather from within the individuals themselves. Thus, following Bar-Tal's definition, the "acts of compassion" investigated by Wuthnow are altruistic. But if we adopt a more restrictive definition of altruism and exclude any rewards, be they external or internal, then these acts are not altruistic.

Concerning the solidarity movement, the question is whether involvement in this form of political altruism is also a way to express one's own individuality. Is helping populations in Third World countries, giving immigrants support, mobilizing on behalf of other people whose fundamental rights are being violated a way to "feel better," to find personal fulfillment? Is participation in the solidarity movement consistent with the Western society's dominant cultural values of individual freedom, personal success, and self-interest? Or, on the contrary, does this type of political engagement raise a *cultural paradox*? A related set of questions, furthermore, asks whether participation in the solidarity movement is a genuine expression of political altruism. Do activists involved in this movement receive any rewards at all? Which motivations push people like Eva, our activist in favor of asylum-seeker rights, to invest time and effort on behalf of other people? Do they "feel better" after such "acts of compassion"?

The second paradox raised by the solidarity movement relates to the theory of collective action, and brings us to Olson's well-known *Logic of Collective Action* (1965). Olson maintains that it is irrational for individuals to do something for the production of collective goods. The peculiarity of such goods is that they are to be shared by all individuals in a community, that is, all individuals in that community will benefit from them, regardless of their participation in its production. Therefore, individuals would have no reason to pay the costs of obtaining goods from which they would benefit anyway. Moreover, the action of a single individual is so marginal that it would not affect the likelihood that the public goods be produced. This paradox, also emphasized by Downs (1957) in relation to voting behavior, is all the more relevant and problematic in the case of altruism: people will get the fruits of mobilization whether or not they participate in the movement, for the outcome of mobilization is addressed to others.

Thus, the question is: How can we make sense of political altruism with the theoretical tools offered by Olson's analysis of collective action and, more generally, following a rational choice model? In his groundbreaking book, Olson has little to say about this type of contentious collective action, arguing that individuals who work on behalf of other people are irrational. He suggests, therefore, that we use other heuristic tools to explain this kind of behavior, namely those developed by psychology. In other words, he suggests that we go back to psychological models put forward in the early twentieth century and later elaborated by collective behavior theorists. Yet, in the light of fundamental criticisms addressed by resource mobilization and political process approaches to collective behavior models (e.g., McAdam 1982; McCarthy and Zald 1977; Tilly 1978; Tilly et al. 1975), this does not seem to be a promising path. According to resource mobilization and political process theorists, collective action is a rational effort to obtain certain goals rather than, as proponents of the collective behavior perspective maintain, the product of psychological reactions to the social stress stemming from macrostructural changes in society.

As Olson's suggestion to refer to psychological models in order to explain political altruism cannot reasonably be taken into account without denying the intention-oriented nature of this type of political behavior, how can we then grasp the logic of political altruism? Does it follow a logic of mobilization different from that of self-oriented actions? Do the patterns of individual participation in the solidarity movement differ substantially from those in other movements? Is the process of mobilization influenced by the movement's orientation? In brief, is political altruism governed by a distinct logic of mobilization? Furthermore, we can wonder whether the two paradoxes mentioned above, which refer to the micro level of analysis, have some repercussions on the macro level as well. Do the organizations of the solidarity movement use different forms of actions in order to mobilize people on behalf of others? Does political altruism have its own action repertoire? By the same token, do actors involved in the solidarity movement use distinct discursive strategies? Specifically, do they need to link altruistic claims to particularistic interests in order to facilitate individual participation in the movement? It is in these and related questions that lies the theoretical challenge posed by the solidarity movement and political altruism.

The paradox raised by Olson in the 1960s leads us to a broad reflection on the heuristic tools that social scientists can use to study political altruism. In order to examine this matter in a more systematic fashion, we propose to discuss three dominant paradigms in social science and see what they can bring to the study of political altruism. Table 1.3, which is largely inspired by a recent assessment of the study of comparative politics by Lichbach (1997), tries to sort out the respective features of these paradigms and to assess their major strengths and weaknesses for the study of political altruism. The three major research schools in social science—rationalist, culturalist, and structuralist (e.g., Lichbach 1997)—rely on different ontological perspectives based on their different perceptions of the social world. We shall review the ontological basis of each of these research traditions, then study the specific focus of their analyses by putting them in the context of the study of political altruism, and, finally assess their strengths and weaknesses in relation to an understanding of political altruism.

The rationalist paradigm sees the world from an individual angle. Collectivities have no specific status; they are understood by means of individuals' behaviors. Rationalists interpret individual action from its motivation. In other words, they put individual intentions at the center of their theories. Individual desires and beliefs motivate action. On the micro level, rationalists focus on the actors' decision; on the macro level, on collective choices and strategies. Thus, rationalist theorists stress individual motivations, desires, beliefs, and rewards to understand participation in altruistic collective action. In addition, they emphasize the collective choices of forms of action as well as discursive strategies that lead individuals to join altruistic collective action. The major strength of the rationalist paradigm lies in the view of political altruism as motivated human behavior. In fact, rationalists have two ways to examine political altruism: either they judge, as Olson did, a priori that altruistic actions are not rational, and then they must study them with other heuristic tools; or they look at intentions that bring individuals to commit themselves to political altruism. In the latter option, the rationalist paradigm can offer social scientists an important avenue of research into individual motivations, political goals, group strategies, and the like. This perspective lends itself to the study of people who engage in altruistic collective action and of strategies by political groups that benefit directly from their actions, as in the case of the solidarity movement. While individual motivations are crucial to a better understanding of political altruism, this approach has its weaknesses. Rationalists' studies have often been criticized on various grounds (e.g., Green and Shapiro 1994). Without getting into the details of these criticisms, we can say that one of the major difficulties in this approach stems from its

TABLE 1.3
Three Paradigms for the Study of Political Altruism

	Rationalist	*Culturalist*	*Structuralist*
Ontology	• Rational actors • Intentional explanation • Methodological individualism	• Rules among actors • Intersubjectivity • Common knowledge and values • Social constructivism	• Relations among actors • Institutional frame • Structural realism
Focus of the analysis Micro level	• Actors' decision to participate	• Individual values and beliefs • Identity formation • Identification processes	• Social constraints • Location of actors in the social system and social networks
Macro level	• Collective choice of forms of actions and discursive strategies	• Value system • Cultural framings	• Mobilizing structures • Political opportunity structures
Explanatory power Strengths	• Political altruism as rational, intentional, and goal-oriented behavior	• Political altruism as meaningful action • Social construction embedded in a cultural context • Space/time variations	• Political altruism as not merely voluntaristic behavior or the product of cultural conditioning • Impact of institutional context • Space/time-varying process
Weaknesses	• Instrumental rationality • Mechanical view of social action	• Tautology • Voluntarism absent	• Deterministic view • Voluntarism absent

narrow view of the human being. Rationalists perceive individuals as being interest-oriented and hence behaving to meet or maximize their private interests. The role of the larger social environment, which impinges upon individual interests, is neglected. This leads rationalist theorists to have a "mechanical-behavioral view of subjectivity and adopt a particularly anemic or thin version of intentionality, rationality, and interests" (256). In this perspective, the study of political altruism is reduced to an analysis of rewards. Yet, in the study of collective action, rationalists have tended to go beyond such a thin version of intentionality by taking into account the role of the social environment and the social construction of subjectivity (e.g., Gould 1993; Marwell and Oliver 1993). The study of political altruism should learn from this lesson.

The culturalist paradigm looks at society through the lens of norms and intersubjectivity. In contrast to the rationalist approach, individuals have no existence outside their communities, which are at the center of their analyses. Culture forms the intersubjective link between individuals. Individuals belonging to the same community share common knowledge, understandings, beliefs, values, cognitions, and identities. Thus culture is seen as a social construction. Culturalist theorists focus basically on the construction of values and beliefs, the formation of individual and collective identities, and the identification of value systems and collective frames. Due to their different view of social reality, culturalists highlight other sides of political altruism. They define the role of cultural factors leading to political altruism—either at the micro level, by stressing the specific values, beliefs, and identities that facilitate participation in this type of collective action and by stressing the processes of socialization and identity formation that allow one to participate; or at the macro level, by understanding the cultural frames and narratives that give shape to altruistic behaviors. One of the strengths of the culturalist approach lies in its view of political altruism as a meaningful action and as a construction, in contrast to rationalists, who do not study where interests come from and how they emerge. The process of formation of individual interests are at the core of culturalists' analyses. A further strength of this paradigm is that it allows explanation of variations in the forms of political altruism from one society to the other, from one country to the other. Rationality varies among cultures. It is likely that certain cultural settings or repertoires facilitate political altruism by offering a language for its emergence. As Wolfe (1998) has put it: "Because [altruism] is not latent in human genes, it has to be activated, and the degree of activation varies across time and space. Some historical periods manifest more altruistic behavior than others, and some countries tend to be more altruistic than others" (41).[9] Indeed, in our brief overview of patterns of mobilization of the solidarity movement, we have seen that, depending on the salience of cultural cleavages, it is stronger in certain countries and weaker in others. On the other hand, the tendency of culturalist theorists to neglect the role of individuals is a major weakness of this approach. While, as Lichbach (1997) has put it, "rationalists sacrifice the subject and surrender the self, undoing the community and unmaking the collectivity" (257), the culturalists do exactly the opposite and tend to deny all forms of individual voluntarism. A further weakness of this paradigm lies in its problematic capacity of hypothesis falsification (Lichbach 1997). Culturalists are put in an uncomfortable position to explain the link between norms, or cultural standards, and action, thus running the risk of tautology.

The ontological basis of the structuralist paradigm lies chiefly in the institutional frames and the interactions among the various parts of a system. At the micro level, the main focus of the analysis is on social interactions and on the location of actors in the social system and in social networks. At the macro level, structuralists stress mobilizing structures and political institutions, which provide both constraints and opportunities for the emergence of political altruism. The major strength of the structuralist approach is its attention to the institutional and relational contexts as structural conditions for the emergence of political altruism. At the same time, it allows for comparisons across time and sector for this type of collective action. Once again, our discussion of the patterns of mobilization of the solidarity movement has highlighted the role played by institutional factors. As in the case of the other two paradigms, the structuralist approach has a number of weaknesses, particularly in the study of political altruism. Structuralists and culturalists share the same weakness with regard to their conception of the human being. Actors are absent from their view of the social world. To use Lichbach's (1997) apt phrase, "[s]tructuralists thus produce a bloodless social science: People are the victims of and silent witnesses to history" (258). In other words, individuals belonging to the same system, to the same category or to the same network play the same game; their intentions are missed in structural explanations. Similarly, structuralists are prisoners of a deterministic view of society, in the sense that specific structural or relational settings are bound to provoke a specific type of outcomes.

To summarize, in spite of inevitable problems and weaknesses, each of the three paradigms for the study of political altruism reveals specific aspects of the social phenomenon at hand. The rationalist paradigm emphasizes the *motivations* that lead to political altruism. This perspective allows us to ascertain whether actions defined a priori as political altruism, such as those of the solidarity movement, are genuine "acts of compassion." Moreover, the rationalist paradigm reveals the collective strategies of groups acting on behalf of others. The culturalist paradigm stresses the *cultural repertoires* that make the activation of political altruism possible. This can be done at the individual level, by examining their role in the formation of individuals beliefs and cognitions, and at the collective level, by looking at discursive repertoires, narratives, and cultural frames of political altruism. The structuralist paradigm focuses on *structural constraints and opportunities* which yield individual or collective conditions that facilitate political altruism.

As we have noted, each tradition has substantial limitation in explaining political altruism in its complexity and multifaced aspects. While in the past, social scientists have tended to lock themselves in one theoretical tradition, today many authors turn to more eclectic explanations of social and political phenomena (e.g., Alexander and Giesen 1987; Archer 1995; Berger and Luckmann 1989; Bourdieu 1977; Coleman 1990; Giddens 1984; Habermas 1984; Lichbach 1997). As Wolfe (1998) has emphasized in his discussion of the various theories that have contributed to the study of altruism, we need to grasp the complexity and multiplicity of human behaviors, and go beyond monocausal explanations. We still have too little systematic research on political altruism for excluding one of those traditions in favor of the other two. At this stage of our knowledge of this subject matter, we will be better off if we take into accounts the strengths and promises of all three perspectives. We will surely benefit from their different approaches to gain a better understanding of political altruism.

Notes

I thank Charles Tilly for his helpful criticisms of an earlier draft.

1. For a cross-national comparison of voluntary associations, see Salamon and Anheier (1998).
2. See also Barber (1984), Putnam (1993), and Wuthnow (1991, 1995).
3. For definitions of claim-making and social movements, see Tilly (1978, 1995a) and Tarrow (1998).
4. See also Lipset and Rokkan (1967).
5. This is one of the main contributions of resource mobilization theory (e.g., Gamson 1975; McCarthy and Zald 1977). This approach stresses the role of resources for the emergence of social movements, thus criticizing "breakdown theories" (Tilly et al. 1975) such as the theory of collective behavior (e.g., Smelser 1962; Turner and Killian 1957).
6. This argument has received strong empirical support (Cotgrove and Duff 1980; Inglehart 1990; Kriesi 1989, 1993; Passy 1998).
7. This is particularly true for the United Nations, which remains a weak aggregate of states rather than a genuine and powerful supranational political entity.
8. The method they used is protest event analysis. For details on this method, see the appendix in Kriesi et al. (1995) as well as Rucht, Koopmans, and Neidhardt (1998).
9. For instance, Jegstrup (1985-86) has shown that the rescue of Jews during World War II in Denmark was inspired by cultural reasons.

2

Do Unto Others

Charles Tilly

Puzzling Behavior

After the fact, civil rights activists called June-August 1964 "Freedom Summer." On 21 June, the second group of volunteers for Mississippi voter registration drives and related educational projects was arriving in Oxford, Ohio, to receive training before entering the field. Near Philadelphia, Mississippi, that same day, first-batch volunteer Andrew Goodman joined staff members James Chaney and Michael Schwerner to investigate a church bombing. Local police arrested the three on traffic charges, detained them past nightfall, then released them. The three civil rights workers disappeared. The next day, passersby found their incinerated station wagon near a swamp.

The public would not know until August that someone had murdered Chaney, Schwerner, and Goodman, then buried their mangled bodies beneath an earthwork dam. But the Oxford volunteers sensed that their co-workers in Mississippi had met foul play. They could hardly have received a more vindictively violent warning of dangers to come. Other activists had died in the line of duty. Yet Mississippi's violence continued. "In just the first two weeks of the summer project," Charles Payne reminds us, "in addition to the murder of Mickey Schwerner, James Chaney, and Andrew Goodman in Philadelphia, Mississippi, there were at least seven bombings or fire-bombings of movement-related businesses and four shootings and a larger number of serious beatings" (Payne 1995, 301).

On 26 June, volunteer Stuart Rawlings wrote in his journal:

What are my personal chances? There are 200 COFO volunteers who have been working in the state a week, and three of them have already been killed. I shall be working in Forrest County, which is reputedly less violent than Neshoba County. But I shall be working on voter registration, which is more dangerous than work in Freedom Schools or Community Centers. There are other factors which must be considered too—age, sex, experience, and common sense. All considered, I think my chances of being killed are 2 percent, or one in fifty (McAdam 1988, 70-71).

Shocked and frightened, some volunteers left Oxford for home. Most, however, stayed with the group. "And with the decision to stay," reports Freedom Summer chronicler Doug McAdam, "their commitment to the project and attachment to the 'beloved community' grew as well" (McAdam 1988, 71).

Why did they stay? More generally, why do people incur serious costs— here including the risk of beating, bombing, and death—on behalf of other people's welfare? Stated as an individual choice to act before the deliberated action occurs, figure 2.1 clarifies what we have to explain. (Later sections of the chapter, however, will point out how this very statement of the problem as individual choice *ex ante* misleads us.) What differentiates situations in which a given actor (a) gains benefits while another actor sustains harm (*egoism*), (b) gains benefits while another actor likewise gains benefits (*co-operation*), (c) sustains harm while another actor likewise sustains harm (*destruction*), or (d) sustains harm while another actor gains benefits (*altru-ism*)? Egoism and cooperation have attracted enormous attention in the form of public goods problems, prisoners' dilemmas, and the like (Shubik 1993). Steadfast rational action theorists (e.g., Hardin 1995) have typically sought to show that actions appearing to qualify as cooperation, destruction, or altruism actually reduce to egoism once we detect the incentives to which actors respond. Within the zones of interstate war, civil war, industrial conflict, and inter-ethnic conflict, rational action theorists (e.g., Lake and Rothchild 1998) have often argued that destructive *outcomes* characteristically stem from initial situations of egoism in which participants fail to recognize that their interaction will lead to losses for all. In such cases, improved advance information about likely outcomes would presumably prevent the conflicts from occurring at all.

Rational action theorists have often found allies among evolutionary biologists (e.g., Clutton-Brock et al. 1999) who interpret ostensibly altruistic animal behavior as a form of individual self-preservation. Clear thinking institutionalists (e.g., Greif 1994; Ostrom 1998) have commonly joined rationalists in denying the existence of destruction and altruism but have also insisted that certain normative, institutional, and network arrangements promote cooperation even in cases in which strictly self-seeking behavior would yield greater short-run benefits. They thereby interpret short-term altruism as long-term egoism or cooperation.

In the statement that put "resource mobilization" in play as a way of analyzing social movements, John McCarthy and Mayer Zald (1977) distinguished between *beneficiary* and *conscience* constituents of movement organizations. By definition, conscience constituents contribute resources to an

FIGURE 2.1
Individual Choices among Harm and Benefit for Actor and Other

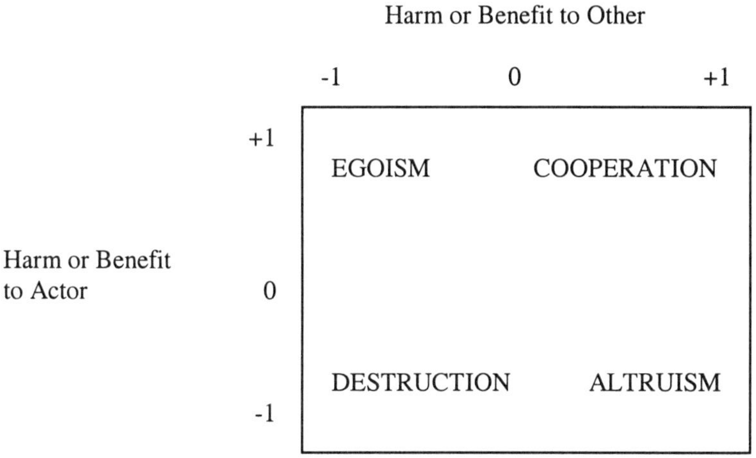

Harm or Benefit to Other

	-1	0	+1
+1	EGOISM	COOPERATION	
Harm or Benefit to Actor 0			
-1	DESTRUCTION	ALTRUISM	

organization's actions but gain no resources from realization of the organization's goals; superficially, then, they resemble our altruists. Speaking of contemporary American social movement organizations, McCarthy and Zald describe conscience adherents as generally more affluent and well connected than beneficiaries. Conscience adherents therefore prove attractive to social movement entrepreneurs. But they also pose risks for organizations and entrepreneurs because of their propensity to withdraw support from the cause when the going gets rough or new interests come along. Although McCarthy and Zald never quite explain why conscience constituents participate at all, they imply strongly that (a) their participation costs them relatively little and (b) they participate because (and only so long as) it gives them self-satisfaction. They actually participate for net benefits. Thus McCarthy and Zald, too, end up converting altruism—at least this mild form of altruism—into egoism or cooperation.

Similarly, students of volunteer work (e.g., Wilson and Musick 1999) generally assume or argue that providing care for others under the auspices of churches and voluntary organizations (as distinguished from care given within households and kin groups) falls under our heading of cooperation: when working properly, it gives net benefits to donor and recipient alike. After acknowledging that some volunteers harm themselves by overdoing it, Robert Wuthnow offers advice:

> Millions of Americans, as we have already seen, provide useful services to the needy *and* gain a sense of personal enrichment and fulfillment from it. The trick

is to develop skills that allow us to show compassion and at the same time take care of our own needs (Wuthnow 1991, 193).

"Personal enrichment and fulfillment," then, constitute net benefits for most volunteers. Indeed, Wuthnow calls his book *Acts of Compassion*, but subtitles it *Caring for Others and Helping Ourselves.*

For analyses of thoroughgoing destruction and altruism, we must therefore turn away from students of voluntary organizations and back to students of contentious politics. Even there, destruction and altruism have received much less attention than have egoism and cooperation. But they are the two locations within the diagram we must describe and explain.

Genuine cases of destruction and altruism exist. They include the range of contention that Doug McAdam calls "high risk activism" and others call "sacrifice for the cause" (Fernandez and McAdam 1988; Hirsch 1990; Loveman 1998; McAdam and Paulsen 1993). They also include terrorism and the sort of activism—usually lower risk—elicited by environmental movements. Although terrorists' enemies often label them as egoists on the ground that the terrorists gain pleasure or profit from other people's harm, much mayhem ends up as net loss for its perpetrators. Terrorists and self-immolators typically declare that they are sacrificing themselves in order to benefit other members of their cause. During such campaigns as antislavery, ecology, and animal rights, campaigners may gain self-satisfaction, revenge, or spite, but on the whole they incur significant costs for benefits reaped chiefly by others—or perhaps by no one at all (d'Anjou 1996; Drescher 1986, 1994; Swedberg 1999). If they actually occur, destruction and altruism deserve close attention because they challenge individual-level cost-benefit accounts of participation in contentious politics.

Let us narrow our focus to the special cases of destruction and altruism in which action of Actor X *causes* detectable consequences for both the actor and for some distinct other. Destruction then refers to collective action in which an actor inflicts net losses on another actor while enduring net losses itself, regardless of possible benefits or losses for third parties. Altruism refers to collective action in which an actor produces benefits for another actor while enduring net losses itself, again regardless of possible benefits or losses for third parties. These are, of course, matters of degree. An action qualifies as just barely altruistic by imposing small net losses on the actor and causing small net gains for the beneficiary, as when activists attend a few too many meetings in moderately effective expressions of support for prisoners' rights. It qualifies as extremely altruistic by imposing large net losses (for example, death or exile) on the actor while producing large gains (e.g., liberation) for the beneficiary. To clarify the issues, let us concentrate on relatively clear cases of destruction and altruism, cases in which the actor bears significant costs.

How is it that some participants in some kinds of contentious politics (e.g., suicide bombers) end up simultaneously producing harm for themselves and others? How is it that other actors (e.g., self-sacrificing protectors of endangered species) end up taking losses while producing benefits for others? The most commonly available answers run as follows:

1. *Secret Satisfaction*: X is actually receiving net benefits because participation, sacrifice, and/or the other's welfare provides X with satisfaction
2. *Side Benefits*: X is receiving selective incentives that compensate for visible losses
3. *Social Security*: X sustains short-term losses in support of relationships that promise benefits over the long run
4. *Ideology*: Commitment to a cause, belief, and/or illusion leads X to disregard costs of risky actions and/or provides intrinsic rewards
5. *Group Pressure*: Collective processes obscure or override X's computation of likely costs and benefits from various possible courses of action
6. *Habit*: X obeys customary authorities and/or continues customary routines without calculation of outcomes
7. *Accident*: Net losses to X result from unlikely or unpredictable consequences of X's action

Except for Habit, Accident, and some versions of Group Pressure, these common explanations all assert that destruction and altruism are actually egoism and/or cooperation in disguise. For Freedom Summer volunteers who went to Mississippi despite the Goodman-Chaney-Schwerner killing and other warnings of danger, someone might argue accordingly that (1) they gained self-satisfaction from the experience, (2) solidarity with other volunteers more than made up for the danger, (3) they were adopting a way of life for which the current risk was a reasonable cost, (4) they were self-selected zealots, heedless of cost, (5) they shamed each other into staying, (6) college had taught them to conform, or (7) they failed to see connections between Mississippi violence and their own futures.

To be sure, these explanations do not exclude each other; one can easily argue, for example, that ideologues (case 4), unlike habitual conformists (case 6) derive direct satisfaction (case 1) from sacrifice. All seven declare that, *ex ante*, the diagram's bottom half is empty: no actor will deliberately undertake action whose foreseeable consequence is net loss. But the cases that interest us here are precisely those in which participants do sustain losses in contention, and not by inadvertence. Such episodes as Freedom Summer establish that genuine cases inhabit our diagram's lower reaches: even if explanations 1 through 7 apply in part, we find significant instances in which—by any ordinary assessment of costs and benefits—actors bear major costs from which they benefit little or not at all, while others stand to gain substantially.

Why, then, would anyone ever choose a costly action from which someone else would be the sole beneficiary, or from which no one would benefit at all? The last few decades' work on collective action and contentious politics identifies the very question as seductive but misleading. The question is seductive because it maps so neatly into the short-run individualistic explanations of social processes that prevail in everyday stories about political life. It is misleading for exactly the same reason. Looked at closely, contentious politics turns out to include very few moments of stark, "make or break" individual choice between helping self and helping others. Like social life in general, it involves many unanticipated consequences—processes in which participants would never have engaged if they had made cool decisions beforehand with respect to the outcomes that actually occurred (Tilly 1996). It includes many situations in which relations to other actors make all the difference. Relations to third parties, furthermore, often matter more than relations between the actor and the action's immediate object.

Figure 2.1 therefore identifies a challenging range of phenomena after the fact, but obscures our explanatory problem. It assumes that people make individualized yes/no choices in anticipation of predictable costs and benefits. In order to explain destructive and altruistic forms of contentious politics, however, we must look for relational processes that promote self-sacrifice—whether or not participants recognize the risks they face at the outset. This chapter pursues such a search.

If this chapter does its work well, it will:

- establish that genuine cases of destruction and altruism exist, and thus require explanations other than that they are really egoism or cooperation in disguise
- raise doubts whether individual level cognitive causal mechanisms alone can explain participation in destruction and altruism
- make a case for the impact of relational causal mechanisms on propensities of different groups to sacrifice on behalf of others
- show that individual decision-making mechanisms articulate closely with such relational mechanisms
- relate sacrifice-inducing processes to network structure and political identity formation
- argue that destruction and altruism occur through similar causal processes, the difference between them depending chiefly on relations of actor and object to third parties
- suggest (but not argue or demonstrate) that the same sorts of mechanisms also explain egoistic and cooperative forms of contention

In order to accomplish those objectives, the chapter will wander a bit among topics that at first glance connect poorly with destruction and altruism: compliance, stories, identities, conscription, mutiny, war, revolution, strikes, and contentious politics in general. By the end, connections among these disparate topics should be clear.

Margaret Levi's Contribution

Despite reasoning mainly in an individualistic mode, Margaret Levi has recently made an important contribution to answering our questions about sacrifice. She astutely chooses to analyze resistance to and compliance with military conscription—a quintessential case in which individuals face the choice of bearing large costs on behalf of benefits they will share little or not at all, and to which their participation will make little difference. Conscription does not descend all the way down into our diagram's destruction or altruism corners because conscripts ordinarily belong to the citizenry on whose behalf they serve. (Levi makes valuable observations on how military service qualifies people for citizenship and thereby reshapes citizenship itself; see also Tilly 1995b.) Conscripts therefore stand to benefit, however slightly, from their own military service. But the case comes close enough that we might hope to learn from Levi about destruction and altruism.

Levi self-consciously builds her analysis on game theory (Levi 1997, 7-8). She thereby commits herself to single actor explanations of social behavior: individuals make decisions that affect other individuals in response to incentives operating within constraints. She moves beyond bare rational actor formulations, however, in two significant ways. She first identifies relations with others as significant constraints on individual decision-making and, second, sketches histories of the institutions that shape constraints, including relations with others. Repeatedly, as a result, she reaches beyond the self-imposed limits of her models to examine interactive processes such as continuous bargaining. Concretely, she analyzes situations in which potential soldiers, governmental agents, and other subjects of the same government bargain out consent to military service or resistance to that consent.

Levi's model of "contingent consent" states that individual citizens are more likely to comply with costly demands from their governments, including demands for military service, to the degree that:

1. citizens perceive the government to be trustworthy
2. the proportion of other citizens complying (that is, the degree of "ethical reciprocity") increases, and
3. citizens receive information confirming governmental trustworthiness and the prevalence of ethical reciprocity (Levi 1997, 21)

More loosely, Levi argues that citizens consent to onerous obligations when they see their relations to governmental agents and to other citizens as both reliable and fair. Fairness and justice matter (Jasso 1999; Moore 1979; Shklar 1990; Vermunt and Steensma 1991; Young 1990). Levi does not specify what mechanisms produce these effects; she treats them as empirical generalizations to verify or falsify. She implies, however, that the effective mechanisms are individual because they involve individual calculations of likely consequences of compliance or resistance. "Contingent consent requires," she declares, "that an individual believe not only that she is obliged to comply but also that others are or should be obliged to comply" (Levi 1997, 205). Like other rational action theorists, she centers her explanations on cognitive processes.

The counter-hypotheses that Levi means to refute include (1) habitual obedience, (2) ideological consent, and (3) opportunistic obedience (Levi 1997, 19). Each of these identifies a different cognitive orientation of subjects to authorities. Opportunism, as Levi defines it, can respond to a variety of incentives including secret satisfaction, side benefits, and social security; the only two of the seven explanations enumerated earlier that Levi ignores are therefore group pressure and accident. (In fact, as we will see, she eventually incorporates group pressure as well.) Her evidence from the United States, Canada, the United Kingdom, France, New Zealand, Australia, and Vietnam concerns differential compliance with demands for military service according to period, population segment, and character of war. Observed differentials challenge habit, ideology, and opportunism accounts while confirming Levi's empirical generalizations summarizing contingent consent: on the whole, compliance with conscription was greater in situations of relatively high trust, and so on.

Institutions, organizations, and social relations enter Levi's explanations as background variables—not as direct causes of compliance, but as shapers of the perceptions and information that themselves explain compliance. Thus Canada's sharp division between anglophones and francophones helps explain both the readiness of the Anglo majority to impose conscription on the entire country and the greater resistance of the French-speaking minority to military service (Levi 1997, 163-64). Institutions, organizations, and social relations also affect available courses of action and their relative costs. Thus French history, with its long tradition of a nation in arms and its weak development of pacifist sects, made conscientious objection much less available to draft resisters in France than in Anglo-Saxon countries (Levi 1997, 191-92).

Toward the end of her analysis, Levi offers a larger opening to social structure: she argues that third-party enforcement strongly affects the actual likelihood of other people's compliance, hence any particular individual's perception of fairness (Levi 1997, 213). Governmental coercion of potential defectors significantly affects not only those recalcitrants themselves, but also others who become more willing to serve when they know that others will have to serve as well. At this point in Levi's analysis, networks of interpersonal commitment start playing a significant and fairly direct part in the generation of social action. Levi offers another opening to social structure by recognizing how significantly governmental performance affects compliance; poorly or erratically performing governments receive less compliance. (This very problem led Albert Hirschman to distinguish exit, voice, and loyalty as alternative responses to governmental failure, but Levi does not follow up that lead.) By this point, interactive processes are doing an important part of Levi's explanatory work.

Levi's two overtures to social structure deserve a whole opera. We have, for example, some evidence that in wartime workers strike more frequently and soldiers desert in larger numbers when their country's military forces show signs of losing badly (see, e.g., Lagrange 1989). For North Carolina's Confederate forces in the American Civil War, Peter Bearman (1991) has shown that ordinary individual-level characteristics tell us little or nothing about propensity to desert, but that collective properties of fighting units made a significant difference. Early in the war, locally recruited companies tended to stick together, while geographically heterogeneous companies suffered relatively high rates of desertion. As the war continued, however, the pattern reversed: after the summer of 1863, members of geographically homogeneous companies became more likely to desert the cause. "Ironically," notes Bearman, "companies composed of men who had the longest tenures, who were the most experienced, and who had the greatest solidarity were most likely to have the highest desertion rates after 1863" (Bearman 1991, 337). Bearman plausibly accounts for this surprising shift as the result of a relational process: Confederate recruiters originally concentrated on forming companies locally, but deaths and tactical reorganization eventually made some companies geographically heterogeneous. Early in the war, commitment to a locality and commitment to the Confederate cause as a whole aligned neatly. As the war proceeded, however, overall losses introduced increasing discrepancies between national and local solidarity; collective connection to the same locality simultaneously activated commitments to people at home and facilitated collective defection from the national military effort.

Variable desertion connects closely with another phenomenon: a tendency of strikes, rebellions, and revolutionary situations to concentrate in immediate postwar periods (Tilly 1992, 1993). One Levi- and Bearman-style component of the phenomenon is that governments pursue major wars by imposing tightened central controls and accumulating large debts, but by so doing they also expand their commitments to all collaborating parties. During the war, signs that governments are losing capacity to meet those commitments induce collaborators in the war effort to press claims for immediate advantages and/or to withdraw their effort. After the war, few governments actually retain the capacity to meet their wartime commitments; in Levi's terms, they suffer declines in trustworthiness. The worse their losses in war, the more they lose capacity and suffer discredit (cf. Schumpeter 1947, 354). Disappointed political creditors respond by accelerating their demands and/or withdrawing their compliance with the government's own demands. These are not mere mental events; they involve genuine changes in relations among important actors within a regime. Levi gives us two structural processes to examine seriously: (1) alterations in networks of interpersonal commitment, and (2) changed relations between governmental agents and citizens.

These processes become all the more interesting when we recognize how crucially they affect prospects for democracy. Consider trust, defined as the placing of significant enterprises and resources at risk to other people's malfeasance. However we define democracy, it depends on two kinds of trust: (1) that significant others, including governmental officials, will meet their current commitments, and (2) that if a political actor loses in the current round, it will get another chance (Przeworski 1997).

Less obviously, democracy depends on a degree of articulation between public politics and networks of interpersonal commitment organized around trade, religious practice, kinship, and esoteric knowledge. In networks of these kinds, people carry on long-term, high-risk activities whose outcomes depend significantly on the performances of others; in that sense, they qualify as trust networks. Through most of human history, subjects of states insulated all such networks from political interference as best they could. Where subjects succeed in protecting their trust networks, they fight off state intervention, subvert state capacity, offer minimum consent to state demands, and withdraw effort from production of public goods under state auspices. Sympathetic to insulation and protection of trust networks, James Scott (1985) calls many of these strategies "weapons of the weak." A necessary (if by no means sufficient) condition of democracy, however, is enough state capacity to meet governmental commitments, defend constituted political actors, and enforce agreements among them. If the weak prevail in this regard, paradoxically, democracy suffers.

Well-insulated trust networks erect almost insuperable barriers to state capacity. In Reformation Europe, for example, the formation of ties among ordinary Protestants greatly inhibited the rule of princes who did not themselves convert or make firm compacts with Protestant leaders (te Brake 1998, 81-90). In nineteenth century Switzerland, only the weakening of separate trust networks embedded in Protestant and Catholic congregations provided an opening to democratization in a country racked repeatedly by civil war between 1798 and 1847. Democratization always involves the formation of new *modi vivendi* between trust networks and governmental agents, whether directly or through powerful political actors such as parties, churches, and special interest associations.

Levi's formulations brush against these phenomena, but do not quite capture them. In all of them, locations within interpersonal networks, rather than unmediated relationships between individuals and authorities, significantly affect people's commitment to collective enterprises. The effect is even more general. We have good reason to believe that collective action on a large scale depends heavily on commitment to subgroups within the acting population rather than directly to the enterprise as a whole (Sandell 1998). That is, of course, the implication of Doug McAdam's findings concerning the effects of network integration on participation in Freedom Summer.

From Social Interactions to Destruction and Altruism

Let us take advantage of these openings to think more generally about destruction and altruism. We continue to assume that cognitive mechanisms affect individual compliance in the manner that Levi argues. But we shift (as does Levi herself) from Levi's initial terrain of individual compliance to the overlapping territory of contentious politics: the collective making of claims that would, if realized, significantly affect the interests of others. We investigate the dynamics of relations that appear as static constraints in Levi's initial consent model.

Accepting provisionally Levi's account of individual-level mechanisms that promote compliance, we can inquire into interpersonal processes that facilitate or activate the mechanisms in question. Under what conditions, why, and how do social interactions encourage people to take significant losses—individual and/or collective—in pursuit of collective claims? Does it make any difference whether those losses are shared with objects of claims (destruction) or taken exclusively by the claimant while some other party benefits from the claims (altruism)? Does the existence of ties that participants regard as reliable and fair promote readiness to engage in destruction or altruism?

These ways of putting our question make clear that with her moves toward "group pressure" Levi has opened up three promising lines of explanation for destructive and altruistic forms of contention:

1. outright coercion by other parties
2. mutual coercion within an acting group
3. by-product commitments

Take coercion first. Levi rightly argues that no polity operates entirely by means of harm and threats of harm. Yet some do a great deal of their work that way. Vast Mongol empires, for example, maintained themselves for centuries through large applications of coercion (Barfield 1989; Johnston 1995; cf. Scott 1998; Stanley 1996; Tilly 1999a; Wolf 1999). More generally, exploitative systems make involuntary altruists of their victims. As seen from the victim's side, exploitation consists of taking losses for another's benefit. Exploitation always depends, at least in part, on coercion (Bottomore 1983,

157-58; Roemer 1982; Stinchcombe 1995; Tilly 1998a, ch. 4). Under a wide range of circumstances, coercion produces compliance and loss.

Mutual coercion, furthermore, occurs within acting groups. With high exit barriers and little opportunity for communication among disgruntled members, many a sect or conspiracy maintains control over its members even when numerous participants privately prefer rebellion or escape (Gamson, Fireman, and Rytina 1982; Zablocki 1980). Similarly, Roger Gould (1999) identifies a process by which clans whose individual members would much rather stay alive engage in self-destructive feuding as internal coercion increases in response to external threat. Mutual coercion promotes a wide variety of destruction and altruism.

By-product commitments probably play an even larger part in collective destruction and altruism than does coercion. Social ties entailing significant rights and obligations grow up from a wide variety of activities: birth, common residence, sexual relations, mutual aid, religious practice, public ceremonial, and more. Some of those ties ramify into networks of identity and trust: sets of social relations providing collective answers to the questions "Who are you?" "Who are we?" and "Who are they?" They also become sites of high-risk, long-term activities such as reputation building, investment, trade in valuables, procreation, and entrance into a craft. Trade diasporas, *Landsmannschaften*, credit circles, lineages, religious sects, and journeymen's brotherhoods provide salient cases in point.

Networks thus formed and reinforced acquire strong claims over their members. Gossip, shaming, and threats of expulsion multiply their effectiveness in such networks. Since the very connections among members become crucial resources, external threats to any member become threats to the high-risk, long-term activities of all members. As a result, external repression operates on networks of identity and trust in two rather different modes. It damps collective action when it concentrates on raising the cost of any new action, but incites collective resistance when it threatens survival of the network and its associated identities (Khawaja 1993; Lichbach 1987; Olivier 1991). Collective resistance, furthermore, can easily turn into collective aggression, or into simultaneous damage of self and other, in the course of strategic interaction.

Lest these observations seem distant from the questions about destruction and altruism with which we began, consider the process Charles Payne describes:

Mrs. Annie Devine played a crucial role in the movement in Canton, Mississippi. CORE's Rudy Lombard speaks of a meeting where "She looked me in the eye and said 'Rudy, I *know* you won't deny us your talents in Canton this summer. I'm depending on you.' I knew I was trapped. No way I could turn that woman down." The organizers and the local people who took to them were in a positive feedback loop, in which the courage and humanistic values of one side encouraged a like response from the other. "They were gentlemen," said Mr. Larry of the McComb organizers, "and around them we were gentle." That would be even more true in reverse (Payne 1995, 239-40).

Rudy Lombard implies that without Mrs. Devine's moral pressure he never would have run the risks he actually ran of behalf of the cause. But Mrs. Devine's moral authority did not depend on personal charisma alone; it operated within a previously established network of mutual awareness and commitment. It depended, at least in part, on Lombard's and Devine's relations to third parties. Through just such interactive processes by-product commitments promote sacrifice. Models of self-directed individuals who respond to incentives within constraints may capture crucial instants of decision or indecision, but they misrepresent the interactive social processes that generate and transform such instants. They cannot deal with the dynamics of interpersonal commitment.

Notice where we are going. Within contentious politics, actions that observers and participants retroactively interpret as consequences of deliberate individual choice almost always turn out to result from interactive processes. Some of those processes occur abruptly (for example, one person shouting, "Fire!" and other people running), and some of them proceed quite incrementally (for example, day-by-day modulation of an acquaintance from distant to friendly). In order to explain destructive and altruistic contention, we must make four related moves in our representation of social processes:

- from individuals to networks
- from individual beliefs to shared stories
- from personal cognition to conversation
- from action to interaction

Participation in contentious politics consists of conversational interaction within networks in the context of collectively constructed stories. Although individual mental events explain some aspects of contentious conversation, much of its dynamics results from alterations in networks, stories, or the course of conversation itself (Emirbayer 1997; Emirbayer and Goodwin 1994; Emirbayer and Mische 1998; Goodwin et al. 1999; Polletta 1998a, 1998b; Somers 1992, 1994; Tilly 1998b, 1998c, 1999b).

Here we encounter a major difficulty in contemporary analyses of contentious politics (see Cerulo 1997, 393-94). This is the difficulty: Humans live in flesh-and-blood bodies, accumulate traces of experiences in their nervous systems, organize current encounters with the world as cognitions, emotions, and intentional actions. They tell stories about themselves in which they acted deliberately and efficaciously or were blocked from doing so by uncontrolled emotion, weakness, malevolent others, bad luck, or recalcitrant nature. They tell similar stories about other people. Humans come to believe in a world full of continuous, neatly bounded, self-propelling individuals whose intentions interact with accidents and natural limits to produce all of social life. In many versions, those "natural limits" feature norms, values, and scripts inculcated and enforced by powerful others—but then internalized by self-propelling individuals.

Closely observed, however, the same humans turn out to be interacting repeatedly with others, renegotiating who they are, adjusting the boundaries they occupy, modifying their actions in rapid response to other people's reactions, selecting among and altering available scripts, improvising new forms of joint action, speaking sentences no one has ever uttered before, yet responding predictably to their locations within webs of social relations they themselves cannot map in detail. They tell stories about themselves and others that facilitate their social interaction rather than laying out verifiable facts about individual lives. They actually live in deeply relational worlds. If social construction occurs, it happens socially, not in isolated recesses of individual minds.

The problem becomes acute in descriptions and explanations of contentious politics. Political actors typically give individualized accounts of participation in contention, although the "individuals" to which they attribute bounded, unified, continuous self-propulsion are often collective actors such as communities, classes, armies, firms, unions, interest groups, or social movements. Even such sensitive analysts of political interaction as Doug McAdam and Charles Payne generally cast their accounts one actor at a time. Analysts and participants alike attach moral evaluations and responsibilities to the individuals involved, praising or condemning them for their actions, grading their announced identities from unacceptable (e.g., mob) to laudable (e.g., martyrs). Accordingly, strenuous effort in contentious politics goes into contested representations of crucial actors as worthy or unworthy, unified or fragmented, large or small, committed or uncommitted, powerful or weak, well connected or isolated, durable or evanescent, reasonable or irrational, greedy or generous.

Meticulous observation of that same effort, however, eventually tells even a naïve observer what almost every combat officer, union leader, or political organizer acknowledges in private. Public representations of political identities and other forms of participation in struggle proceed through intense coordination, contingent improvisation, tactical maneuvering, responses to signals from other participants, on-the-spot reinterpretations of what is possible, desirable, or efficacious, and strings of unexpected outcomes inciting new improvisations. Interactions among actors with shifting boundaries, internal structures, and identities turn out to permeate what in retrospect or in distant perspective analysts portray as actor-driven wars, strikes, rebellions, electoral campaigns, or social movements. Hence the difficulty of reconciling individualistic images with interactive realities. Margaret Levi's valuable analysis of consent never quite escapes the difficulty.

Interactive Political Identities

In response to that difficulty, let us stress social interaction as the locus and basis of contention. Let us recognize that political identities consist of public representations of relationships: us to them and us to us. Let us further recognize that much of contentious politics directly involves identity claims: we speak as X, we claim a certain relationship to Y, our being Xs gives us the right to Z, and so on. We can then draw on analogies between political contention and argumentative conversation, which follows a dynamic that is irreducible to the initial intentions of the conversationalists (see, e.g., Duneier and Molotch 1999). Above all, let us break with the common assumption that intentions—or, worse yet, reasons given by participants after the fact—explain social processes. Yet, ironically, we will end up observing that assertions of unitary actors and performances to validate those assertions play central parts in a great variety of contentious politics. The assertion of self-propelled unity turns out to be both a socially organized illusion and a profound truth of contention.

Who, then, are the actors? What sorts of people are likely to engage in contentious politics? What sorts of people, that is, are likely to make concerted public claims which involve governments as objects or third parties and which, if realized, would visibly affect interests of persons outside their own number? In principle, any connected set of persons within a given polity, to whom a definition of shared stakes in that polity's operation is available, qualifies. In practice, beyond a very small scale every actor that engages in claim-making includes at least one cluster of previously-connected persons among whom have circulated widely-accepted stories concerning their strategic situation: opportunities, threats, available means of action, likely consequences of those actions, evaluations of those consequences, capacities to act, memories of previous contention, and inventories of other likely parties to any action.

In practice, furthermore, such actors have generally established previous relations—contentious or not—to other collective actors; those relations have shaped internal structures of the actors and helped generate their stories. In practice, finally, constituent units of claim-making actors often consist not of living, breathing whole individuals but of groups, organizations, bundles of social relations, and social sites such as occupations and neighborhoods. Actors consist of networks deploying partially shared histories, cultures, and collective connections with other actors. The volunteers who trained in Oxford, Ohio, during June 1964 were joining and transforming a well-articulated network of activists.

Such actors, however, almost never describe themselves as composite networks. Instead, they offer collective nouns; they call themselves workers, women, residents of X, or United Front Against Y. They attribute unitary intentions to themselves, and most often to the objects of their claims as well.

They recast social relations and network processes as individuals and individually deliberated actions. What is happening here? Identities in general consist of social relations and their representations, as seen from the perspective of one actor or another. They are not durable or encompassing attributes of persons or collective actors as such. To bear an identity as mother is to maintain a certain relation to a child. The same person that bears the identity of mother in one context easily adopts the identities manager, customer, alumna, and sister in others. A crucial subset of identities are categorical; they pivot on a line that separates Xs from Ys, establishing distinct relations of Xs to Xs, Xs to Ys, and Ys to Ys. Black-white forms an important pair in the United States, but so does male-female, Jew-gentile, worker-boss, and welfare recipient-social worker. Each pair defines not only a boundary but also a locally variable set of relations across that boundary.

Seen as social relations and their representations, all identities have a political side, actual or potential. Whether husband-wife or black-white, each categorical pair has its own historically accumulated forms of deliberation and struggle. Much identity-based deliberation and struggle raises questions which, when generalized, become problems of the common good: questions of inequality, of equity, of right, of obligation. Public debates and private ones often interact, as when women and men enact in their daily lives the issues and terms of great public struggles over gender inequality. Finally, all polities leave room for some claim making on the basis of shared identity, and all polities build some identities explicitly into public political life. Demands in the name of a religious minority illustrate the first phenomenon, and installation of legal distinctions between citizens and aliens the second. Recognizing the ubiquity of identity politics in some senses of the term, we can nevertheless call identities explicitly *political* when they qualify in one or both of these last two regards: when people make public claims on the basis of those identities, claims to which governments are either objects or third parties.

Identities are political, then, insofar as they involve relations to governments. Obvious examples are officeholder, military veteran, citizen, imprisoned felon, and welfare recipient. Identities such as worker, resident, and woman likewise become political in some regimes, either where governments actually rule by means of such identities or where any set of people who subscribe to the same program have the right to voice collective demands. Over the long run, American political struggles have inscribed the identity pair black-white more definitively into public politics than has been the case in Brazil, although not so comprehensively as in South Africa (Marx 1998; see also Fredrickson 1997). But in all three countries black activists have repeatedly divided over whether they should make demands in their capacity as blacks, as citizens, as workers, as women, or perhaps as some combination of these categories (see, e.g., Jenson 1998; Seidman 1993, 1999).

Or consider the politics of Hindu-Muslim divisions in India. One of the most hotly debated questions in current Indian politics is whether, if it came to full power, the increasingly influential Bharatiya Janata Party (BJP), with its origins in Hindu nationalism, would inscribe religious categories into the previously secular Indian national governmental structure. In the present Indian system, people who share routine religious identities already have the right to form parties of their own, so long as they represent themselves as embodying distinctive cultural traditions rather than creeds as such. Authorities currently contest any such right in Turkey, Algeria, Tanzania, Afghanistan, and parts of the former Soviet Union. To that extent, many religious identities are already political identities in India.

Indeed, in some regards the Hindu-Muslim pairing operates across South Asia chiefly in relation to government rather than as an organizer of everyday social relations; in routine social interaction, caste, class, community, and gender tend to prevail (see, e.g., Brass 1994, 1996, 1997; Copland 1998; Tambiah 1996, 1997). Hindu-Muslim designates a political distinction rather than separating two well-defined, unitary, transcendental world views from each other. To an unknown but probably large degree, shared orientations of category members result from, rather than cause, recurrent political relations between members of different categories (Laitin 1999; cf. Turner 1982, 69-70).

Over the course of contentious politics, actors take action in the names of identities. Identities define their relations to specific others. Their actions actually consist of *inter*actions with those others, interactions that center on claim-making. They put on a performance of mutual, public claim-making by paired identities. In the name of their asserted collective identity, interlocutors for actors demand, command, require, request, plead, petition, beseech, promise, propose, threaten, attack, destroy, seize, or otherwise make claims on assets that lie under someone else's control. When interlocutors for others reply in the name of their own political identities, an episode of contentious politics has begun. As the process continues, relevant identities often modify. From the perspective of local power holders, COFO volunteers arrived in Mississippi as alien invaders; although they never became friends of the white power structure, they and their staff organizers became significant actors in local politics. One way or another, clusters of civil rights activists established recognized, collective, identity-framed relations with local and national holders of power. That those relations were rarely cordial does not gainsay the point. Warfare and strike activity, after all, also involve contentious politics among well defined parties.

Dynamics of Altruism and Destruction

Armed with an interactive, identity-based understanding of contentious politics, let us return to the explanation of altruism and destruction. Recall that
destruction refers to collective action in which an actor inflicts net losses on
another actor while enduring net losses itself, regardless of possible benefits
or losses to third parties. Altruism, then, refers to collective action in which
an actor produces benefits for another actor while enduring net losses itself,
again regardless of possible benefits or losses to third parties. Several different mechanisms promote one variety of self-sacrifice or another. The first is
outright external compulsion. As in Levi's cases of mass conscription, a
government's readiness to coerce reluctant soldiers drives unwilling individuals to undertake lethal risks. The second mechanism is mutual coercion
within a network, a process that gains efficacy with high barriers to private
communication and exit, as well as with prior organization of that network as
the site of high-risk trust and wide-ranging identity.

Following Levi's analyses, we can reasonably suppose that mutual coercion will also gain efficacy with:

- public enforcement of fair treatment within networks of potential activists
- third-party enforcement of previously-made public commitments
- guarantees of network durability
- guarantees of mutual support among network members
- signaling of determination among potential participants in risky actions
- central coordination of identity-sustaining action within trust networks

To the extent that these mechanisms converge, we can even expect suffering
to become a badge of worthiness, a proof of commitment—in some respects,
a reward in itself.

We must move beyond Levi's analyses, however, to recognize the signifi-
cance of two other causal mechanisms that promote destruction and altruism.
One is the activation of shared stories with which defection is incompatible
(McAdam and Paulsen 1993; Polletta 1998b). As we have seen, people integrate political identities with shared stories about those identities. Such stories crystallize answers to these sorts of questions: "Who are we?" "What are
our rights and obligations?" "What do we intend?" "Who are they?" "What
are their rights and obligations?" "What do they intend?" Those stories con-
strain participants in contention thrice: by setting limits on what sorts of joint
interaction they consider, by influencing their collective self-presentation,
and by embodying standards of proper individual performance. If stories
about who "we" and "they" are include imputations of courage, shared fate,
and exposure to hostile outsiders, those stories in themselves raise the self-

imposed costs of self-seeking behavior. They increase estimated costs of alternatives to mutual defense.

The other causal mechanism is an external threat to the survival of shared identities and trust networks. To the extent that people have invested their futures in such networks and cut themselves off from opportunities to exit, external threats to any part of the network become threats to the whole. Thus people will die defending their networks against heavy odds. Freedom Summer volunteers joined a beleaguered minority of activists in hostile territory. Each threat to their collective survival increased the salience of their shared identity, and reduced the likelihood of individual defection. To be sure, reversal of the other crucial mechanisms—in the form of panic among leaders, sharp division within the cause, or open challenges to shared stories—raises the probability of helter-skelter exit. But over a wide range, activation of external threats to shared identities and trust networks promotes common defensive efforts, even to the point of substantial net losses for participants.

These arguments finally bring us to distinctions between destruction and altruism. One version of destruction resembles altruism: if a shared identity and trust network come under serious external threat, under some circumstances a set of actors incur large costs for themselves and inflict large costs on others for the benefit of third parties with whom they share an identity and trust network. Thus some targets of genocide may attack the perpetrators in order to distract their attackers from other family members. A second version involves even more general losses, as cornered members of a trust network may destroy themselves and their attackers rather than submit to the subjugation or defilement that is likely to follow their surrender. In both scenarios, relations to third parties make a large difference: in the first case, because third parties of similar identity stand to gain from destructive action; in the second case, because the absence of third-party monitors with relations to both parties increases the likelihood of destruction.

Altruism, by the same reasoning, becomes more feasible in the presence of (1) identity-trust ties to the object of self-sacrificing action, (2) threats that relatively limited actions can reduce, and (3) third parties that are likely to intervene on the beneficiary's behalf once self-sacrifice alerts them to the threat faced by the trust network at large. Conversely, in the absence of extensive identity-trust ties, both destruction and altruism should be rare or nonexistent. The line of reasoning brings us back to a kind of agreement with rational action skeptics about destruction and altruism: cases of apparent self-sacrifice for others unlike themselves—trees, the environment, endangered species, and unknown foreigners—will ordinarily turn out to depend on mechanisms operating within groups of activists. Mutual coercion, third-party enforcement, and other mechanisms from Margaret Levi's well-stocked tool kit will explain those cases. In the final analysis, they will not involve isolated individual decisions to take substantial net losses for the benefit of others. Instead, they will result from by-product commitments and interactive processes.

If these sorts of arguments apply to destruction and altruism, they ought likewise to account for egoism and cooperation. In egoism and cooperation, by definition, actors receive (or at least can anticipate receiving) net benefits from their interactions with others. Straightforward satisfaction-seeking therefore probably plays a part in egoism and cooperation that it does not in genuine destruction and altruism. Yet here, too, we should find that relations to immediate others, as distinguished from the cause as a whole, significantly affect participation and its satisfactions (see Bowles and Gintis 1998; Goldstone 1994; Hechter 1987; Nesse 1999). No doubt full analyses of egoism and cooperation would also require identification of further mechanisms. We should, for instance, search out mechanisms that make it possible for an egoistic actor to benefit by inflicting harm on others, and other mechanisms altering the categorical distinctions and relations currently available to participants in contention (see Tilly 1998a). For the moment, however, it will suffice to examine how well this chapter's analyses apply to concrete cases of destruction and altruism.

Assertion is not proof. Single-actor accounts of contentious politics have held such sway in recent years that we have far too little evidence to assess the plausibility or implausibility of my speculations. At least those speculations have the virtues of concreteness and novelty. Where, then, do we stand? We have identified these clusters of causal mechanisms as likely contributors to collective destruction and collective altruism:

1. application of straightforward coercion by outsiders
2. application of mutual coercion within pre-existing networks, especially if barriers to exit and to private internal communication are high
3. public enforcement of fair treatment within networks of potential activists
4. third-party enforcement of previously-made public commitments
5. guarantees of network durability
6. guarantees of mutual support among network members
7. signaling of determination among potential participants in risky actions
8. central coordination of identity-sustaining action within trust networks
9. activation of shared stories with which defection is incompatible
10. external threats to survival of trust networks

Let no one misunderstand: such a list of ten extremely general relational mechanisms falls far short of constituting an all-purpose explanation for altruism and destruction. In any particular case, we should expect to find different combinations and sequences of such mechanisms, hence significantly different trajectories and outcomes. The list simply points explanations of altruism and destruction in a certain direction: away from simple *ex ante* decision matrices, toward relational processes.

The proposed mechanisms have the virtues of being observable and being widely documented in actual accounts of high-risk contentious politics. Doug McAdam sums up his network-oriented interpretation of Freedom Summer:

> Activism depends on more than just idealism. It is not enough that people be attitudinally inclined toward activism. There must also exist formal organizations or informal social networks that structure and sustain collective action. The volunteers were not appreciably more committed to Freedom Summer than the no-shows. Their closer ties to the project, however, left them in a better position to act on their commitment. Those volunteers who remain active today are distinguished from those who are not by virtue of their stronger organizational affiliations and continued ties to other activists. Attitudes dispose people to action; social structures enable them to act on these dispositions (McAdam 1988, 237).

McAdam's summary moves in the direction of this chapter, but from the vantage point of the individual participant rather than the collective process. We need to know more about collective processes that generate commitment, collaboration, and sacrifice. My conclusion, then, is simple: the ten mechanisms we have uncovered provide crucial causal connections among individual experiences, social structures, and high-risk contentious interaction. Their convergence sets altruism or destruction in operation. The mechanisms probably play significant parts in lower-risk egoism and cooperation as well. The challenge is to detect those mechanisms, examine their sequences, concatenations, and outcomes, then determine exactly how they work.

Notes

I have adapted a few passages from a preliminary draft of *Dynamics of Contention*, by Doug McAdam, Sidney Tarrow, and Charles Tilly, a book in progress for Cambridge University Press. For criticism of earlier drafts, I am grateful to Karen Barkey, Peter Bearman, Mario Diani, Marco Giugni, Jack Goldstone, Margaret Levi, Doug McAdam, Johann Peter Murmann, Florence Passy, Francesca Polletta, Marc Steinberg, Richard Swedberg, Harrison White, and Viviana Zelizer.

Part II

National Dynamics

3

Dynamics of Commitment in the Sector Known as "Solidarity"

Methodological Reflections Based on the Case of France

Olivier Fillieule

Introduction: A Boom in "Solidarity" Activism in France?

> They offer their time, their know-how and, when they can, their money. "They create: associations, movements and new forms of action. They reject: exclusion, poverty, fatalism. For them, solidarity isn't merely a watchword: it is a reality they experience daily. . . . It is thus that all over France, support associations have proliferated and notions of "generosity," of "charity," of "compassion," have taken on their true meaning again.

The above is taken from the introduction to a recent feature in the magazine *Le Nouvel Observateur* on "the political activism of solidarity" entitled: "The French are truly impressive. Millions of uncategorizable political activists."[1] It offers an exemplary illustration, along with several others, of an increasingly resonant discourse in France around the idea of a revival of solidarity— of a concomitant development of associations known as "solidarity," at the expense of more traditional forms of political involvement (particularly political parties and trade unions).

And, in fact, if one believes the opinion polls periodically conducted on the issue of solidarity, this notion has never been so popular. In 1995, 55 percent of those polled in France displayed a high approval rating for the expression "solidarity."[2] In 1997, the expression elicited highly positive responses in 57 percent of the sample polled,[3] and 92 percent of them claimed to be highly favorable to the notion of solidarity with people in need.[4]

In addition, the proportion of the French population prepared to get involved in this type of movement is four to six times higher than for political parties and two to four times higher than for trade unions (Ysmal 1995). It is hardly surprising, then, that from 1993 to 1996 the number of volunteer workers increased by 10 percent, bringing to 10 million the total number of French people who have "worked" for an activist voluntary organization (called *associations* in France)—one in four adults. Finally, although over the same period donations to charitable associations and those which help people in difficulty (e.g., disabled, the elderly, poor families) have fallen by 20 percent, nonetheless they remain high (1.6 billion francs in 1996), representing 15 percent of total donations, exceeded only by those to the church and health-related charities (Archambault, Bon, and Le Vaillant 1991; Archambault and Boumendil 1994).[5]

At the same time, countless analyses demonstrate a transition from political and trade union activism toward involvement in associations, which are better able to support an individualistic and rational collective mobilization, and to represent those whom traditional institutions have forgotten or excluded. This development concurs in many respects with that which occurred in the early seventies concerning "new social movements" (Touraine 1973; Inglehart 1977; Melucci 1980). Both movements invoke radically new forms of activist investment and draw support mainly from the "new salaried middle classes."

Finally, this wave of political activism is said to have spread through all levels of society. Several studies indicate that this "solidarity activism" is neither the monopoly of a bourgeois class (like traditional charitable engagement) nor merely the province of the "salaried middle classes." The voluntary worker today is likely to come from an enlarged middle class, the "working classes," blue- and white-collar workers, all increasingly involved in volunteer activity (Ferrand-Bechmann 1992). On the other hand, age would seem to constitute a differential criterion, the most active participants being between 35 and 44 years old, followed by those of 18 to 24. This preponderance of the younger age groups is congruent with a relationship to the political world generally marked by great distance and distrust, and a pronounced taste for causes with moral connotations (Muxel 1996; Baugnet 1996).

However it remains the case that "solidarity activism" seems primarily left-wing. The type of causes often coincides with the Left's universalistic and egalitarian values, and professional managers in this "solidarity activism," except in religiously-inspired associations, tend to come from left-wing organizations. It is significant that the tendency to rate highly the expression "solidarity" increases in proportion to the extent to which the respondent aligns himself with the Left, moving from 35 percent of National Front voters to 63 percent of Communist voters and 73 percent of Green party voters. Religious belief, traditionally predictive of a very positive response to the notion of solidarity, seems decreasingly decisive. Although 58 percent of

Catholics react positively to the expression "solidarity," so do 64 percent of those professing no religious faith.[6]

How can one explain the apparently huge development of such forms of involvement at a time when most discussion, in the social world as in the social sciences, is more inclined to analyze our contemporaries in terms of the "rise of individualism"? From one sector to the other, from one author to another, responses vary; however, all agree on the decisive role of the state's retreat from urban affairs.

Since the mid-seventies, in effect, the welfare state has been profoundly brought into question—in terms of social protection (the increasing burden of the nation's social expenditure), employment (with the increase in unemployment and employment insecurity), public intervention (the state increasingly disengaging from its mission to produce, via denationalization, and to innovate), and social structuration (society's increasing atomization, weakness of the "intermediary bodies," and disaffection toward traditional social organizations such as political parties and trade unions).

The integrating mechanisms that were established since World War II do not function as effectively as they did in the past. New forms of integration and new mechanisms have been, or will be, put in place: new, more precarious forms of employment; a more modest role for the state, as a simple "band leader," leaving the market to ensure social regulation; more targeted, contractualized, and territorialized social policies; an undertaking of responsibility for the social fabric by civil society, through the family, the market, or the tertiary sector; and a trend toward the politics of personal choice as motivation for involvement in collective movements. Consequently, the questioning of traditional forms of solidarity would seem to call for the construction of new modes of production for social solidarities, in which voluntary organizations would play a central role.

Can one leave it at that, and conclude that in France there has been a growth of a relatively specific sector, that of "solidarity activism"? (The term may be defined as a particular form of political activism in which people who suffer, socially and/or physically, are defended by people other than themselves, altruistically, with no ulterior motive.) Do the activities of the associations embodying this political activism manifest new solidarities, and are they building the foundations for a new social citizenship?

In this chapter, we would like to show that notions of "solidarity activism," and the tendency of many scholars to identify a specific field of "solidarity," constitute one of the first methodological obstacles to analysis. To state it another way, we would like to demonstrate that the persistent habit of considering the "field of solidarity" as an object naturally endowed with sociological reality is misleading. It is this very phenomenon which ought, at least initially, to be the object of research. Based on many case studies carried out by the Groupe d'étude et de recherche sur les mutations du militantisme (GERMM), we propose a different approach to the issues of involvement in what is known as solidarity movements, one that considers the wider context of social, individual, and political interactions.[7]

The discussion is organized around three arguments. Firstly, avoiding a substantialist approach, we have to recognize that the notion of solidarity is a *social production*. Secondly, it is illusory to seek to understand how voluntary groups and involvement in them function if one remains attached to an objectivist definition of the groups as undivided unities. Thirdly, because the definition of solidarity differs among various actors involved in the movements under study, we suggest that the oppositions between *volunteer worker* and *beneficiaries* and/or between *volunteer workers* and *paid professionals* be central dimensions to investigate.

The Notion of Solidarity as a *Social Production*

One must be conscious, at the outset, that the concept of solidarity is a *social production*, as Jacques Lagroye stresses:

> One can easily reject the substantialist ambition which endeavors to grasp the significance of solidarity's practice and attitudes ahistorically. As if "solidarity" existed in itself, and merely saying: "this is solidarity, that isn't" would suffice to grasp its significance. From this perspective, which everything leads us to reject (the expression does not always have the same meaning, being itself the object of controversy between those involved in its promotion), it is as if the researcher was able to find "the correct significance" despite the divergences and oppositions that can be observed amongst those who "practice solidarity" (Lagroye 1996).[8]

In other words, one must take into account the fact that the distinction between that which "is" solidarity and that which "isn't" really (charity, good works, self-help) is, first of all, an effect of demarcation strategies between associations.

Solidarity Label and Demarcation Strategies

Within a general context of supposed disaffection with politics, it is not insignificant to observe that a number of associations have begun claiming the "solidarity" label to characterize activities previously presented in other ways. This is because, in the competition for donations and state recognition (which translates into grants), the solidarity label has every chance of proving effective by distancing itself from traditional politics. So there is every possibility that the observable growth of the solidarity sector in France is less a sign of a transformation in forms of involvement in social causes than of a change in the strategies of self-presentation of associations seeking social legitimacy and subsidies.

The antiracism sector in France, and particularly SOS-Racisme, provides a paradigmatic example of the importance of taking into account demarcation when classifying groups as part of the "solidarity sector" or not. In his thesis dissertation, Philippe Juhem demonstrates how—under the pressure of changing political conditions (mainly the election of François Mitterrand in 1981 and a decade of socialist administration, but also the changing of the media sector in the same period)—a new public discourse emerged about antiracism and pro-immigrant movements, relying on an appeal to solidarity with those who suffer and not on political and ideological ideas and convictions (Juhem 1999).[9] In that respect, the emergence of a "new antiracism" movement in the 1980s, linked to the decline of the traditional pro-immigrant movement and to the rise of an anti-National Front movement, illustrates a general shift from political discourse to ostensibly apolitical claims, in a context of a disaffection toward traditional politics in the media as well as in public opinion.

The rise of anti-AIDS movements in France is another example of the adoption by associations of the "solidarity" label (Fillieule and Duyvendak 1999; Fillieule and Broqua, forthcoming). At the beginning of the epidemic, during the years 1981-88, homosexual associations got involved in a hidden way in the fight against AIDS. If the campaign associations were created and sustained, at arms-length, by homosexuals for self-help, they fostered a public image removed from any element of gay activism, and, in good republican tradition, without reference to homosexual identity. The anti-AIDS movement, at that time, relied on an appeal to solidarity with the sick, on a humanitarian stance. Things only began to change after 1989, after anti-AIDS associations underwent a dual process of differentiation and institutionalization. On one side, there was a multiplication of associations oriented toward specific groups of people (hæmophiliacs, blood-transfusion patients, drug addicts, and children), and on the other side a new-found professionalization of which AIDES was undoubtedly the most striking example. These changes produced several effects. The most striking was that homosexual groups, within and outside these associations, started to feel a sense of dispossession—as much from the growing de-homosexualization within the associations as from the fact that AIDS sufferers had been deprived of a direct voice in deference to professionals speaking on their behalf (one starts speaking of an "AIDS establishment" and of the "AIDS business" (Patton 1989). For that reason, new associations were born in 1989, with the objective of giving the sick back their voice and of clearly establishing a link between homosexuality and AIDS, rejecting at the same time any public framing in terms of solidarity. This organizational regeneration had the effect of building a new opposition between a "general" model and a model based on identity and community which, responding to movements on the other side of the Atlantic, embraced the politics of minorities based on the claim to a specifically HIV-positive and/or homosexual identity. The founding of the Paris branch of Act Up constitutes a clear illustration of that process.

This second example illustrates the gap between public discourse regarding a movement and what it actually is or not. At the very moment AIDS movements began to experience a process of *desingularization* and of *heterosexualization*, which in that case means the arrival of women,[10] they also started to present themselves as self-help movements, a "strategic" identity that was increasingly contradictory with the changes in their own constituencies.

Solidarity Label and External Agents

One must also take into account the strategies of a whole group of agents— civil servants, at a local and national level, journalists, "experts," sociologists—who have, over the last few decades, contributed to the development of a discourse propounding associations as the appropriate intermediaries for a state failing in its social mission, guaranteeing flexibility, proximity, a capacity for innovation and adaptation. This discourse is not unrelated to the growth of decentralization which began in the early 1980s, when local authorities began relying heavily on the voluntary sector to implement their local policies within the community (CNVA 1993, 1996). In other words, a whole set of agents with divergent interests plays a crucial role in the collective defining of the "solidarity" sector.

In this context, the distinction between that which pertains to the "field of solidarity" or not, between altruistic or self-help initiatives, relates back, as Pierre Bourdieu suggests in relation to the legitimacy of the strike, to "a strategy of self-interest which science ignores at its peril. There is political manipulation of the definition of the political. What's at stake in the battle is the battle at stake" (Bourdieu 1984, 258).[11]

The Intellectual Poverty of Single Actor Models

It is questionable that the criterion of involvement "for others" is alone sufficient to define a particular type of involvement in social causes. Such a statement can only be made at the end of a research project, and one should refrain from reducing *a priori* involvement in the movements known as solidarity to the general category of "moral political activism" (Raynaud 1980), a practice very much in favor in the current literature on political activism.[12] In effect, concepts of "solidarity sector," "field of solidarity," "solidarity political activism" are problematic in that they subsume highly differentiated activist realities to unequivocal and homogenous categories. From this point of view, it is by no means certain that there is much in common between, on the one side, antiracist and pro-immigrant rights groups and, on the other, those who support the weakest and most vulnerable members of society (the new poor, the underclass). The mere memory of the weaknesses of analyses of "new social movements," still fashionable, should suffice to prevent us falling for a label which conceals more than it reveals of what it purports to describe. From this perspective, it seems important to raise further points.

Determinants, Motivations, and Reasons

When one considers the question of distinguishing between involvement "for others" or "for self," one must be careful to distinguish the aforementioned classification of collectives (such and such an association being, or not being, a solidarity or self-help organization, for example) from the ways in which the agents themselves describe and/or experience their individual involvement. If such a distinction is not made from the start, one is condemned to behave as if all the agents involved in the movements known as "solidarity" held the same altruistic motivations. At the same time, involvement in other segments of the social movement would inevitably require some explanation in terms of utilitaritarian motives.[13] The idea that the agents in a given movement would have an undifferentiated perception of their motivations, or of the cause they are fighting for, is strongly objectivist. Each time one seeks to understand "solidarity" activism or "altruistic" behavior specificities by comparing social characteristics of the people involved, in or out solidarity movements (usually by statistical comparisons along numerous dimensions), one condemns oneself to find no significant differences in the process of individual involvement and participation.

In order to resolve the question of distinguishing between involvement "for others" or "for self" (in terms of determinants as well as in terms of sociological characteristics), one must adopt a micro-sociological perspective. One must take into account that, beyond the observable similarities one can observe at a macro-sociological level, an in-depth analysis of support mechanisms points up the coexistence of different activists profiles, outlining for each movement considered homogenous sub-groups from the standpoint of their positions and interests, linked by a common involvement which makes up only one aspect of their social being. To understand this heterogeneity of activist profiles within the same organization, one must relate them to the development over time of the movements' public image, which one can hypothesize as encouraging the coexistence—by the stacking, so to speak—of different categories of individuals with various motives, notably with regard to justification in terms of interest or of altruism.[14]

Such an orientation also implies that we define more clearly than is usually the case what we mean by "determinants of participation." The first mistake to avoid here is the usual confusion between sociological *determinants* and *motivations*, the latter being more a sort of rationalization/justification of participation. Each time one analyzes at the same level a set of sociobiological characteristics (such as sex, age, occupation, level of education) and opinions about the reasons for joining a group, or the expected rewards, one condemns oneself to mix implicitly various types of data (objective social characteristics and opinions), sociological determinants, and discourses of justifications by the actors themselves, initial and actual motivations (depending on the very moment when the questionnaire is issued).[15] The second mistake to avoid is to use the concept of *motivation* without making any effort to define it. In our own research, we prefer to use the term *reasons* to characterize why people join an organization, since the word *motivation* (and, to some extent, the word *motives*) carries the implication of inner drives, of impulses within the person that impel some behavior. Apart from the fact that we are not very convinced by such a psychological construct, what we are seeking is the kind of justifications people give when they join a movement and what is the share, among the variety of reasons invoked, of altruistic justifications.

One clear message of our survey of volunteers in anti-AIDS movements, and more precisely of AIDES, whose public image is clearly that of a self-help group (Fillieule and Broqua, forthcoming), is that no one reason appears to explain why people do AIDS volunteer work. The same act of volunteerism apparently derives from different reasons for different people. That identical behaviors in the same movement reflect different underlying motivations illustrates a fundamental lesson for the student of social movement, namely, that people engage in what appear to be the same actions for very different reasons.

Without going into the details of these results,[16] at the end of the analysis two categories of reasons are clearly opposed. In one group, reasons are expressed in terms which clearly refer to commitment to others, hence conceived as "giving of oneself," of a will to be useful. It is in this group that the terms "solidarity" and "in solidarity" are found, embedded in a vocabulary of sharing, support, and meeting. Alongside is a proliferation of personal pronouns ("me," "my") which, when one adds to them words expressing pursuit of an experience "for oneself" ("wish," "desire," "experience," "want") indicate an involvement experienced in terms of strong personal implication, of a desire to reach out to the other and thereby gain something mutually enriching.[17] The composition of this group is characterized by a higher proportion of heterosexuals (and women in fact), a link to religious belief (but a distance from religious institutions), and relatively recent membership (1995-98). Here one finds this minority of activists, having arrived at the association through the desingularization of the AIDS cause, and whose involvement is not so far removed from that in other charitable causes (soup kitchens, etc.).

In the other group, reasons spring from a traumatic experience of the disease, a vocabulary dominated by references to death, loss (death/to die; decease/to pass on; loss/lost), associated with mention of experience of the disease (hospital, disease /sick, epidemic, body). Closely associated is the vocabulary of family relationships (son, brother, child, mother, parent) and links of friendship and love (lover, friend, companion, pal). Hence what comes across is a realm of involvement resulting from a personal or emotional proximity to the disease, marked by grief, distress and solitude, but also sometimes "guilt" and the desire to "bear witness." The reasons here seem mainly means of mourning or dealing with uncertainty (fear) of a death fore-told.[18]

Logic of Giving versus Logic of Interest?

One should try to avoid the pitfalls of a simplistic opposition between the logic of giving and the logic of interest—an opposition whose intellectual poverty Jon Elster's work has long since demonstrated. However one looks at it, the issue of the rewards of activism cannot provide a clear distinction between that which pertains to a logic of interest from that which doesn't. Attempts to surpass the well-known paradox of collective action, notably through the notion of selective, then symbolic (i.e., nonmaterial), rewards, have only obscured the debate, to such an extent that it is worth wondering whether a sociology of interest is of any continuing interest whatsoever.[19]

If, however, one does not confuse an approach of looking at "interest" with a utilitarian and economist approach, we think it is possible to move toward a sociology of differentiated investments by the agents in the causes they defend, starting by looking into the rationality of their action.

That means initially that the reasons for action cannot always be reduced to *conscious self-interest* on the agents' part. In other words, the social agents have strategies which only very occasionally are guided by a real strategic intention. Here we encounter Pierre Bourdieu's notion of *illusio,* used to demonstrate the extent to which individuals are *caught* in social games which they internalize as natural and whose rules, although they might have mastered them in practice, escape their conscious awareness:[20]

> The agents who fight for [such and such] ends . . . may be possessed by those ends. They may be prepared to die for those ends, regardless of consideration of specific rewards, lucrative, career, or other. Their relation to the end concerned is not at all the conscious calculation of utility attributed to them by utilitarism, a philosophy one applies willingly to others' actions. They know how to play the game; for example, in games in which one must be detached, "disinterested," in order to win, they can achieve, in a spontaneously disinterested manner, actions in line with their interests (Bourdieu 1994 [our translation]).

Depending on the place, time, and group in which they are carried out, then, social actions can present themselves as legitimately motivated or, on the contrary, naturally take the form of disinterested acts. Therefore, every time the sociologist concentrates on the observation of social actions without relating these actions to the specific constraints of the contexts in which they operate, particularly in terms of legitimacy, he prevents himself from grasping the practical rationales which organize them. For example, in societies where giving is the constitutive basis of social exchange, the practice of giving refers to a belief system and incorporated values which reflect their insertion in a given society.[21] Concretely, that implies one is making an *externalist analysis* of social actions which articulates four orders of determination:

- on the one hand, that of the characteristics of *the space in which the social actions under consideration operate*. The value attributed to disinterestedness is highly likely to vary in relation to the social and temporal sphere. Also, in the case under consideration, one must relate the motivations of activists in movements known as solidarity to the transformations in the solidarity landscape, i.e., its public image and its social and numerical composition, as well as to developments in the set of social movements and political mutations;[22]

- that, on the other hand, of *the group in which the social actions operate*. The associational contexts in which the social agents evolve also determine, to a greater or lesser degree of legitimacy, acts conceived as a form of disinterestedness. Given, as we said earlier, that reference to solidarity and altruism is also a weapon in the competition which governs relationships between associations, one might expect that the public image promoted by a given association might tend to impose itself as the actual guiding principles for their practice. As Pierre Bourdieu suggests, "one cannot simply get away with incessant invocations of virtue, because one is caught up in mechanisms and there are sanctions, which recall the obligation to disinterestedness" (Bourdieu 1994, 164 [our translation]).

- that, next, of the *predispositions* of agents and conditions of production of these predispositions; in other words, all that which, in each individual's history, enables the realization of a greater or lesser predisposition to the giving of self, to disinterestedness;

- that, finally, of the agents' *personal histories*. Involvement in social causes, as well as the meaning it confers upon the person involved, cannot be understood as a simple reflection of a social position. The mediations between predispositions and action are numerous and one must relate the analysis of reasons—and thus the tendency to think of one's involvement in terms of disinterestedness or not—to biographical events. If taking into account the space in which social actions operate (cf. supra) fulfills, in part, this need to factor in biographical history, through consideration in particular of effects of historical era and generation, one must still add in the role that can be played by particular events, at an individual level (for example, in anti-AIDS movements, the experience of loss and self-diminishment).

Volunteer Workers, Paid Professionals, and Beneficiaries

The debate surrounding solidarity and disinterestedness constitutes one axis structuring the divisions even within the associations themselves. In other words, the meaning given and/or lent to social activities by various individuals relates to oppositions between *volunteer workers* and *beneficiaries*, and between *volunteer workers* and *paid professionals*.

Volunteer Workers and Beneficiaries

The relationship between volunteer workers and beneficiaries contains a tension between a model of charitable action, seeking to reduce the beneficiaries of support to the role of helpless actors kept in a state of paternalist dependency (Laville and Sainsaulieu 1997, 288), and a model in which the beneficiaries are also, and at the same time, actively involved in the association. The example of Secours Populaire Français, with its 72,000 volunteer workers, is a perfect illustration of this tension. The volunteer workers (called "collectors")[23] must encourage the beneficiaries to become collectors themselves, i.e., to also participate in the provision of solidarity.[24] Now, as Marc Castille, one of the twelve national secretaries of the organization, suggests, the problems accruing from this ambition come first of all from the volunteer workers: "[T]elling volunteers to get the beneficiaries of support to get moving is not well understood. The volunteer worker is frightened of the 'other:' it's better if the beneficiary remains on the other side of the generous gesture. Conversely, the good volunteer worker will no longer enjoy the prestige of generosity if he finds himself partnered with the excluded" (cited in Rebelle and Swiatly 1999).

In other words, even the definition of solidarity is the object of diverse, indeed contradictory, intrepretations, which suggests once again the diversity of meanings invested in this concept by people involved in "solidarity activism."

In a number of associations, the volunteer workers-beneficiaries tension arises from the fact that it is difficult, indeed impossible, to clearly distinguish between these two categories. This is the case with anti-AIDS associations in which it is difficult to distinguish between those who are suffering effectively and/or affectively from the others. Another striking example is that of the Restos du Coeur (a form of soup kitchen), studied by Bertrand Ravon and Roland Raymond, who write:

> One cannot disassociate the vulnerable position of Restos du Coeur beneficiaries (whose eligibility depends on criteria close to the state definition for obtaining the minimum benefit paid to those with no other source of income) from that of volunteer workers. In effect, a total of over 80 percent of non-working people comprise the volunteer workers at the Restos du Coeur, if one adds to the unemployed or young people at risk the other non-workers, not counting students. Cross-indexed with information on socio-professional background which indi-

cates a substantial majority of volunteer workers are or were blue- or white-collar workers, this data attests, for many of them, to the vulnerability or precariousness of their social status. And if one examines the situation further, beyond the material insecurity of their conditions of existence, the social places where a stable position in society, and social utility and public recognition are no longer assured, a number of volunteer workers may be described as "useless to the world," "supernumerary," "floating in a kind of social no man's land"[25] (Ravon and Raymond 1997, 105-106).

This example confirms once again the extent to which the autonomization of a "solidarity sector" is highly problematic because the distinction between involvement for self and for others is extremely difficult to make, depending on the type of group and type of population one is dealing with.

Volunteer Workers and Paid Staff

The relationship between volunteer workers and paid professionals must also be examined in the context of an increasing professionalization of associations. Relationships between the two groups are characterized by forms of specific competition on the question of disinterestedness. The full-time workers on paid contracts often are suspicious of interference from volunteer workers, all the more so since the latter often claim greater legitimacy by working without pay. In addition, in the context of a crisis of the salaried classes and growing unemployment, it is difficult for paid workers not to see their professional activities threatened by volunteer workers who are sometimes just as, if not more, competent. Volunteer workers often reproach permanent employees for pursuing their material and bureaucratic interests rather than the association's ideals, as if gaining material benefits from their political commitment should *restrict them* to the world of economic exchange. This perception is known to arouse suspicion generally in many voluntary action groups.

One must place the suspicions that all too often surround professional solidarity activists within the current context of a growing loss of confidence in institutional policies, as Jacques Ion and Bertrand Ravon have rightly stressed:

> As soon as institutional policies are denounced for their mistakes, when they become the bureaucratic apparatus, going beyond the initial reasons for action, the institutional dimension specific to contemporary activist involvements is also to be understood within the framework of the relationship of mobilized individuals to the political sphere . . . the current commitment can be understood as an uneasy game of offers of institutional participation coming from political-association leaders or as a response to institutionalized devices deemed at the very least insufficient if not actually discriminatory. . . . In addition, it can be compared to new forms of political action which acquire meaning within a detailed critique of the everyday political process and its compromises. . . . It is a

question of tearing oneself free from institutional influence, from the logic of the apparatus. Denunciations of personal interest or of being used by institutions, the ineffectiveness of multiple meetings or the power games linked to the activity of representing the group: as many restrictions on the possibilities for action and the autonomy of activist involvement (Ion and Ravon 1998, 65).

Several observations (for example, Hamidi 1997;[26] Madelin 1998; Fillieule and Broqua, forthcoming) converge around this idea that perceptions of the political process inform the way individuals regard their involvement in associations. Through a kind of homology of perception, the power games, politicization, hierarchy, and personal interests that are denounced in the political world are replicated within associations. At the same time as it creates a remoteness from the rules of politics, the invocation of a *truly* altruistic investment on the part of a minority of volunteer workers also appears as a possible explanation for a compensatory strategy—offering either a way to lessen the difficulty of experiencing a position of weakness and being dominated within the association, or of translating a resentment into acceptable terms vis-à-vis those who occupy enviable positions because they confer status or simply because they are remunerated.[27]

Conclusion

To conclude and summarize, we would like to reiterate three basic points. First, it is important to avoid taking conceptions of the "field of solidarity" or "solidarity sector" as relevant categories for analysis. To avoid any danger of naturalization and reification of collectives, it is better to start from the idea of an ill-circumscribed locus of struggle, whose boundaries cannot in any case be identified in what is precisely at the basis of the struggle.

Second, rather than confine ourselves to an organizational analysis which would be limited to the groups' public image, it is necessary to posit the question of the existence and/or the specificity of solidarity involvement starting with a micro-sociological analysis which concentrates on individual reasons. Everything in the analysis above tends to demonstrate the extent to which it is illusory to seek to understand how voluntary groups and involvement in them function if one remains attached to a substantialist definition of the groups as undivided unities. Against this fiction of a unity of the collective and models with single actors (Tilly 1986b; Dobry 1986; Fillieule 1997), the results gathered by the GERMM reported here highlight the coexistence in a same temporality of different orders of rationality for activists' investment, thus preventing us from using categorizations in terms of solidarity, of altruism or of interest, as the point of departure for the research.

Third, reasons are to be understood in a dual logic of relationship to the social and associational contexts in which they are located and of individual histories which owe as much to predispositions as to biographical experiences.

Notes

1. *Le Nouvel Observateur*, 18-24 December 1997, 10-25.
2. CEVIPOF (Centre d'étude de la vie politique française) exit poll, May 1995, N=4078, cited in Mayer (1997).
3. CEVIPOF/CIDSP (Centre d'informatisation des données de science politique)/CRAPS (Centre de recherche administrative politique et sociale)/*Libération* exit poll, 26-31 May 1997, N=3010, cited in Mayer (1997).
4. SOFRES Poll for Secours Populaire, Fédérations Mutuelles de France and A2C, 7-8 November 1997, N=1000, cited in Mayer (1997).
5. At the same time, the number of associations created every year is increasing dramatically (Barthélémy 1994; Laville and Sainsaulieu 1997; MAUSS 1998): in 1975, 20,000 new associations were counted, 47,000 in 1985 and 65,000 in 1994.
6. SOFRES poll for the Secours populaire, the Fédérations mutuelles de France and A2C, 7-8 November 1997, N=1000, cited in Mayer (1997).
7. The GERMM (Groupe d'étude et de recherche sur les mutations du militantisme, or Study and Research Group on Mutations in Political Activism) is a research group of the Association Française de Science Politique which I have been co-chairing with Nonna Mayer since October 1994. It brings together researchers working on political activism within associations which have in common the fact of being built on other solidarities than professional or political ones, specializing in defending causes such as the fight against AIDS, humanitarism, the fight against social exclusion, antiracism, and defense of immigrants. A questionnaire was sent to the following groups: Ligue des Droits de l'Homme, FASTI, SOS-Racisme, MRAP, Ras L'Front, Manifeste contre le Front National, CIMADE, France terre d'Asile, Droit au Logement, Act Up, AIDES, Restos du Cœur, Amnesty International, and pro-choice and antiabortion movements. The question of solidarity is currently the object of a research project funded by the Ministry of Social Affairs and the Fondation de France, entitled "producing new solidarities." I would like to thank Nonna Mayer, Christophe Broqua, Sophie Duchesne, and Camille Hamidi with whom I am conducting this research.
8. "On écartera facilement l'ambition substantialiste qui s'efforce de saisir la signification des pratiques et des attitudes de solidarité de manière anhistorique. Comme si la 'solidarité' existait 'en soi', et qu'il suffisait d'en appréhender la signifcation pour pouvoir dire: 'ceci est de l'ordre de la solidarité', 'ceci n'en est pas'. Dans cette perspective, que tout conduit à écarter (la signification du terme n'est pas la même en tous temps, elle est elle-même objet de controverses entre des acteurs intéressés à sa promotion) on fait comme si le chercheur était en mesure de trouver 'la bonne signification' en dépit des divergences et des oppositions repérables chez ceux qui 'font' de la solidarité" (our translation).
9. See also Siméant (1998) on the history of the *sans-papiers* movements in the 1970s and the 1980s.
10. If before 1987, 90 percent of volunteers in AIDES were male, by 1993, only 57 percent of activists were men. The rise in the number of women in AIDES compares to the proportionately weaker proportion of homosexual men and women in Act Up (44 percent against 62 percent). Women are in effect 85 percent heterosexual, against only 15 percent men. This phenomenon is explained by an altruistic commit-

ment to AIDES and by an influx of volunteers from the health and social services fields, a strongly feminine sector directly involved with sick people.

11. "Une stratégie intéressée que la science ne peut pas reprendre à son compte sans danger. Il y a une manipulation symbolique de la définition du politique. L'enjeu de la lutte est un enjeu de lutte" (our translation).

12. The term "moral political activism" is habitually used to designate, on the one hand, the forms of involvement which purport to be disinterested, in the sense that they are directed toward the support of others or of the community as a whole, and, on the other hand, groups characterized by the promotion of interests which are precisely not material interests but which refer in a normative manner to a morality relative to the organization of society (Agrikoliansky 1997, 14).

13. One can thus avoid repeating another common mistake in the literature on new social movements, which for a long time consisted in wanting to reserve for this type of group such or such qualities and/or orientations, such as, for example, the centrality of identity, which are, however, just as present in the worker's movement.

14. Such an orientation means an appeal to a better integration of psychological concepts and methods in the study of social movements. In that respect, the work currently done by Bert Klandermans shows one seminal direction (Klandermans 1997).

15. The multiple methodological questions raised by the study of motivations are largely dealt with in psychology, but rarely in the field of social movements. For example, experts in this area have cautioned that data on motivation may be biased due to the tendency toward socially desirable responding. Stated motives may be more revealing of people's expectations about what they are supposed to say than of the actual past experiences, needs, and goals that prompted people to join an organization.

16. The responses to an open question in our survey ("What led you to join or support this association?") were submitted to a lexical analysis. We used ALCESTE computer software. The classification and regrouping of responses in terms of proximity between units of lexical context results in a certain number of distinct types of discourse "lexical worlds."

17. The following responses give a good idea of this type of motivation: "My desire to make myself useful, also to use my life to help men and women who maybe haven't have the luck I've had"; "The need to give one's time, one's affection, which until then I'd devoted to my family"; "I've been through a lot of difficulties in my life which have given me a certain amount of experience. I needed to offer this experience to those who asked for it, with the aim of giving a deeper aim to my life"; "Above all, a need to help someone who really needs me. To feel that I'm contributing to something, being useful."

18. As the following responses illustrate: "My being HIV positive, the distress of the sick at the hospital, the promise made to a friend who died, the need to find cohesion, a community expression"; "Fear, guilt, to have a clear conscience following the decease of my HIV positive brother and my friend of sixteen years who became positive four years ago"; "And then there was one day, I didn't know it would be the last. I don't have the courage to describe what happened next. Over the course of Claude's five hospitalizations, I got to know other sufferers, also people close to me."

19. To borrow the title of an article by Alain Caillé: "La sociologie de l'intérêt est-elle intéressante? A propos de l'utilisation du paradigme économique en sociologie"

(1981). Cf also Caillé (1994) for an explanation of the paradigm of giving used by this writer.

20.   Which doesn't only mean that individuals stick to thinking their motivated actions are disinterested. The *illusio* mechanism also functions inversely, from the reappropriation into the social world of the tools used in research, the volunteer workers often tending to justify their actions by explicitly interested motivations (on this point, suggested to us by Sophie Duchesne, cf. Paugam 1997).

21.   See for example, Godelier (1996). Florence Passy says the same thing when she notes that "altruism is not an act inherent in human nature but is a cultural construction . . . . The significant rootedness of activists in solidarity movements in Christian networks, where helping one's peers is a constitutive element of Christian cosmology, allows us to predict that there is such a cultural anchorage of altruistic action around which the solidarity movement in western Europe has organized" (Passy 1998, 241). See also Elias (1985) on the extravagant behavior of the ancien régime nobility and Bourdieu (1972) on codes of honor in Kabyl society.

22.   This is what we suggested earlier in *Stratégies de la rue* (1997) when we invoked the necessity of thinking structurally about political involvement, i.e., not to study a type of involvement or demands independently of the system of other involvements and demands, just as it is important not to study any particular element from a repertoire, or such a repertoire, independently of the system of available instruments of struggle. For the same approach in French monographs on movements, see Agrikoliansky (1997), Siméant (1998) and Juhem (1999) who reposition the groups they study in all their historical and contextual depth.

23.   The term "collector" refers to the fact that the volunteer workers have nothing to distribute, the only thing they have to offer having to come from themselves: to give of one's time, to take children from poor families to the seaside, to work in reception, etc. This information is taken from Rebelle and Swiatly (1999).

24.   For example, the Secours populaire organizes rag sales rather than handouts. The visitor to the sale is thus both assisted (the products are very cheap) and at the same time a contributor: he or she participates in funding specific solidarity actions through his/her purchases (Rebelle and Swiatly 1999).

25.   Castel (1995, 412 and 424).

26.   The latter, in her survey on representations of young second-generation immigrants, shows that some see associations as a different way of being politically involved, i.e. in a more "concrete" manner, "closer to peoples concerns." Politics is thus defined negatively, and highly critically, as something abstract and distant; the representational relation between the people, particularly immigrants, and politicians, is questioned.

27.   This can be best observed when associations recruit paid employees from their volunteer workers, thus setting up a competition among equals who are very soon frustrated by a failure that is experienced as a denial of competence, as a questioning of their sincerity and the depth of their commitment. In the groups we have studied this is one of the reasons for the sudden withdrawal of particularly committed activists.

4

Altruism in Voluntary Organizations

Mobilization and Transformation of Voluntary Action in Italy

Costanzo Ranci

Introduction

This chapter analyzes processes of mobilization and organization of voluntary action in nonprofit organizations which pursue aims in the public interest by providing services and protecting disadvantaged social groups and at times by exerting political pressure to obtain benefits for the beneficiaries of the services provided.

Therefore, attention is concentrated on organizations whose goal, as opposed to other types of organization that act in the public interest, is to obtain advantages exclusively for persons who are clearly distinct from their membership. Their action is furthermore focused more on the supply and distribution of services rather than on political action aimed at obtaining new social benefits. The action performed by these organizations can therefore be considered as a form of social altruism, a type of action that takes "the form of a generously offered gift" (Mauss 1950), although offered on an organized basis.

The presence of an altruistic goal distinguishes this type of collective action from that performed in pursuit of a collective good even when it involves a relative disadvantage for those involved resulting from free riders (Olson 1965). In this sense, participation in a pacifist or environmentalist organization does not constitute a form of altruistic voluntary action because the action is performed in pursuit of a benefit which would be available to all. Action may be classified as altruistic voluntary, however, when it assumes no direct return, when it is an action that excludes any direct advantage being obtained for the persons who participate.[1]

On the other hand, this form of action is also distinct from political altruism, which characterizes the basic orientation of what are defined in this book as solidarity movements. The action of nonprofit organizations that pursue altruistic goals differs in two respects from that performed in solidarity movements: it concentrates on providing services and not on political activity (even if this sometimes accompanies the supply of services) and it does not, except in very rare cases, produce any form of social or political conflict since its basic orientation is decidedly that of integrating and cooperating with public authorities. However it must not be forgotten that most nonprofit organizations are founded on clearly distinguishable collective identities and values, which may at times be opposed to those of public institutions.[2]

The problems of analysis raised by the recent increase in this form of action are numerous. In the first place, one must ask what are the causes of the recent diffusion of these organizations. They are mainly connected, as will be seen later, with the crisis of social citizenship and the emergence of an altruistic cultural orientation common to solidarity movements. The second factor, especially—the emergence of altruistic goals—remains without an adequate explanation. A second question concerns the mechanisms by which organizations composed exclusively or prevalently of *conscience constituents* are mobilized. What forms of recruitment are adopted and what type of participation is developed within these organizations? In what sense do they differ from those characteristic of social movements?

In this chapter an attempt is made to provide answers to these questions on the basis of an analysis of the Italian case. First, explanations that have been supplied to justify the persistence, if not the diffusion, of this form of action in contemporary society are considered. A scheme of interpretation is then proposed, identifying the elements of novelty that have emerged in this form of action in recent decades. Finally, an attempt is made to reconstruct the basic mechanism for the "mobilization of altruism" that these organizations adopt.

The Determinants of Voluntary Action

Interpretation not merely of the persistence but of the renewed diffusion of voluntary action in contemporary society has only just begun, even if authoritative contributions are already part of the international tradition in the social sciences (Beveridge 1948; Titmuss 1971).

The most recent analyses have concentrated on the system determinants of voluntary action, concerned above all about locating its development in the context of the crisis and transformation of modern welfare systems (Kramer 1981; Paci 1987). These approaches see the distinguishing feature of voluntary organizations as their ability to activate mechanisms which allocate services differently from those prevalent in the public and private sectors and which are particularly suited to meeting post-materialist needs. The recent revival of voluntary action can be traced to the emergence of social needs which find adequate answers neither from the public nor from the private sectors and for which one observes both a "state failure" (Weisbrod 1977) and a "market failure" (Hansmann 1980). According to Weisbrod (1977), the voluntary sector, not being obliged to seek to satisfy the preferences of the median voter, is more able than the state to provide services to subgroups of the population which are undersupplied. According to Hansmann (1980), goods and services for which the supply determines an "asymmetry of infor-mation" to the disadvantage of consumers (e.g., all those personal care serv-ices the quality of which is difficult to verify by the recipients in advance), are produced more reliably by nonprofit organizations which, since they are not profit seeking, do not expose consumers to the propensity of profit seek-ing organizations to exploit their information advantage.

The main limit of these interpretations is that they only consider demand factors and not also supply factors, giving no importance to the conditions in and mechanisms by which voluntary action is produced. There is no doubt that the crisis of mature welfare systems, and the ample variety of material need and ethical demands that it leaves untouched, constitute the structural and cultural context within which contemporary voluntary action has grown. However in various countries this same crisis has fostered not just a redis-covery of voluntary action but also a withdrawal of commitment toward and responsibility for the public good, a mistrust of public welfare systems and a return to the values of the market. These contrasting signals require a com-plex explanation of the conditions and mechanisms that constitute voluntary action.

Supply-side explanations insist on the altruistic motivation of individuals or on the emergence of moral and religious beliefs which attribute ethical or "redeeming" values to philanthropic practices. James (1989) explains the greater diffusion of voluntary organizations in some countries on the basis not only of the existence of unsatisfied social demand but also of the presence of "religious entrepreneurs," a foundation of benefactors with strong ethical or religious motivations. Other authors (Donati 1993) have identified the causes of the growth of voluntary organizations in the emergence of new cultural orientations that developed as a reaction to the interruption of chan-nels of communication between "life worlds" and the welfare system, and which offer themselves as new sources of ethical values for reconstructing a sense of civic responsibility.

These interpretations undoubtedly have the merit of showing that voluntary action is mobilized on the basis of norms and values that are different from those of for-profit and public sector action. Furthermore, they put the accent on the accompanying socio-cultural dynamics of the emergence of organized altruism in contemporary society. Nevertheless, little has been done to explore the specific ways in which the presence of ethical or religious values is activated in society to produce specific organized action with altruistic purposes.

In addition to structural determinants and belief systems, it thus becomes important to pay attention to the organizational processes that lie at the basis of the development of voluntary action (Knoke 1990). The main condition for the diffusion of voluntary action lies in the existence of a stable organizational foundation and a source of collective identity; in other words, by the existence of organizations that "attract" altruistic motivations and organize them to produce a service of public usefulness. In this duality—the construction of a collective identity and the provision of a service—is found the genuine peculiarity of new voluntary organizations pursuing altruistic goals.

A New Form of Altruism

Voluntary organizations can be considered as one of the most important forms, in mature welfare systems, for mobilizing altruistic attitudes present in civil society. The recent diffusion of these organizations seems to contradict the contention that the concentration of altruistic "resources" in a few specific organizations has the effect of "atrophying" the availability in primary groups and local communities. My starting point is the idea that a voluntary organization is the main channel for the activation of these resources in differentiated societies. This mobilizing channel nevertheless brings with it definitions of altruistic action which are not basically opposed to the universalistic model of citizenship that historically has legitimized modern systems of welfare.

Modern welfare states have developed as substitutes for social protection systems founded on altruism and charity (Alber 1982). Nevertheless, modern citizenship does paradoxically require a form of altruism as basis for the diffusion of civic responsibility. According to Titmuss (1971) the concept of social rights embraces also the "right to give" in nonmaterial as well material ways. The altruism developed in welfare systems is a rational altruism, independent of religious and moral convictions, aimed at pursuing egalitarian and redistributive social objectives. It is a sort of recognition of the equality of rights of all members of society. This was the crucial condition for citizens to adopt responsible behavior (expressed, for example, in correct fiscal behavior) and must be inscribed in a context of social integration that guarantees the equality of all citizens and the reciprocity of individual altruism (Titmuss 1971). The universalism of the welfare state has thus constituted a *sine qua non* for the development of altruism among citizens.

Furthermore, the altruism of citizens is a bond established between strangers. In Titmuss' well-known analysis of blood donors (Titmuss 1971), it is the very anonymity of the voluntary donation that makes the English gratuitous system superior to that of the United States, dominated by the market. An "impersonal" act of altruism must be based on the guarantee of reciprocity of the other, and in a more general sense of belonging to the civil community. On the other hand, it is only the rule of anonymity that guarantees that the public blood transfusion service is provided in an egalitarian and undifferentiated manner for all citizens. An altruistic action is therefore "civic" when it is aimed at total strangers, not as the recipients of an affective investment, but because this action is the essence of civility (Walzer 1995).

Different factors have contributed to the crisis of this form of altruism. They are correlated both with the weakening of the sense of citizenship and the growing inadequacy of support provided on an impersonal basis. This impersonality, typical of altruism between citizens, constitutes a requisite suitable to assistance offered independently of a direct and personal relationship between donor and beneficiary, as well as on the idea that anyone may benefit from it. (It was not by chance that to illustrate the potential of altruism in society, Titmuss analyzed the donation of a good, such as blood, that is relatively easily transferable.) These necessary conditions have virtually excluded all the services based on the recognition of a particular need and a specific relationship from the circuit of altruism between citizens (Seligman 1991). Faced with the diffusion of post-material needs, the altruism obtained by citizenship thus shows its limits of extent and effectiveness.

The new altruistic practices found in voluntary organizations are very different from civic altruism that is developed in social citizenship. What characterizes these new practices is: (1) the discretionary nature of the altruistic action (it does not originate on the basis of recognized rights so much as on voluntary choices on the part of volunteers; (2) the construction of a *bond of exclusive belonging* between those who practice altruism that does not include the beneficiaries; (3) the provision of help and support *that does not require any reciprocity*. In many developed countries these practices are widespread and organized to the extent that they designate what has been defined as a "third sector" beyond state and market (Salamon and Anheier 1996) or a new "*économie solidaire*" (Laville 1994).

The diffusion of these practices does not seem to be explainable in adequate terms by considering it as a reaction to the limits of growth of welfare citizenship. On the contrary, it suggests a possible overturning of the relationship between public and private spheres. In contemporary societies the common good depends more on the capacity to activate *private virtues* than it does in modern societies (Etzioni 1993). Compared to modern citizenship, the altruism of voluntary organizations has a more accentuated unilateral and asymmetric character. It emerges in social contexts which, because of their degree of internal fragmentation, do not easily allow altruism based on expectations of reciprocity.[3]

The persistence of social altruism in contemporary societies is then related to the importance that problems of identity assume in them. In a social system in which giving no longer forms part of a social ritual, altruistic practice becomes an act that not only confirms social bonds, but also procures and attributes new identities (Wuthnow 1991). It may establish bonds of equality and equal dignity, but it more easily gives rise to differences and inequalities that are difficult to close. In a context of considerable social differentiation and a great weakening of reciprocal ties, we can expect the unilateral and asymmetric nature of altruism to become increasingly more accentuated. As opposed to the altruism of citizenship, the asymmetric altruism practiced by voluntary organizations is the reflection of differences and identities that are increasingly segmented and difficult to unite. This makes it intrinsically particularist and discretionary in character, a resource for creating ambivalent relationships of help and power.

Recent Changes in Voluntary Action

The existence of voluntary organizations providing services in the public interest is certainly not new historically. Nineteenth-century philanthropy maintained more or less the same unidirectional and asymmetric form of help. The progressive expansion of state intervention during the twentieth century weakened these forms of action, confining them to particularism and privatism. Today voluntary action is nevertheless assuming a new dimension as the expansionist phase of the welfare state begins to wane. In fact, the current scenario sees these organizations playing not so much a role complementary to government provision as that of a partner specializing in the supply of primary services.

This change of role has coincided with a profound transformation in the forms of management and organization of voluntary action. As we will see later, the demise of the privatism characteristic of traditional philanthropy coincided with the secularization and the growing autonomy of voluntary organizations from the control of the church, and was accompanied by a propensity to develop more structured and rational forms of organization. One far from negligible effect of these processes was, in more recent times, the professionalization of voluntary organizations and their fully qualified inclusion in the public welfare system.

This section focuses on the main changes that have occurred in Italy in the forms of action of voluntary organizations with altruistic goals. Most of these transformations occurred in the mid-1970s when there was a considerable expansion of voluntary action, particularly in the area of welfare services.[4] This wave of mobilization was accompanied by a distinct change in the forms and content of the action.

The course of the phenomenon, though difficult to reconstruct due to the lack of empirical data prior to 1983 and the fragmented nature of the available data, can be summarized in general terms as follows. In the middle of the 1970s new voluntary groups started to appear, mainly of religious inspiration but independent of the ecclesiastical hierarchy. Many of these developed rapidly into organizations specializing in providing social services (Colozzi and Rossi 1985; Ranci 1985). A national survey carried out in 1983 confirmed the considerable presence of recently-formed voluntary organizations, indicating a rising trend that started in 1975.[5] A second survey performed ten years later (in 1993) confirmed the diffusion of the phenomenon (an increase from 7,200 organizations surveyed in 1983 to 9,200 in 1993), again disclosing a considerable number of recently-formed organizations (32 percent of them were set up between 1985 and 1990). A third, still more recent survey (carried out in 1997) showed a further increase in the phenomenon (13,000 organizations surveyed) and again the recent formation of a substantial proportion of the organizations (24 percent were set up between 1990 and 1995), as well as confirming the existence of a considerable leap in the number of organizations during the five-year period 1975-80.[6]

The data confirm that a diffusion of voluntary organizations occurred in Italy starting in the mid-1970s and that the diffusion continued to increase during the 1980s and 1990s. At a distance of more than twenty years since the start of this increasing trend, this development has resulted in the widespread diffusion of a much larger number of stable organizations than existed in the past, but which maintain a fluidity that characterizes the phenomenon. Apart from the "explosion" in voluntary action that occurred between the end of the 1970s and the beginning of the 1980s, the data show that a proportion of the voluntary organizations overcame the spontaneous and fragmentary character of their "birth phase" and gave life to established organizations.

An explanation of the change that characterized voluntary action in Italy must therefore demonstrate why the wave of new voluntary action that emerged in civil society was channeled from 1975 onwards into new organizations rather than into those already in existence. Secondly, it must show the processes that supported the organizational stability of some voluntary organizations.

The Exit from Traditional Philanthropy

The traditional presence of voluntary organizations in Italy was for a long time characterized by a "charitative" orientation. It was the orientation of Catholic philanthropic and charitable associations with a nineteenth-century tradition. The social context in which these organizations worked for decades was marked by residual government intervention in social welfare and by an extensive proliferation of private institutions dedicated to offering welfare services. In this situation, the work of charitable organizations developed alongside that of private organizations and shared the same religious and "charitative" inspiration.[7]

The basis of the "charitative" orientation lay in the ethical concept of voluntarism: it was founded on the "moral duty" of those who gave help and not on the "right" of the poor to welfare. Charitable work was done for the purpose of performing "acts of compassion" (Wuthnow 1991) for individuals identified as in a state of need. On the basis of this conception, heavily imbued with religious values, voluntary action translated into traditional charity (the purpose of which was to redistribute the "superfluous") aimed at edifying the morale of the volunteers.

The diffusion of voluntary organizations that started in the mid-1970s occurred in a profoundly changed social and cultural environment. The ending of the social movements of the 1960s and 1970s left room free for social activism that was no longer dominated by "strong" ideological concepts. At the same time, the demand for social rights by these movements spread through society, expressed as a demand to widen and consolidate the rights of citizenship. On the other hand, the welfare state commenced a stage of maturity and explicit recognition of universalistic objectives.[8]

The diffusion of new voluntary groups reflected this changed scenario. The old charitative philosophy was abandoned in favor of action aimed to "fight against emargination," in which voluntary action became a form of tutelage and representation of social groups excluded from the benefits of public welfare. The duty of volunteers then came to be based on recognition of the social right of the emarginated to assistance and reintegration into society. The action of new groups did not consist of protest and representing rights so much as setting up services in local communities to offer the emarginated a chance of reintegration. Voluntary action thus undertook an ambitious task: "sharing with the last" was proposed as a new model of social commitment, antagonistic to institutional approaches.[9]

The cultural area in which the new forms of voluntary action grew was very distant from traditional philanthropy. The difficulty of filling old organizations with the new content was also increased by the heavy centralization of those organizations. Control of these organizations had long remained concentrated in the hands of a religious leadership that guaranteed respect of principles dictated by ecclesiastical authorities. The leaders of new groups, meanwhile, came mostly from local initiatives, started during the period of the social movements, which then converted from political and ideological protest to providing services (Melucci 1996). They used their existing network of contacts to mobilize and coalesce disillusioned militants and new members around the new project. The decisive move came, however, from grassroots religious groups, who rediscovered new possibilities for action independent of the ecclesiastical hierarchy after a long period of restiveness.

The growth of the new voluntary action has been determined by a composite set of factors: the diffusion of new values as a basis for social commitment; the rigid centralization of traditional organizations; and the simultaneous presence of local networks and capacities inherited from social movements that were harvested and dominated by spontaneous groups from a Catholic background. The room for initiative thus created was occupied by groups with a new identity whose action, although not aimed at conflict with public policies, very soon showed up the limits to growth of the Italian welfare system.

The Tendency to Specialization

From 1985 onwards, studies on the voluntary sector unanimously registered the passage from a "pioneer" phase of experimentation to progressive specialization and professionalization of a substantial number of voluntary organizations (Ascoli 1987; Borzaga 1991). Specialization was the result of a selective process which allowed only organizations with greater resources to survive; the others were either marginalized or destined to disappear.[10]

Specialization reproduces a tendency already observed in voluntary organizations in other countries (Kramer 1981). The Italian case is striking because of the rapidity of the process, especially considering the initially nonspecialist and informal character of voluntary organizations. The passage from the tumultuous start-up phase to that of proper well-organized services actually occurred in the course of a few years. To understand the reasons behind this rapidity, we must consider that the new voluntary groups started up services which were extremely innovative and identified social needs not yet recognized by the public sector. The provision of "primary" services (Kramer 1981) brought voluntary organizations to an "overload" crisis within the space of a few years, as they sought to meet needs that had become visible and recognized, but not adequately covered by direct state intervention. Local authorities also proceeded very quickly to recognize the welfare function of voluntary organizations and contract out services with them.

The spread of new voluntary initiatives, which continued throughout the 1980s, reflected this emphasis on specialization. The range of activity widened. In addition to social assistance and therapy-rehabilitation services, there was a diffusion of first-aid intervention, safeguarding of rights, specialist assistance, and so on. There emerged a "specialist" model of voluntary action that identifies organizations providing high-standard services requiring specialist training. A basic peculiarity of these organizations is that they reward competence. Altruistic commitment does not originate with ethical or sociopolitical attitudes, but with a professional vocation that is placed at the service of society. The meaning of voluntary work is seen not so much in terms of ethics and intentions, nor more general social effects, as much as in the effectiveness of the solutions provided in responding to specific needs.

The gradual specialization of voluntary organizations indicates the completion of a passage from forms of altruism based on ethical motivations to collectively produced services based on technical competence. The transition

from a charitative to a specialist model of action also makes voluntary organizations an interesting opportunity for new middle-class professionals
who were previously inactive in this field, attracting more skilled volunteers
than in the past.

Specialization nevertheless caused a radical change in the process of mobilization as well as in the definition of the role of the volunteer. Voluntary
work did not appear adequate to the task of providing increasingly specific
and sophisticated services. The new services required individuals with specific skills willing to make substantial professional investments; they required
a figure closer to that of the professional rather than the traditional figure of
the volunteer. The process of partial professionalization that had been set in
motion created at the same time a demand for finance to pay personnel and
also to bring facilities and equipment up to the new standards.

The consequences of this new situation for organizations were considerable. First of all, there was a drastic reduction in the number of volunteers.
The increase in larger financial transactions and the rationalization of work
required an internal administrative system. Control over organizations by
volunteers tended to diminish, while control by skilled and professional
workers increased. Finally, organizations became more dependent on outside
resources for finance. Maintaining organizations required steady flows of
cash, but this could only be achieved by finding regular purchasers for their
services. Hence the increasingly dense network of financial and economic
relations with state institutions.

The Relationship with Public Authorities

The 1980s and 1990s were characterized by the spread of strategies seeking
to involve voluntary organizations in public policies, particularly on the part
of local authorities. In a period of reduced public expenditure, a tendency to
delegate welfare service provision to voluntary organizations prevailed in
exchange for substantial financial support.

Responsibility for running services of public interest was accompanied by
strong appreciation and approval of the work of voluntary organizations to
the extent that in 1991 national legislation acknowledged their work as "in
the public interest" and regulated their financial dealings with public administrations. Discussion of a growing interdependence between voluntary and
public sectors raised the prospect of an increase in the number of public contracts awarded and of increasing cooperation between the two sectors.

The greater attention of public authorities toward the voluntary sector was
due to the desire of the former to widen the supply of welfare services beyond the state supply alone. The strengthening of the voluntary sector
throughout the 1980s was thus assisted by the support of public administrations. That they left their "separateness" behind them should be fully recog-

nized as one of the most salient characteristics of the "new" voluntary sector.[11] In many cases, public funding was essential to guarantee continuity to the organizations and to support their professionalization.

The presence of substantial public funding has created a certain dependence. However, examination of individual cases raises two points. First, organizations have maintained considerable leverage over public authorities because of their monopolistic position; each cut in finance produces an equivalent cut in services to the population. Second, regulations governing the awarding of public contracts do not provide for effective control by public authorities, nor do they give precise rules for implementing projects. Public funding is therefore supplied under a regime which Kramer (1981) defined as "pragmatic cooperation" which allows considerable respect for the autonomy of voluntary organizations.

The increased flow of public funds to the voluntary sector does not seem to have greatly affected the forms of action and of mobilization of organizations. Nevertheless, government interest in voluntary action has undoubtedly caused them to accelerate the process of specialization. This effect, however, was not caused so much by the forms of public control as by the mechanism of transferring social responsibility from public institutions to voluntary organizations.

Public funding has, in fact, allowed many voluntary organizations to develop their activities in areas in which there was no direct public provision.[12] For a certain time, the development of innovative services allowed these organizations to avoid standardized management of services, but at the same time it pushed them onto a frontier beyond the reach of public sector intervention. The lack of alternative services consequently set in motion a process whereby these organizations became socially responsible, inexorably transforming the original motivations of the commitment. Faced with the urgency of the social needs, ethical or political considerations counted less than the ability to provide effective and professional answers. Providing an indispensable service became increasingly less dependent on the discretion of altruism.

The partial professionalization of the voluntary sector constitutes, then, the perverse outcome of a pioneering initiative which, since it could not find institutional actors capable of taking direct responsibility to meet the needs, was obliged to "take over" the area of needs which it had helped to bring to public attention. Cooperation with public institutions thus assisted the passage from mobilization of altruism on an ethical basis to one on a specialist basis, and the channeling of this form of action toward professionalization.

The Mobilization of Volunteers

The picture outlined confirms the idea that the recent diffusion of voluntary organizations coincided with considerable variety in the content and the logic of the action. Although at the beginning the new forms of altruistic voluntary action assumed characteristics typical of spontaneous groups, they quickly had to face a rapid process of specialization. Consequently, after the explosive growth that occurred in the 1970s and 1980s, many voluntary organizations went beyond the spontaneous and fluid stage typical of the *statu nascenti* phase of collective behaviors and developed established organizational structures. In order to understand which organizational processes allowed these organizations to survive it is necessary to reconstruct the processes of mobilizing members and the forms of participation. The following section looks at these two aspects.

Who Are the Volunteers?

The mobilization base of voluntary organizations appears very diversified both in terms of social background and of age, sex, and marital status. As found by other research studies, volunteers consist mainly of members of the middle and upper classes and have received higher education (Ascoli 1987; Dekker and van den Broek 1998). Composition by age and sex, however, is more heterogeneous: there are a large number of males and young people alongside large numbers of middle-aged married women. Furthermore, the data on employment show on the payrolls a considerable number of persons quantitatively exceeding the more traditional figures of housewives and female pensioners (Frisanco and Ranci 1999).

Some differences emerge when different models of voluntary action are considered. Charitative associations have the most homogeneous and most traditional recruitment base, dominated by the figure of the middle-aged to elderly woman from the upper classes in a family role (housewife or pensioner). In the new voluntary organizations, students and workers predominate. For these people voluntary action constitutes a sort of "apprenticeship" to the profession, or a supplement to or extension of a professional role already acquired. The dominant role that these figures assume in the more specialist organizations also modifies the characteristics of their voluntary commitment in terms of motivations, time given to the organization, technical qualifications, and prospects of personal and career progress connected with the voluntary commitment. In general, the more recent insertion of these new voluntary figures—young people, workers with jobs, individuals without work—shows that the capacity of organizations to attract volunteers has gone beyond the traditional "reservoirs" of the parishes and religious associations, to reach groups that traditionally have shown little interest in this type of action.[13]

Recruitment

The great variety of motivation behind the mobilization of volunteers requires the construction of a homogeneous and shared framework of principles (Snow et al. 1986). The recruitment model that prevails in voluntary organizations is what might be defined as an "experimental-rational" model (Long and Hadden 1983): membership occurs not so much by sharing a consistent and integrated system of beliefs, as by immediate practical involvement within an organizational network of the association. The "recruitment strategies" adopted by voluntary organizations show (apart from the significant exception of the "fight against emargination" organizations) that the most important requirements for membership relate less to specific ideological convictions than to a general willingness to make an altruistic commitment and a set of skills of direct use in providing a specific service. By not tying membership to a strong adherence to collective beliefs, this depends more on the results achieved in the short term than on the accomplishment of overall goals.

The studies that have been done on the recruitment of volunteers show the voluntary action as an area of participation that is completely foreign to the more "political" forms of social and civic involvement.[14] Research carried out in Italy shows an almost total absence of connections with political parties, trade union bodies, and protest organizations (ecology groups, advocacy associations, etc.). Moreover, only a small minority of volunteers have been militants in trade union or party organizations (Ranci 1992; IREF 1998; Frisanco and Ranci 1999). There is, however, a much greater participation in other voluntary organizations operating in the welfare and cultural and recreational fields. This is connected with a high level of interest in society, shown by high exposure to media.

Religious beliefs are generally considered as one of the main factors facilitating the mobilization of volunteers. Empirical research shows the existence of a dense network of connections between voluntary organizations and the Catholic world (Ascoli 1987). Studies generally find that a substantial proportion of voluntary organizations is actively assisted by the church and that approximately two-thirds of organizations cooperate with church bodies.[15] The Catholic world is therefore a "privileged" area of recruitment, in which many organizations can select volunteers whose motives are already congruent with their objectives. The cultural and organizational closeness of the Catholic world to many voluntary organizations also facilitates block recruitment; a large segment of volunteers has previously been involved in church groups and religious organizations.

A large proportion of volunteers are nevertheless recruited without any previous experience in other voluntary organizations. While the closeness of many charitable organizations to the church provides them with a rich reserve of volunteers who are already socialized into the values of the group, many more-specialized organizations enlist a great number of middle class specialists never previously involved in collective action. In such cases, recruitment draws people from weak relationship networks involved in the same field of action. In Milan, the extension of these weak ties seems significant: 10 percent of volunteers not active in other organizations had assisted before recruitment in providing services in the same field of work as that of the voluntary organization; 19 percent said they had frequently been involved previously in the same type of problem, and on joining the group were able to be involved in a more organized fashion (Ranci 1992).

Membership of a voluntary group does not involve any great cost or risk.[16] In organizations that develop non-conflictual forms of action, recruitment is mostly based on the specific interest in the actual task performed and is valued on the basis of the results obtained in a short time. However, the role played by "conviction" requirements is still important, as shown by the fact that many voluntary organizations recruit from a culturally homogeneous base in which the value of altruism is widespread and supported by religious beliefs. Catholic values are found in a recognized secular setting. Moreover, most voluntary organizations have grown and professionalized, weakening their institutional and cultural ties with the church hierarchies. Therefore, it can be said that the progressive specialization of voluntary action has been accompanied by religious beliefs changing from regulatory principles to a resource for mobilizing volunteers.

Participation and Forms of Voluntary Commitment

What distinguishes voluntary organizations from solidarity movements is that membership entails providing a service to persons who do not belong to the organization itself and that the group is not involved in political action. This gives rise to two unique characteristics: on the one hand, much of the voluntary work does not necessarily involve contact with other members of the organization, but is performed through a relationship with the beneficiaries of the organization; on the other hand, it assumes the character of service provision and is assessed along parameters such as effectiveness and the continuity of the work performed.

At the organizational level this situation gives rise to specific problems. The survival of an altruistic voluntary organization depends on the difficult combination of two demands that can come into conflict, and even lead to organizational dilemmas (Sills 1957): on the one hand, the demand to encourage voluntary participation and, on the other, to ensure the provision of an efficient service. The conflict between participation and efficient functioning is intrinsic to the existence of groups that base their identity on providing a service. The capacity of organizations to maintain a stable and active participation of volunteers depends on how this conflict is resolved (Pearce 1993).

In general, voluntary organizations adopt an organizational structure that lies halfway between a democratic association and a professional team. The driving nucleus is generally concentrated in a decision-making body composed of the founding members and the supervisors of the operating groups. The most important decision-making functions concerning the planning of work, finance, relations with local institutions, and the management of internal relations are centralized in this body. The elected nature of this body does not prevent its members from keeping their posts for a long time and from changes being made by co-opting new members.

Volunteers participate in two ways: by working to provide the service and by attending periodic assemblies, which are also generally attended by the "contributor members" who finance and promote groups from the outside. While in the less structured organizations, the vote of an assembly maintains a certain power of direction and control, in most cases it constitutes a symbolic occasion and functions as ritual to confirm the identity of the organization.

The balance between participation and administration is therefore achieved by concentrating decision-making in a very small body and by clearly distinguishing between operating functions and democratic legitimization. Officially all voluntary associations have a democratic organization based on the election of officers. The actual functioning of organizations helps considerably, however, to maintain the permanence of the managing group and to equip it with the power needed to keep a close guard on the collective identity of the organization.

The distinction between operational and legitimization functions results in three main forms of membership: the active participation and very strong identification with the association of the members who assume responsibility for running the organization; the commitment of the volunteers who actually provide the service; and the symbolic membership of the contributor members. As a rule, these three levels of commitment may each develop independently of the others.[17]

The participation of most volunteers consists exclusively of working to provide the service, with no involvement in running the organization. Consequently, incentives for this form of participation come from the relationship established with the beneficiaries.

As opposed to volunteers, active members constitute a nucleus that identifies very strongly with the collective goals of the organization and are regularly involved in decision-making. Assuming a leadership role imposes considerable cost to the individual due to the strong concentration of the decision-making and administrative processes. Power and willingness to invest in collective action tend therefore to coincide. This is one effect of the scarce power differentiation in these organizations, but it also tells us that running an organization requires a large investment of time and energy. It shows us the costs connected with the position of leader and explains why the position is not particularly sought after in these organizations.

The capacity to mobilize volunteers is tied to the centralization of decision-making and the adoption of an "inclusive" and pragmatic recruitment model. The limited participation of volunteers in defining strategies, nevertheless, leaves this form of mobilization vulnerable to fluctuations in the attitudes of society. A favorable or unfavorable social climate may affect the flow of volunteers, and it may also encourage specific forms of action, independently of the seriousness or urgency of the needs which they meet. Furthermore, this model of participation does not appear adequate to generate changes in the mechanisms of social exclusion. These objectives, which lie at the basis of the "fight against emargination" developed by organizations formed in the first half of the 1980s, require more selective recruitment and more intense and costly involvement in running the organizations.

Voluntary Action between Identity and Service

The persistence of voluntary action in a society with a developed welfare system cannot be interpreted as the simple effect of the survival of pre-modern forms of social altruism. Considerable empirical data show the constant vitality and new features of this phenomenon. This dynamism of voluntary action also coincides with profound changes in the processes of mobilization and organization toward forms more adequate to the conditions of a differentiated and pluralistic society.

The direction that voluntary action is taking may be interpreted as progressive differentiation and specialization. It marks the passage from traditional philanthropy, motivated by religious convictions or community ties, to organized voluntary action, or pragmatic activity performed using associations and based on rational principles and specific goals.

The emerging mobilization model is inclusive in the sense that altruistic commitment in voluntary organizations does not require the adoption of ideological values, nor does it imply a strong commitment to the organizational goals, but is needed to perform some immediate action. If it is easily facilitated by the existence of religious and civic beliefs that attribute a particular value to altruism (whether understood as a redeeming action or as a civic duty), mobilization nevertheless does not occur so much for the purpose of spreading the values of altruism in society as it does as an opportunity to take concrete action. Alongside traditional ethical and religious motives, the decision to participate is also increasingly affected by career considerations and social opportunities. Voluntary commitment is no longer considered as an alternative to paid employment, but as an activity that is adjacent or complementary to a paid job.

The process outlined could be interpreted in terms of progressive bureaucratization of voluntary action, in line with the dynamics already observed in other research (Kramer 1981). From this viewpoint, the recent expansion of the voluntary sector in Italy may be considered the premise for the development of a well-developed professional nonprofit sector, capable of guaranteeing efficient and effective services to substitute or supplement state services, but also exposed to greater institutional homogenization and to a preference for non-innovative lines of action (Barbetta 1997).

The considerations made so far nevertheless suggest a less evolutionary interpretation of transformations in the voluntary sector. The hypothesis of progressive bureaucratization contains the risk of an uncritical application of analytic models that were formulated with reference to professional organizations and of paying insufficient attention to the specific nature of voluntary organization with altruistic aims.

Their peculiarity lies in combining the characteristics of spontaneous associations with those of service provision agencies. Two parallel structures of responsibility and power exist side by side within them, legitimated by two organizational visions that produce values, norms, and preferences that at times conflict. The typical structure of a service agency is seen in the way it produces a service, while the typical structure of an association manifests itself in the way people adhere to the mission of the organization. The internal organization is thus based upon two processes that tend to diverge: the mobilization of a membership of conscience constituents and the provision of a specialized service.

The mobilization of conscience constituents requires, first of all, nonmonetary incentives: social reputation, sense of belonging, compatibility with value systems. Secondly, it requires that the organization have diversified forms of participation in response to varying degrees of commitment and involvement. Finally, it requires rituals and symbol systems aimed at feeding and cementing bonds among members and at keeping the collective mission alive. The purpose of this organizational activity is to strengthen the fundamental spirit that constitutes the collective identity of the organization, though at times this may act to the detriment of functions intrinsic to achieving the organization's practical aims.

Providing a service, however, requires adopting forms of control over the work of volunteers. Furthermore, the need to maintain high management standards requires material incentives to attract people with a high level of skills, the development of a "professional culture" to encourage greater specialization, and the introduction of measures of efficiency and effectiveness both in actual service provision and in decision-making processes. Finally, the consequent need to maintain constant flows of cash makes cooperation with state institutions and social and political legitimization of the organization crucial.

The simultaneous presence of different functional demands lies at the basis of what Billis (1993) calls "the ambiguous nature" of voluntary organizations. This ambiguity reveals itself in the vast number of tensions and conflicts that afflict these organizations. The areas of management where conflict mainly occurs are the formulation of the mission, the control of resources crucial to the organization and the running of service provision. In light of studies carried out by Kramer (1981; Kramer et al. 1993), the greatest conflicts occur between the governing body and the management.[18] However, conflicts between the demands of running the organization and those connected with the participation of members,[19] as well as between different levels of official membership, appear to be equally important.

The ambivalence between identity and service may be considered one of the salient characteristics of an organization caught in the middle of the change from an associative organization to a service agency. If this viewpoint is taken, then the existence of an organizational isomorphism (DiMaggio and Powell 1983) must be assumed, leading virtually all voluntary organizations to take on the features of a service agency.[20] This position appears, nevertheless, weakened not only by research showing the continued existence of a vast area of voluntary organizations that are still capable of mobilizing volunteers, but also by the observation that often it is precisely the ambiguous nature of voluntary organizations that enables them to tackle problems whose solutions elude the private sector and public administrations (Seibel 1989).

It can be stated that the ambivalence between service provision and identity is intrinsic to the existence of organizations that base their identity on the provision of a socially useful service. How this ambivalence is dealt with in organizational terms determines both the internal structure and the capacity to meet the needs and the social responsibilities undertaken by the organization. To put it briefly, the functioning of a voluntary organization consists of drawing up a set of mechanisms designed to hold together and to balance the functions of identity and service provision.[21]

A large variety of organizational solutions have been found to bind together this ambiguity. Voluntary organizations do not adopt homogeneous organizational models, but find quite a diverse balance and mix among the various functions that must be performed. *Both* functions must nevertheless be present for a voluntary organization to maintain its identity. Hence the inevitable tensions that run through most of these organizations. Reaching a point of equilibrium between identity and service provision constitutes a field of choices and strategies, where values, practical orientations, and professional cultures confront each other. According to Billis (1993), the tensions arise because each choice connected with internal functioning must be measured in relation to the "cultural roots" of the voluntary organization, or the set of principles and orientations that make up its cultural ground.

It is precisely the existence of this field of tensions that allows voluntary organizations to play their role of mobilizer and organizer of a resource—the altruistic voluntary commitment of many citizens—which, if it were not inserted in a stable organization that assigns roles and sets goals, would end up being temporary or confined to the area of private relationships.

Notes

1. It is therefore performed by organizations composed of "conscience constituents," according to the definition proposed by McCarthy and Zald (1977).
2. See also the introduction of this book for a discussion of the difference between political altruism and voluntary action.
3. Sahlins (1965) introduced the notion of generalized reciprocity to indicate a complex network of giving acts through which it is possible to guarantee equality of rights and treatment in a large community.
4. A number of studies show similar trends in other European countries. See Gaskin and Davis Smith (1995), Evers (1995), Kramer et al. (1993).
5. The data are obtained by comparing the results of the three main surveys performed on a national scale: the first commissioned by the Ministries of Labor and the Interior in 1983, the second and third performed in 1992 and 1998 by the Fondazione Italiana per il Volontariato.
6. A full 24 percent of the organizations in existence in that year were founded between 1975 and 1980, and 28 percent during the 1980-85 period.
7. Traditional voluntary organizations shared their religious roots with the human rights organizations described by Passy in the introduction of this book.
8. See della Porta (1996) on the evolution of social movements in Italy between 1960 and 1995.
9. In this respect, the emergence of this new voluntary action is part of the change in action repertoire of the solidarity movement that occurred in the 1960s and the 1970s (see Passy in this volume).
10. Several studies showed a process of polarization during the 1980s between organizations able to specialize and set themselves more specific goals, and groups tied down to the choice of informality (Ranci, De Ambrogio, and Pasquinelli 1991; Kramer et al. 1993).
11. The Fivol study of 1996 found that 75 percent of voluntary organizations had contacts with local administrations to obtain finance or cooperation between services operating in the same field.
12. The fields where the impact of voluntary organizations is greatest are those of assistance to persons suffering hardship, such as the elderly, the poor, the handicapped, drug addicts, AIDS sufferers, immigrants from outside the European Union.
13. See McPherson, Miller, and Rotolo (1996) for an ecological approach to mobilization in voluntary organizations.
14. See Knoke (1990), McPherson et al. (1996), Gaskin and Davis Smith (1995), Dekker and van den Broek (1998).
15. According to a recent Fivol study of more than 10,000 voluntary organizations (Frisanco and Ranci 1999), approximately 40 percent of them espouse Catholic beliefs

and another 30 percent work on a permanent basis with church bodies although they declare themselves to be nonreligious.

16.   Nevertheless, this is only partially true for the groups that I have defined as "fight against emargination" organizations, which act on the basis of egalitarian beliefs and in close contact with heavily stigmatized social groups. For these groups, recruitment takes on a character similar to that traditionally attributed to protest movements: large resort to interpersonal networks, a high level of agreement on group values, selection based on "convictions," and—inevitably—a smaller mobilization base.

17.   Many organizations formally distinguish the role of volunteer from that of official member. Volunteers are individuals who provide a service in the name of the organization, while members are those involved in the administration of the organization and have a right to vote. Promotion from volunteer to member is achieved by demonstrating loyalty and a constant commitment.

18.   While the governing body is generally more concerned about adherence to the original mandate, the management responsible for service provision generally requests innovations to increase the dimensions and quality of the services.

19.   Often decisions designed to make service provision more efficient act as disincentives to wider participation, just as measures designed to strengthen the participatory climate at times tend to affect the efficiency of service provision.

20.   See Horch (1994) and Powell and Friedkin (1987) on organizational change in voluntary organizations.

21.   It could naturally be claimed that a for-profit agency or a state bureaucracy must tackle the same task. However, what makes a voluntary organization different is that the two functions—identity and service provision—exist in it together with a reciprocal relative autonomy and without either of the two dominating the other. This renders any strategic decision particularly susceptible to conflict and dilemma.

5

Different Issues, Same Process

Solidarity and Ecology Movements in Switzerland

Florence Passy and Marco Giugni

In the social science literature, altruism is often seen as a phenomenon *sui generis* which requires specific theoretical tools to be analyzed (e.g., Greven and Willems 1994; Olson 1965; Rucht, forthcoming). We do not share this view. Just as different forms of collective protests, from social movements to revolutions, can be brought under the same rubric of "contentious politics" (McAdam, McCarthy, and Zald 1996a), we think that individual participation in social movements follows similar processes, regardless of the type of movement and regardless of the beneficiaries of the action. In the end, the distinction between altruistic and "egoistic" behavior depends on the presence or absence of self-interest. Political altruism, by definition, does not rely on private interest. The goal is not to provide individual benefits for oneself, but rather to improve the situation of others. As a consequence, if one admits that these two kinds of political behavior are different, the difference stems precisely from the self-interest involved and the possibility to achieve individual gains for oneself. As a great many authors have shown (e.g., Gould 1991; Klandermans 1997; Marwell and Oliver 1993; McAdam 1986), the process leading to participation in social movements is much more complex, involving a number of crucial factors and going through a number of stages. We reject a monocausal explanation of individual participation which focuses on one key decision based on self-interest. While rational decisions to take part in a social movement do play a role, other factors affect participation: above all, the activists' position in the social structure, their value system, and their embeddedness in social networks. If that is true, altruistic and "egoistic" political action, as Charles Tilly argues in this volume, do not stem from different processes, but rest on similar causal mechanisms.

In considering how to study political altruism, the problem with a *sui generis* view is that it is based on a purely rationalist perspective which focuses almost exclusively on the individual benefits one gets from getting involved. In other words, the basic theoretical problem is that, if one appears to get no benefits whatsoever, then altruistic behavior cannot be grasped with a rationalist approach. At this point, scholars have opted for one of two solutions. On one hand, most have expanded the notion of rational behavior. They have broadened the concept of selective incentives to include not only material incentives, but also moral and purposive ones, as well as other individual rewards (e.g., Opp 1985, 1989). This solution seems not very viable in the light of criticisms from students of collective action (Chazel 1986; White 1976). The danger of falling into tautology and the failure to make empirical statements that can be falsified suggest abandoning this path. Alternatively, as Olson proposed to do, the rational-choice model might be abandoned in favor of other theoretical perspectives in order to account for altruistic behavior. Yet interests do play a role in the process of individual participation in social movements, at least as expressed in the actors' intention to act. Most importantly, if we expunge interests from our explanations, there is the risk of denying that those who act on behalf of others do so out of a rational willingness to act. In other words, there is the risk of overlooking the purposive nature of human action and of falling into an overly deterministic view of political behavior.

In sum, in this chapter we question two mistaken ideas: that altruistic behavior—and, more specifically, political altruism—is a form of human action in its own right which, consequently, requires specific analytic tools to be grasped; and that it ultimately depends solely on the actors' decision to act altruistically. The latter point can be generalized to say that the process leading to individual participation in social movements cannot be reduced simply to de-contextualized interests, intentions, and decisions, but involves contextual and relational factors, that is, social structure and networks. Political altruism, as any other form of contentious politics, is a product of social relations.

Research Strategy

To empirically illustrate our argument, we propose to compare participation in two social movements that differ in the altruistic orientation of their claims: solidarity and ecology movements. The latter cannot be defined *prima facie* as an instance of altruistic behavior, as participants stand to benefit directly from the outcomes of their actions. Our strategy consists of comparing two movements that belong to the same family (the new social movements family) in order to isolate the effect of the principal variable of interest (altruistic versus self-oriented mobilization) on individual participation. In addition, we control for the political context by focusing on a single country: Switzerland. The main difference between solidarity and ecology movements concerns the benefits of successful mobilization. Actions carried by the solidarity movement benefit other persons; those by the ecology movement produce gains for participants as well.

We focus on two social movement organizations: the Bern Declaration (BD) and the World Wildlife Fund (WWF). The BD emerged out of Protestant milieus in 1970 and belongs to the development-aid branch of the Swiss solidarity movement. Unlike charity organizations, which provide direct aid to Third World countries, it seeks to inject social justice into economical and political relations between the North and the South. This organization, which has about 18,000 members, is run by a small staff of professionals (fewer than ten persons) on a relatively low budget. The Swiss branch of the WWF was created in 1961. At the beginning it dealt primarily with nature conservation. Activists were engaged in traditional areas such as endangered animal species, forest destruction, water pollution, and so forth. However, the organization soon expanded to new areas and added new political interests to its agenda. Specifically, it came to incorporate a political ecology dimension. The WWF has developed steadily since its founding to become one of the largest organizations in the Swiss ecology movement. With more than 210,000 members, almost 100 employees, and an annual budget of 28 million Swiss francs, the WWF is not only one of the major organizations of the ecology movement today, but one of largest social movement organizations overall in Switzerland.

To analyze individual participation in the BD and the WWF, we use survey data on two representative samples of their members. The survey of members of the BD was conducted in 1993 in the context of a study on the process of individual participation in social movements (Passy 1998). The survey on WWF members was made in 1998 with the aim of allowing for a comparison of participation in two distinct movements.[1]

A Model of Individual Participation

Generally speaking, explanations of how and why people get involved in movement activities follow two perspectives. Following the route paved by Mancur Olson (1965), a number of scholars explain participation in social movements by underscoring the key role of individual interests, intentions, and decisions (e.g., Chong 1991; Hardin 1982; Macy 1991; Opp 1989; Sandler 1992). Rational choice theorists stress individual preferences as the critical moment along the path leading people to join a movement. Their accounts focus on the last stage of the process of individual participation, namely the actors' decision. In contrast, scholars in another theoretical tradition have criticized rational choice explanations and stressed instead the role of social structures and networks (e.g., della Porta 1988; Kriesi 1993; McAdam 1982, 1988). According to them, participation does not stem from a single key decision; rather, it is the product of social relations. Both approaches have proved insightful, for they have shown, on the one hand, that individual preferences have an important impact on participation and, on the other hand, that social norms and values, structural locations, and social networks are crucial push-factors. However, this theoretical divide has encountered many criticisms from scholars who try to link social relations to the actors' decisions in an attempt to go beyond a fragmented view of individual participation in social movements (e.g., Gould 1991, 1993; Klandermans 1997; Marwell and Oliver 1993).

We start from these criticisms to go a step further, arguing that both the actors' decisions and their embeddedness in social networks must be seen as part of a broader process in which each factor intervenes at different moments in time. Specifically, we maintain that the process of movement participation unfolds in three stages. First, individuals come in *cultural proximity* with the movement, that is to say, they share norms, values, and a structural location which make them belong to its mobilization potential. Second, they come in *social proximity* with the movement, a process that is largely facilitated by the embeddedness in social networks. Such embeddedness, in turn, strengthens the cultural affinity and the identification with the movement. Furthermore, it establishes a direct contact with the opportunity to participate and hence allows individuals to translate their willingness to act into actual action. Third, before getting involved, potential participants assess a number of cognitive parameters in order to *decide* if they will join the movement and with what intensity. Thus, before they reach the stage of deciding whether to participate or not, individuals go through a complex process of construction of the willingness to do so. Social relations play a crucial role in this process, one that has largely been overlooked by rational choice theorists.

Cultural Proximity

Cultural proximity evokes the concept of cleavages. As Rokkan (1970) shows in his seminal work on European political parties, political conflicts are rooted in cultural and structural cleavages. Social change produces the structural bases for the emergence of political conflicts, but the politicization of the conflicts results mainly from mobilization (Bartolini and Mair 1990). Thus political parties, interest groups, and social movements all contribute to the politicization of cultural and structural cleavages. Following the way charted by Rokkan, Kriesi (1989, 1993) argues that after World War II a new cleavage has emerged in Western Europe[2] which reflects two major contradictions of post-war societies: the growth of control over the population and the development of new technological risks that can potentially destroy the planet (e.g., nuclear power, genetic technology, industrial pollution). Much the same as for traditional cleavages, new sectors of the population mobilize around this new cultural and structural divide, claiming individual autonomy and emancipation, citizen oversight on the state, democratic control of high-risk technology, and a democratization of society in general. New social movements draw their human resources largely from the new middle class (Cotgrove and Duff 1980; Eder 1993), in particular among the social-cultural specialists (e.g., teachers, social assistants) (Kriesi 1989). In addition to having a specific position in the social structure, people who join these movements display a value system that favors individual emancipation and a leftist political orientation (Cotgrove and Duff 1981; Inglehart 1990; Kriesi 1993).

According to the cleavage hypothesis, individuals who belong to the new middle class—and, even more specifically, to the social-cultural specialists—and who have a value system emphasizing emancipation and a leftist orientation form the *mobilization potential* of new social movements. We can then plausibly argue that if members of the BD and the WWF share a similar structural position and a similar value system, the nature of protest (altruistic versus self-oriented) should not have a great impact on the first stage of the process of individuals participation. Table 5.1 largely confirms this expectation, and allows us to make a first step toward a rejection of the *sui generis* hypothesis of political altruism. Participants in solidarity and ecology movements have a similar location in the social structure. The new middle class, in particular, is over-represented in both organizations as compared to the Swiss population. While 14 percent of the Swiss belong to the social-cultural specialists, they represent respectively 59 percent and 45 percent of the members of the BD and the WWF. In addition, table 5.1 shows that the working class is largely under-represented in both organizations, especially in the BD. The under-representation of the working class in new social movement organizations is a well-known phenomenon (Kriesi 1989, 1993; Passy 1998), and confirms that the mobilization potential of these movements is socially determined. However, while the BD attracts social-cultural specialists in high numbers, the WWF has a somewhat more heterogeneous stock of members, for it tends to draw less from social-cultural professionals and more from the working class. This difference might be due to a particular strategy of the WWF, which often organizes summer camps for children that provide financial support for low-income families. This program would enable the WWF to expand its mobilization potential.

Participants in altruistic contentious politics not only have a similar struc-

TABLE 5.1
Distribution of BD and WWF Members by Class
(Compared to the Swiss Population)

	BD Members	WWF members	Swiss population [a]
Bourgeoisie/old middle class	**14**	**11**	**19**
Free professionals (independent)	9	7	8
Employers/craftsmen	4	3	7
Peasants	1	1	4
New middle class	**76**	**66**	**48**
Social-cultural specialists	59	45	14
Technocrats	16	19	14
Managers	1	2	20
Labor class	**12**	**23**	**34**
Specialized workers/employees	3	6	23
Nonspecialized workers/employees	9	17	11
Total	100%	100%	100%
N	599	535	2807

[a] Bütschi (1997).

tural location, they also share a value system. If we compare the two main cultural values espoused by new social movements—emancipation and a leftist orientation—we see how the two groups under study resemble each other in this respect. First, both groups are clearly close to leftist parties, in particular those of the "red-green" alliance. About 80 percent of solidarity and ecology movement members declare themselves to be politically close to either the Greens, the Socialists, or both (table 5.2). Second, taking Inglehart's postmaterialism scale to measure an emphasis put on individual emancipation, we see that the number of postmaterialists in the two organizations is perceptibly higher than among the Swiss population. Only 22 percent of the Swiss display postmaterialist values, whereas 89 percent of BD members and 61 percent of WWF members declare a strong affinity with emancipation values (table 5.3). The latter table suggests that participants in the solidarity movement are more postmaterialist than those active in the ecology movement. This variation can be understood in the light of the different years the two surveys were conducted (1993 for the BD and 1998 for the WWF). If we look at the national trend in this aspect of the value system, we observe a sharp decline of postmaterialist values in the Swiss population. As Switzerland encountered economic difficulties, postmaterialist values decreased (Brunner 1999). This trend affected the whole population, including new social movement participants. In fact, a closer look at the four dimensions included in Inglehart's scale shows that participants in the ecology movement

TABLE 5.2
Distribution of BD and WWF Members by Partisan Preference
(Compared to the Swiss Population)

	BD members	WWF Members	Swiss population [a]
Extreme left	5	3	1
Extreme left/Socialist party	3	3	—
Socialist party	33	23	21
Left/Greens	34	33	—
Greens	10	22	6
Left/right	2	3	—
Religious-based parties	5	4	15
Right	3	8	30
Other/no partisan preference	3	3	28
Total	100%	100%	100%
N	566	540	2022

[a] Analyses Vox (no. 49, 51, 53).

privilege the economic dimension rather than that of law-and-order, which explains why 37 percent among them belong to the mixed category on the scale. On the other three dimensions of emancipation values (gender equality, equal opportunities for citizens, and increasing citizen participation), there are no significant differences between the BD and the WWF.[3]

To summarize, we observe no significant difference between altruistic and self-oriented involvement with regard to the first stage of the process of individual participation in social movements. As far as locations in the social structure and value systems are concerned, we cannot distinguish between BD and WWF members; both have a cultural and structural profile similar to that

TABLE 5.3
Distribution of BD and WWF Members by Value Scale
(Compared to the Swiss Population)

	BD Members	WWF Members	Swiss Population [a]
Postmaterialist	89	61	22
Mixed, prevailingly postmaterialist	7	22	28
Mixed, prevailingly materialist	4	15	31
Materialist	0	3	19
Total	100%	100%	100%
N	547	469	2416

[a] Bütschi (1997).

of participants in other new social movements, which is a pre-condition of mobilization.

Social Proximity

Social networks perform a variety of functions in the process of individual participation (Gould 1991; McAdam and Paulsen 1993; Passy 1998). First is their cultural function intervening in the political socialization of potential participants. Previous participation in social networks provides individuals with meanings and identities which facilitate involvement in social movements. Second, networks have a structural function in bridging the gap between individuals and a social movement organization. They provide a concrete opportunity to translate individuals' willingness to act into actual action and thus play an important role in the recruitment of new members. Finally, social networks contribute to the definition and evolution of individual preferences. The latter, in turn, lead individuals to decide if they will eventually participate. In our comparison of solidarity and ecology movements we focus on the first two functions of social networks, which correspond to the processes of political socialization and recruitment.

If political altruism and self-oriented contentious politics arise from different processes, social networks should have a varying impact on them. But if they are not substantially different, we should find a similar impact of networks on BD and WWF members. Networks should affect both the socialization and recruitment of members. Social psychologists have long stressed that emotions usually accompany altruistic acts, provoking a favorable reaction from persons in interaction with individuals who act altruistically (Berkowitz 1972; Brehm 1966; Isen and Noonberg 1979; Krebs 1970; Piliavin and Charng 1990; Thorton, Kirchneer, and Jacobs 1991; Wolfe 1998). Thus imitation can facilitate prosocial behavior (see Soule in this volume). As the chances that actions are imitated are higher in intensified face-to-face social interaction, we expect networks (which reflect social interaction) to play a greater role in individual participation in the solidarity movement (which we define as an instance of altruistic contentious politics), independently of their function. Moreover, following the imitation hypothesis, we expect imitation to be more important when individuals are recruited by people who are already involved in the movement. Therefore we think that the role of social networks in political altruism should be particularly important in their recruitment function.

While several social psychologists emphasize the impact of emotions on altruistic behavior, others argue that altruistic acts are motivated by a commitment to principles (Charng, Piliavin, and Callero, 1988; Chaves 1998; Schwarz 1977; Zuckerman and Reiss 1978). Emotions and principles are the two main types of motivations put forward by work in the social psychological tradition to explain prosocial behaviors (Wolfe 1998). Principles leading to altruism develop in specific cultural contexts. Certain contexts yield a greater amount of symbolic and discursive resources which are instrumental in propagating altruistic attitudes. As Wuthnow (1991) points out, cultural repertoires facilitate prosocial behaviors. Relying on survey data, he shows that although Americans have little substantial knowledge of the Bible, half of them were able to relate the story of the Good Samaritan. This percentage is much higher among individuals engaged in altruistic activities. This example suggests that religious institutions are a crucial "reservoir" of symbolic and discursive resources that facilitate the emergence and spread of prosocial behaviors in Western societies. Thus we expect participation in religious networks to be a major factor of socialization to political altruism; individuals who are part of religious networks should be more inclined to join the solidarity movement.

Table 5.4 offers a first empirical test of the impact of networks on political altruism. If we look at the top half of the table, we observe no striking differences between BD and WWF members in the socialization function of networks. In both cases, social networks impact significantly the process of meaning and identity construction which led individuals to join the movement. Only a small part of participants were not previously involved in networks. If we distinguish between formal (i.e., organizational) and informal (i.e., interpersonal) networks, we see that the socialization function is performed mainly by interpersonal networks, or by a combination of both formal and informal ones. Interpersonal networks play a greater role in the socialization of participants in the solidarity movement, whereas for participants in the ecology movement a combination of formal and informal networks seems to be more important. Sixty percent of WWF members were part of formal networks before they joined the organization, and at the same time had a broad network of interpersonal contacts with people sensitive to environmental issues or already engaged in the ecology movement. Only 29 percent of WWF members were exposed to ecology issues exclusively through interpersonal networks. This percentage rises to 44 percent in the case of BD members. Their socialization to Third World issues comes from interpersonal relationships with individuals close to these issues or already involved in the branch of the solidarity movement that deals with North-South issues. Only 36 percent of BD members got socialized through a combination of informal and formal networks.

We can perform a more detailed analysis of the differences between altruistic and self-oriented participation with respect to the socializing role of networks by looking at the type of formal networks in which members were involved before they joined the organization. Our expectation was that reli-

TABLE 5.4
Distribution of BD and WWF Members by Social Network Function

	BD members	WWF members
Socialization		
No networks	11	4
Formal networks only	9	8
Informal networks only	44	29
Formal and informal networks	36	60
Total	100%	100%
N	646	670
Recruitment		
No networks	41	61
Formal networks only	23	5
Informal networks only	23	30
Formal and informal networks	13	4
Total	100%	100%
N	646	670

gious organizations should serve as a key network for the political socialization of participants in the solidarity movement. These networks carry symbolic and discursive resources that might facilitate the emergence and diffusion of pro-social behaviors. Table 5.5 shows the prior formal embeddedness of BD and WWF members, that is, their participation in formal networks before they got involved in the organization. The results do not support the hypothesis. No difference can be observed between the two organizations. In both cases, participants were heavily associated with new social movement networks, less so with conventional political networks such as unions and parties, and even less with religious networks. The important point here is the strong resemblance of the embeddedness of altruistic and self-oriented participants. Contrary to our expectation, religious networks are not a privileged channel for the political socialization of participants in the solidarity movement.[4] The only significant difference between the two groups is the larger proportion of WWF members that were embedded in youth and student associations. This difference is traceable to the holiday camps that the WWF often organizes for youngsters; and many of today's adult members may have taken part in such activities in their childhood.

Turning to the recruitment function of networks, the bottom part of table 5.4 shows that about half of the members in both organizations became involved through this channel. Hence social networks represent indeed an important bridge between individuals who are culturally close to an area of

TABLE 5.5
Distribution of BD and WWF Members by Network Type (Percentages)

	Members of formal networks before joining the BD	Members of formal networks before joining the WWF
New social movements	**50**	**47**
Ecology movement	23	27
Third World organizations	20	20
Human rights organizations	9	10
Student associations	1	8
Peace movement	6	7
Antinuclear movement	4	6
Women's movement	3	2
Asylum/immigration organizations	2	3
Antiracist organizations	1	2
Conventional political networks	**21**	**20**
Unions	19	15
Parties	5	8
Employers' associations	—	2
Religious networks	**11**	**11**
Other networks	**35**	**43**
Youth associations	1	17
Charity associations	5	11
Other associations	3	10
Consumers' associations	4	8
Scientific associations	5	6
Renters' associations	4	5
Neighborhood associations	2	4
Pupils' parents associations	1	4
Patriotic/military associations	—	1
N	646	670

Percentages do not total 100 because data drawn from multiple-choice questions.

interest and the opportunity to participate. Furthermore, these networks play a greater role in recruiting participants in the solidarity movement than in the ecology movement. In the latter case, other channels are more important. For example, a closer look to the various channels of recruitment (the organization itself, the news media, networks, and others) shows that the media are much more important for the WWF than for the BD.[5] This difference stems more from the higher public visibility of the WWF than from the distinction between altruistic and self-oriented nature of mobilization. A simple but significant indication of this explanation comes from a survey showing that the WWF logo is the most widely known in Switzerland after that of Coca-Cola. The wide popularity and visibility of this international organization facilitate recruitment through advertisement in the media, and could explain the difference we observe in the recruitment function of networks.

The bottom half of table 5.4 also suggests that informal networks do not impact strongly on recruitment in the solidarity movement. This finding questions the contention that the function of networks, as regards the mechanism of imitation, is specific to political altruism. Members of the WWF have been recruited mostly through interpersonal contacts (30 percent), whereas recruitment of members of the BD is more variegated and went through formal (23 percent), informal (23 percent), or both (13 percent) types of networks. Thus interpersonal relationships are not prevalent in the recruitment process of participants in the solidarity movement.

In sum, our comparison of ecology and solidarity movements with respect to the second stage of the process of individual participation—that involving social networks—tends to counter the hypothesis that political altruism follows a distinct path. To be sure, some variations can be observed between BD and WWF members. Yet, in our view, they are too small to suggest that altruistic contentious politics follows a distinct route in this second stage of the participation process. That said, it is obvious that no organization resembles another in all respects and no most similar research design can eliminate all differences in the variables one wants to control. The BD and the WWF differ, in particular, as to public visibility. The latter is much more publicly visible.

Perceptions and Intentions

The third and last stage in the process of individual participation concerns the decision to act, made by people who are culturally and socially close to a given area of contention. A great many studies have shown that individual preferences and perceptions are strong predictors of participation in social movements (e.g., Klandermans 1984, 1997; Macy 1991; Marwell and Oliver 1993; Oberschall 1993; Opp 1985, 1989; Opp and Roehl 1990). Drawing from the extant literature, we can identify four cognitive parameters that affect the individual decision to participate: the perceived effectiveness of the action (Klandermans 1984, 1997; McAdam 1986; Marwell and Oliver 1993; Opp 1989), the potential risks of the action (della Porta 1988, 1995; Hirsch 1990; McAdam 1986; Opp 1989; Wiltfang and McAdam 1991), the degree of legitimacy of political authorities (McAdam 1982; Melucci 1989, 1996; Piven and Cloward 1979), and the personal availability of potential participants (McAdam 1988; Marwell and Oliver 1993; Wiltfang and McAdam 1991).

First, the perceived effectiveness of the action refers to the individuals' sense of usefulness of their own action in case they join a social movement organization (individual effectiveness), as well as of the action of the organization as a whole (collective effectiveness). If they perceive positively their and the organization's effectiveness, they are more likely to participate. Second, the evaluation of the risks of the action usually occurs when significant risks derive from participating. Risks increase substantially the costs of the action and tend to form an important barrier to participation. High risks are, in general, absent from activities of solidarity and ecology movements.[6] These two movements make mostly moderate demands and tend to adopt pacific forms of action. Therefore we can ignore this aspect in the present study. Third, when individuals think that the authorities are unable to provide adequate responses to certain problems and that citizens—specifically, organized citizens—are both legitimate and capable political actors, they are more likely to engage in social movements. Fourth, participation in contentious politics depends on personal availability, that is, the amount of time at one's disposal for collective action. We consider both objective (i.e., actual) and subjective (i.e., perceived) availability. People who have, or think they have, more time at their disposal should be more likely to participate.

Do members of the BD and the WWF score differently on these perceptions and intentions? Our data suggest a negative answer to this question. First of all, before they got involved, both BD and WWF members had a strong feeling of the effectiveness of the respective organization to reach its goals. As table 5.6 illustrates, they perceived the organization as very effective, and this influenced their decision to join it. In contrast, their own individual contribution was seen as less relevant in encouraging them to participate. This factor does not seem to decisively affect the decision to get involved in social movements. However, as we shall see below, it does significantly affect the degree of commitment once one has decided to participate. Second, the judgment of the capacity of the authorities to adequately address social problems in North-South relations and environmental protection is less negative than we might expect. Indeed, there is no significant distinction between the evaluation of the authorities' capacity to act and that of the potential contribution of citizens. Table 5.7 indicates that about half of the participants do not grant legitimacy to the role of political authorities for bringing about

TABLE 5.6
Mean of Perceived Effectiveness by BD and WWF Members

	BD members	WWF members
Individual effectiveness	2.71 (617)	3.31 (652)
Collective effectiveness	4.00 (615)	4.02 (657)

5-point scale (1 = no sense of effectiveness, 5 = strong sense of effectiveness); number of cases in parentheses.

TABLE 5.7
Evaluation of Authorities and Citizens' Capacity to Act
by BD and WWF Members

	BD members	WWF members
Delegitimation of authorities/ legitimation of citizens	47	39
Legitimation of authorities/ legitimation of citizens	31	39
Delegitimation of authorities/ delegitimation of citizens	18	16
Legitimation of authorities/ delegitimation of citizens	5	10
Total	100%	100%
N	646	670

social change, while they do grant legitimacy to the role of citizens. However, a third of them do not question either the state's capacity or that of citizens. They think that both are legitimate actors, able to provide adequate answers to the problems that concern them. Finally, as far as personal availability is concerned, BD and WWF members reveal similar constraints. The resemblance is striking concerning professional constraints: about three-quarters of participants in both organizations have a job[7] and more than half of them work full time.[8] Thus participants have quite limited resources of time to be devoted to social movement activities. On the other hand, they do not perceive that as being very important. All said that before they joined the organization they thought they lacked enough free time for such activities.

To sum up, we do not find substantial differences between BD and WWF members regarding perceptions and intentions. While the various aspects we have examined might impact the decision to participate, members of both organizations evaluated these aspects in a similar fashion. This leads us to conclude that altruistic and self-oriented participants do not behave differently in the third and last stage of the process of individual participation in social movements.

High-Cost Participation

Our comparison of members of the BD and the WWF indicates that participants in political altruism do not follow a process of individual participation different from that in other kinds of contentious politics. We observe similarity on three levels: the cultural and structural profile of participants, their involvement in and recruitment by social networks, and the cognitive parameters that affect their decision to participate. However, we may still wonder whether the process of individual participation varies for different levels of engagement. If we take the restrictive definition of altruism which Charles Tilly adopts in his contribution to this volume—that altruism not only implies benefits for the other person, but also significant costs for the actor—we may wonder whether a distinct pattern of involvement characterizes those participants who are most deeply involved (i.e., activists). Activists in the Swiss solidarity movement do not face the high risks implied in the kinds of altruistic behavior Tilly refers to, but deeply involved participants invest much time and energy for the cause. Such commitment is very costly. In-depth interviews with core activists of the BD show clearly that commitment implies high costs for all activists, especially in their private life (Passy 1998). For example, one activist stated that her strong involvement in the movement proved disastrous for her family life.

In the light of the distinction between strongly engaged participants (i.e., activists) and those with a more marginal involvement, we can try to determine whether, when it comes to very costly participation, political altruism is indeed distinct from other types of contentious politics. In other words, do individuals who not only mobilize to provide others with collective benefits, but in addition bear important costs from such mobilization, follow the same process of individual participation as activists in self-oriented movements? Alternatively, is political altruism a phenomenon *sui generis* when it comes to strong commitment? To answer this question we compare once again members of the BD and of the WWF. In both cases, we isolated the group of activists from the whole sample. Activists are participants who enter an active process of participation, either on an irregular or a regular basis (in contrast to participants who simply contribute financially to the organization).[9] We want to ascertain whether the three stages in the process of individual participation discussed above—cultural proximity, social proximity, and perceptions and intentions—differ between the two groups.

Tables 5.8 and 5.9 show the results of logistic regression, respectively of BD and WWF activists, on a battery of independent variables grouped according to the three stages of the participation process. They support the hypothesis that political altruism is not a phenomenon *sui generis* even in the case of high-cost participation. For both solidarity and ecology movements, social relations and the cognitive aspects related to the actors' intention to act are the key factors leading to activism. As far as social proximity is concerned, the findings (model 2) indicate that networks play a key role in engaging individuals with the protest issue and establishing a direct contact with the opportunity to participate. Organizational (formal) networks, especially organizations that are culturally and ideologically close to the movement, are particularly important to socializing individuals to the issue,[10] while interpersonal (informal) networks play a crucial role in the recruitment process. As regards perceptions and intentions, it appears that certain parameters are more important than others (model 3). First, a positive assessment of the effectiveness of their own participation is, by and large, the strongest determinant of both altruistic and self-oriented activism. The finding is especially interesting for the former group, for we see that action is prompted by the interest in bringing about social change and that a positive perception of one's personal effort leads to a higher level of participation. In other words, contrary to Olson's (1965) view, political altruism is performed on a rational basis rather than irrationally. Second, the interest in the issue affects the level of participation. However, as often stressed in the literature (e.g., Klandermans 1997; Marwell and Oliver 1993), it is not the most important factor. Moreover, its impact disappears when we control it for the other determinants of engagement (model 4). Finally, the perception by ecology activists of having free time to invest in collective action leads them to a higher level of participation. This factor is not significant in the case of the solidarity movement. However, here we must note that the measure of this variable differs for the two groups. Specifically, we do not have a good indicator of the perception of free time by BD members because the study measures the lack of free time in the context of not being more active in the organization, whereas in the WWF survey it refers to the perception that individuals held before joining the organization. For technical reasons, therefore, we cannot draw solid conclusions from this finding.[11]

Thus, when we look at social proximity as well as perceptions and intentions, we find no fundamental difference; the role of these two stages in the route leading to activism is comparable for altruistic and self-oriented movements alike. A substantial difference does exist in the impact of cultural proximity, which is much stronger in the case of the WWF (model 1). This divergence could result from the lower degree of homogeneity of this organization. As previously noted, the WWF organizes summer camps for children, and this activity may help the WWF to expand its mobilization potential beyond the new social movements. Whereas the WWF attracts people beyond the cleavage articulated by the new social movements, ecology activists have a structural and cultural profile typical of the potential participants in those movements. Therefore we suspect that the difference in the weight of cultural factors in our comparison is due to a peculiar characteristic of the ecology organization under study, rather than to basically different processes leading to activism.

To facilitate a more consistent comparison, model 5 in tables 5.8 and 5.9 excludes from the analyses the variables pertaining to cultural proximity. This allows us to ascertain whether the two groups of activists show similar patterns of participation when we control for the specificity of the WWF on mobilization potential. The answer is yes. Without going into much detail, we

TABLE 5.8
Logistic Regression of BD Activists on the Determinants of Participation (Odds Ratios)

	Model 1	Model 2	Model 3	Model 4	Model 5
Cultural Proximity					
Social-cultural specialists	2.087			1.211	
New middle class (other)	2.300			3.099	
Workers	1.446			1.339	
Partisan preference	1.355***			1.739	
Postmaterialism	.668			1.419	
Social Proximity					
Embedded in formal networks close to the movement		2.332***		3.525***	3.468***
Embedded in other formal networks		.932		.916	.972
Embedded in informal networks		1.569***		1.474	1.377
Recruited by formal networks		1.615*		2.208	1.543
Recruited by informal networks		3.346***		5.908***	5.591***
Perceptions and intentions					
Interest in the issue			1.803**	1.587	1.545
Individual effectiveness			2.146***	2.239***	2.103***
Collective effectiveness			.777	.763	.729
Delegitimation of authorities/legitimation of citizens			.778	.767	.814
Objective availability			1.353	1.977**	1.850*
Subjective availability			1.146	1.247	1.226
−2 Log likelihood	503.105	614.438	294.695	173.169	204.741
R^2 (Nagelkerke)	.032	.199	.251	.452	.414
N	436	534	264	222	258

* p < .05; ** p < .01; *** p < .001

TABLE 5.9
Logistic Regression of WWF Activists on the Determinants of Participation (Odds Ratios)

	Model 1	Model 2	Model 3	Model 4	Model 5
Cultural Proximity					
Social-cultural specialists	.724			.610	
New middle class (other)	.923			1.326	
Workers	.386			.284	
Partisan preference	3.660***			3.555***	
Postmaterialism	1.746***			1.652*	
Social Proximity					
Embedded in formal networks close to the movement		1.797***		1.249	1.875***
Embedded in other formal networks		.817**		.840	.826
Embedded in informal networks		1.100		1.058	1.014
Recruited by formal networks		1.169		.809	.811
Recruited by informal networks		2.260***		1.890	2.352**
Perceptions and intentions					
Interest in the issue			1.868**	1.446	1.731*
Individual effectiveness			1.701***	1.787***	1.662***
Collective effectiveness			.831	.953	.938
Delegitimation of authorities/legitimation of citizens			1.000	.881	.916
Objective availability			.987	.969	.960
Subjective availability			1.389**	1.607***	1.435***
-2 Log likelihood	444.201	719.065	436.799	317.071	436.799
R^2 (Nagelkerke)	.200	.124	.224	.424	.317
N	508	524	317	231	307

* p < .05; ** p < .01; *** p < .001

can stress two points. First, the findings indicate that altruistic activists do not follow a distinct process of participation. The effect of social networks remains significant, for both the BD and the WWF. Specifically, socialization by organizational (formal) networks and recruitment by interpersonal (informal) networks lead to a stronger engagement. Second, individual effectiveness continues to be significant, meaning that a positive evaluation of one's own contribution continues to be significant and increases the chances of becoming an activist, in both altruistic and self-oriented movements.

Political Altruism: Social Construction or Reality?

Our analysis of the process leading to political altruism in general, and to activism in this type of contentious politics in particular, leads us to conclude that altruistic participants do not follow a distinct process of individual participation. In other words, political altruism is not a phenomenon *sui generis*—a special form of political behavior that rests on distinct causal mechanisms. Specifically, we see that involvement in social movements is not the result of a single key decision in which one assesses the costs and benefits of participation. It is rather the product of a more complex process in which perceptions and intentions do play an important role, but in which social relations also intervene in a decisive fashion. The most important finding for the present purpose, however, is that the nature of the protest issue and the orientation of the movement (altruistic or self-oriented) do not affect the process of individual participation. Such participation occurs through similar causal processes, regardless of the issue addressed and the orientation of the movement. This conclusion calls for further reflection about the supposed altruistic bases of the solidarity movement. Put another way, is the solidarity movement a genuine instance of political altruism? Isn't it simply a disguised form of egoism, as it was often considered in certain theoretical perspectives? (See Tilly's criticism in this volume.) For example, Wuthnow (1991) concludes that "acts of compassion" in voluntary associations are, in fact, a way to gain self-fulfillment. Prosocial behavior would help individuals to "feel better" and to express their own individuality. In this context, therefore, it should be considered an act of disguised egoism. Hence the question: Is the solidarity movement, too, a channel for the self-fulfillment for people who participate to feel better or to obtain some kind of hidden rewards?

A first way to answer this provocative question is examining whether participants get rewards once they are involved in the movement. Table 5.10 shows that members of the BD receive various compensations for their acts of solidarity. Virtually all of them say that their engagement in the organization gives them individual rewards. These rewards are mainly nonmaterial and represent a route toward self-fulfillment. Participation offers them the oppor-

TABLE 5.10
Rewards Received by BD and WWF Members
from Engagement in the Organizations (Percentages) [a]

	BD Members	WWF Members
Has received rewards from engagement	**84**	**92**
Material		
Participate in actions in the field	—[b]	36
Provides outlets for a future job	17	33
Benefit from special offers given to members	—	19
Self-fulfillment		
Acquire skills	72	88
Realize own ideals	—	74
Belong to a group that shares own ideals	33	48
Meet new friends	40	42
Acquire recognition from friends	9	10
Life experience	61	—
Give meaning to life	49	—
N	646	670

[a] Percentages do not total 100 because data drawn from multiple-choice questions.
[b] Not measured.

tunity to acquire and develop new skills, realize their ideals, and gain a life experience. Here again, participants in the solidarity movement are not different from those involved in the ecology movement; both get compensations for their political activities. Political altruism, then, seems to provide rewards. These findings hence support Wuthnow's argument that acts of compassion contribute to self-fulfillment. Do they lead us to revise our view of the solidarity movement as an instance of political altruism?

One of the characteristics of political altruism is to perform deeds without expecting any external reward, but now we see that participants in the solidarity movement do receive rewards. However, we must consider the definition of political altruism more carefully. The definition given in the introduction to this volume stresses that in order to be seen as altruistic, individuals do not have to *expect* any reward before they join the movement. In other words, they do not have to be *motivated* by individual rewards. Table 5.10 indicates, in fact, that BD members receive compensations once they are already involved in the movement; they do not say that they were motivated by rewards to get involved in the first place. Although we lack quantitative data, we have qualitative information suggesting that altruistic participants were not motivated by individual rewards to act on behalf of others (Passy 1998). Activists of the BD said during in-depth interviews that they were unaware beforehand of the potential gains on the private level to be drawn from their participation in the organization. They learned such rewards only after they first got in-volved in the movement. In the light of this statement, we can hardly consider participation in the solidarity movement as a form of disguised egoism.

A second way to answer the question addressed above lies in sociological considerations. It is difficult to imagine that social actors receive nothing in return, whatever the purpose of their actions. Human action is not a one-way ticket, but rather an interactive process (Tilly 1996). Individuals get feedback that either encourages or discourages them to act again, independently of the type of action they are performing. It would be overly idealistic to say that in certain areas individuals receive nothing in return. Both altruistic and self-oriented movement participants receive something from their actions, some-thing we usually call "rewards." Yet this does not allow us to conclude that political altruism is a form of disguised egoism. Every individual performing an action of this sort gets something in return.

Here we might open a broader philosophical debate on the definition of po-litical altruism. We refrain from the temptation to do so, and limit ourselves to a few concluding reflections. To think of altruistic acts in the absence of rewards or compensations is quite difficult in contemporary Western cul-ture.[12] As Mansbridge (1998) points out, "[l]ove (or some feeling of empathy or affinity with a group or individuals) and duty (or some form of commit-ment to principle) are the two known forms of altruism, of which public spirit is a subset" (4). But the definition of the concept of public good (i.e., the public spirit) has been subject to much controversy and to historical as well as geographical variation. Since the time of Christian thinkers such as Augustine and Aquinas in the Middle Ages, altruism has been a difficult idea to grasp, as they clearly held opposing views on the public good and the private good. This conflict was intensified in the eighteenth century by utilitarianism. Ol-son's (1965) theory of collective action fits well into this philosophical and cultural background. Altruism—and, for that matter, any other kind of action lacking individual rewards—cannot be grasped intellectually. Yet this con-ception of public and private goods as two opposed entities was preceded by quite a different view. For example, the ancient Greeks, notably Plato, saw public and private goods as compatible, positing that what is good for the public is naturally good for individuals as well. Similarly, Rousseau, who was strongly influenced by Greek thinkers, did not consider these two entities opposed to each other, for human beings are social actors inclined toward the public good. As a consequence, what is good for individuals is naturally good for people collectively. Adam Smith also saw compatibility between the pub-lic good and private interests, insofar as private advantages are inevitably transformed in public advantages through the "invisible hand."

These examples, borrowed from Mansbridge's (1998) discussion of the contested boundaries of the public good, show that our appraisal of political altruism—which can be defined as a contribution to producing collective

goods without receiving individual rewards—is contingent upon the philosophical view of the human being we endorse. Today we still largely share the
opposition between public goods and private interests which was handed
down by early Christian thinkers and utilitarianism, and which leads us to
think in such terms as: if people do something for the public good, it is because they think they will get something in return, something we usually call
"rewards." Otherwise it is irrational do so. This way of thinking puts us in a
poor position to judge pro-social behavior. It also prevents us from seeing
that individuals may act altruistically driven by hopes of social change, moral
obligations, or another internalized altruistic principle or norm. Instead of
saying that political altruism exists or not depending on what view of the
human being we adhere to, instead of falling into a sterile discussion that
resembles Pandora's box, we think it more fruitful to examine the processes
that lead to this type of behavior with the aim of bringing its peculiarities to
the fore and hence reach a better understanding of social processes in general.

Notes

1. The sample of members of the BD includes 646 respondents who returned a
structured questionnaire sent to 1,200 members of the organization. Subjects were
selected at random in each of the two linguistic regions of Switzerland (German-
speaking and French-speaking). We applied the same research design to the WWF
survey, with one exception: given the small percentage of activists in the WWF as
compared to the large number of members who simply give financial support to the
organization, we inflated the number of activists. The WWF sample includes 670
members.

2. See also Raschke (1985).

3. If we compare the means on these three dimensions, there are no significant
differences between the two groups. On all three dimensions the means vary between
1.20 and 1.64 (1 = for individual emancipation, 7 = against individual emancipation).

4. A further indication of the absence of influence of religion on altruism comes
from a comparison of religious practices by both types of participants, showing no
significant differences. This result is consistent with previous findings that religious
beliefs do not influence altruistic acts (Chaves 1998; Oliner and Oliner 1988; Wuthnow 1991).

5. Participants were recruited through this channel in 30 percent of cases for the
WWF and 18 percent of cases for the BD.

6. Actions by Greenpeace activists and, even more so, by ecoterrorist groups are
obvious exceptions to the general moderation of the ecology movement. Our study,
however, deals with members of a moderate organization.

7. BD members: 75 percent; WWF members: 68 percent.

8. Members of both organizations: 59 percent.

9. Ideally we would have compared only those members who display the stronger
degree of activism by participating on a regular basis (what we may call the "core
activists"), as for them the costs of participation are the highest. Unfortunately we

lack enough cases of this type of members to perform a statistical test of our hypothesis.

10. The formal networks closest in cultural and ideological factors that help socialize potential activists of the solidarity movement are new social movement organizations and churches. The culturally closest networks in socializing potential activists of the ecology movement consist of new social movement organizations, the environmental parties, and student and youth organizations.

11. All the measures in the model of individual participation are similar for the BD and the WWF, except for this measure of subjective availability.

12. Altruistic actions may also stem from coercion or the threat of sanctions in case one does not act. We do not consider these cases in the present discussion.

6

Better Off by Doing Good

Why Antiracism Must Mean Different Things to Different Groups

Ruud Koopmans

In the early 1990s, Germany witnessed a wave of violent attacks by right-wing youth, skinhead and neo-Nazi groups against asylum seekers and other ethnic minority groups, in which several dozen immigrants were killed. Although at first German politics and society reacted hesitantly to these events, ultimately they provoked one of the largest mass movements in German history, involving millions of citizens in rallies, nightly candle-lit marches, and vigils in front of asylum-seeker hostels to protect them against attacks. Many of the larger antiracist demonstrations were actively supported by a wide spectrum of organizations, ranging from antiracist and human rights groups to high-ranking union, church, and government representatives. On 8 November 1992, for instance, more than three hundred thousand people, almost exclusively native Germans, gathered in Berlin and were addressed by, among many others, federal President Richard von Weizsäcker, Chancellor Helmut Kohl, the bishop of the Berlin-Brandenburg Evangelical Church Martin Kruse, and the Chairman of the Central Council of Jews in Germany, Ignatz Bubis. Apart from the Bavarian branch of the Christian Democratic party (the CSU) all parties represented in the federal parliament supported the event. The rally's central slogan cited Article 1 of the German constitution, stating the fundamental human rights principle that "human dignity is unassailable" (*Frankfurter Rundschau*, 9 November 1992).

This and other massive demonstrations against extreme-right violence and racism demonstrate that altruistic collective action is, contrary to what some may want us to believe (e.g., Olson 1971, 2), a far from rare empirical phenomenon. However, this ubiquity makes political altruism more rather than less puzzling for social scientists. As a wealth of research has shown in the wake of Mancur Olson's *The Logic of Collective Action* (1971; first published in 1965), for collective action to occur formidable barriers have to be surmounted even in the pursuit of aims that, if realized, would clearly benefit the mobilizing group. But if such self-interested collective action is so difficult already, how can we explain that millions of individual citizens and a wide range of collective actors take to the streets to defend the interests of a group (immigrants and ethnic minorities) that is not their own? As I will argue in the following section, neither the rational choice model of collective action, nor the alternatives that emphasize the role of values, solidarity, norms, and collective identities, have provided convincing answers to this question. Given the apparent complexity of the matter, I do not aim in this contribution to present a full and conclusive answer, but will present a theoretical argument that may resolve at least part of the puzzle. This argument is tested and elaborated using empirical data on more than two thousand five hundred instances of claims-making against racism and the extreme right in Germany between 1990 and 1997.

The Double Dilemma of Altruistic Collective Action

Although often vulgarized in cursory references in this way, Olson's famous statement of the "dilemma of collective action" in no way presupposes that individuals are solitary egoists uncommitted to collective interests, causes, and ideals. On the contrary, the dilemma arises from the empirical fact that many large groups of individuals share such interests, causes, and ideals, but still find it difficult, and sometimes impossible, to mount the collective action necessary to achieve their common aims. In a sense, then, Olson asks the same question as Karl Marx did long ago when he discussed the difficult transformation of a class "in itself" to a class "for itself." Contrary to Marx and his followers, Olson of course does not identify the cause of the problem as a lack of class consciousness, bourgeois hegemony, or the doings of reformist renegades, but in the individual's propensity to make rational choices. According to Olson's reasoning, in large groups, any single individual's contribution to the provision of a public good—a benefit which, when achieved, cannot be withheld from any member of the group, regardless of her or his participation in the collective action that brought about the benefit—will be imperceptibly small. Moreover, if collective action is successful, the public good will accrue to the individual anyway. Thus, the individual has no incentive to bear the inherent costs of collective action unless she or he derives some selective incentive—one that is different from her or his share in the public good—from participation that only accrues to those who have contributed to the achievement of the public good. For the present purpose, it is important to note that Olson emphasizes that this theory holds regardless of whether or not the individual involved acts selfishly:

> [T]he concept does *not* necessarily assume the selfish, profit-maximizing behavior that economists usually find in the marketplace. The concept of the large or latent group offered here holds true whether behavior is selfish or unselfish, so long as it is strictly speaking "rational." Even if the member of a large group were to neglect his own interests entirely, he still would not rationally contribute toward the provision of any collective or public good, since his own contribution would not be perceptible. . . . The only requirement is that the behavior of individuals in large groups or organizations of the kind considered should generally be rational, in the sense that their objectives, whether selfish or unselfish, should be pursued by means that are efficient and effective for achieving these objectives (Olson 1971, 64-65).

While here Olson seems to claim that his theory applies to collective action regardless of the nature of the public good sought, elsewhere he is skeptical about its applications to collective actors with noneconomic aims.[1] The popularity his theorem gained through the resource mobilization approach in social movement studies must certainly have surprised Olson. He himself, at least, did not see much use in applying the theory to "groups that are characterized by a low degree of rationality," such as "mass movements" operating on the "lunatic fringe," for which "it would perhaps be better to turn to psychology or social psychology than to economics for a relevant theory" (Olson 1971, 161-62).

Olson was also highly skeptical about extending the theory to include collective action for altruistic aims: "The theory is not at all sufficient where philanthropic lobbies, that is, lobbies that voice concern about some group other than the group that supports the lobby, or religious lobbies, are concerned. In philanthropic and religious lobbies the relationships between the purposes and interests of the individual member, and the purposes and interests of the organization, may be so rich and obscure that a theory of the sort developed here cannot provide much insight." In a footnote, which merits to be quoted at length, Olson explains why this should be the case:

> Many theorists simply assume that all individual behavior, whatever the context, is rational . . . . All of the situations analyzed so far in this book require no such comprehensive and questionable definition of rationality. But the application of this theory to *some* noneconomic organizations might require such a comprehensive definition. A charitable organization could best be analyzed if the theory were interpreted in this way; the individual who made a modest contribution to a large nationally organized charity would under this interpretation do so, not from any mistaken belief that his contribution would noticeably augment the resources of the charity, but rather because he got an *individual, noncollective* satisfaction in the form of a feeling of personal moral worth, or because of a desire for respectability or praise. Although in this way the theory can be applied even to

charities, in such a context it does not seem especially useful. For when all action—even charitable action—is defined or assumed to be rational, then this theory (or any other theory) becomes correct simply by virtue of its logical consistency, and is no longer capable of empirical refutation (Olson 1971, 160).[2]

Of course, in applying Olson's theorem to social movements, many resource mobilization theorists have proceeded precisely along this road (e.g., Fireman and Gamson 1979; Moe 1980; Oberschall 1980; Hirsch 1990). By extending the concept of selective incentives to include a whole range of social and moral incentives that are inseparable from the individual's insertion and participation in the group, the theory has been turned into an unrefutable hypothesis at best, or a tautology at worst (see Knoke 1988; Marx Ferree 1992).

Does this imply, as Olson himself suggests, that for the study of social movements, and particularly those with other-regarding aims, we should better forget altogether about the "dilemma of collective action" and solutions to it such as selective incentives? This is certainly the road that has been taken by many critics of resource mobilization theory. Particularly in European studies of new social movements, it has been emphasized that the whole distinction between collective aims or goods and collective action is misconceived in the case of social movements, for which "the medium is the message" (Melucci 1980; Cohen 1985). Contrary to Olson's theory that builds on an instrumental separation of means and ends, participation itself, and the values, solidarities, and collective identities that are forged, shared, and reproduced in it, are seen here as the driving forces behind social movement action. Unlike the Olsonian model, this "identity" approach has little difficulty in incorporating altruistic collective action. If the solidarities and collective identities derived from struggling together for a common cause are what inspires people to participate in social movements, then what would be better suited than a cause that emphasizes the common good and unselfish sacrifice rather than the narrow-minded strife for personal benefits?

Compared to the Olsonian model, the identity approach has the advantage that it fits the empirical ubiquity of (noneconomic) social movements in general, and altruistic collective action in particular. However, in many respects this alternative is as deficient as the Olson theorem stretched *ad absurdam*. For here, too, we are dealing with an unrefutable tautology. Solidarity, identity, and living up to one's values and ideals are no doubt important motivations for social movement participants, as one can learn from any study using personal accounts of movement activists (for altruistic activism, see Passy 1998). But can they contribute to explaining collective action if they are so inextricably intertwined with participation itself that we will logically always find solidarity and collective identity in collectivities that have successfully mobilized, and find them necessarily absent in any groups that have remained latent? Does not the reference to solidarity, identity, sacrifice for the common cause, and similar motivations amount to putting different labels on that which instead needs to be explained—namely collective action?

Recently, another strand of theory has emphasized the importance of social movement organizers' efforts to develop interpretive "frames" in order to mobilize their constituencies. Such frames have to demonstrate the necessity, the possibility, and the legitimacy of improving the social condition which the movement addresses. In order to do so, collective action frames must identify targets for blame, select responsible authorities to which demands can be directed, present solutions to the problem, and convince potential adherents and participants that collective action is both necessary and will be effective in bringing about the desired changes. Snow and his collaborators (Snow et al. 1986) have labeled this type of interpretive efforts as "diagnostic" (defining the problem and attributing responsibility and blame), "prognostic" (presenting demands and solutions), and "motivational" framing (arguing for the necessity and efficacy of collective action for realizing these demands).[3] Still, even if fully successful, such framing only brings us at the doorstep of the dilemma of collective action, not anywhere near its resolution. As Olson has emphasized, even if among the latent group full consensus about the necessity of change and the potential effectiveness of collective action exists, rational individuals would still not contribute to the cost of mounting collective action. Since such a contribution, he explains, will not perceptibly change the chances of success of the mobilization effort, but will—unless the cost of participation is very small, as in the case of voting or signing a petition—have a perceptible cost to the individual (Olson 1971).

Here, too, it is insufficient to point out that movement organizers' framing efforts will include attempts to foster a collective identity or to create a sense of solidarity, which may induce the individual to overcome the dilemma of collective action by defining her or his personal interests as indistinguishable from those of the movement, because again that would be little more than phrasing "mobilization" differently. However, the picture changes, and the explanation becomes scientifically meaningful and empirically refutable if we focus not on aspects that are inextricably linked to the collective action and the collective actor that one seeks to explain, but on the mobilization of *preexisting* solidarities, identities, social networks, values, and norms on which social movement organizers may draw in order to forge a new collective actor. In other words, what successful movements must achieve is to draw *already mobilized groups* into their camp, by arranging alliances with representative organizations, establishing personal links to these groups' networks, and constructing interpretive frames that link these groups' interests, values and norms to the movement's cause. If these preexisting groups have sufficiently developed collective identities, established common values and norms, and a high level of internal solidarity, then the dilemma of collective action can be overcome within them.[4]

This, of course, is not a new idea, and the literature teems with examples of the importance of this type of what Oberschall (1973) has labeled "block mobilization." One example among many would be the Western European peace movement's co-optation of church groups (especially Protestant ones), by framing opposition against weapons of mass destruction as a "Christian duty" and peace as a "Christian value." The point here—one that is usually blurred in the literature referring to collective identities—is that peace movement mobilization success cannot be explained solely by the peace movement having a strong collective identity and sense of solidarity, or by participants seeing opposition to peace as a personal duty and drawing gratification from their sacrifice for the peace cause. Although all this was true and important, it amounts to nothing more than a restatement of the peace movement's mobilization success. A more meaningful (and empirically testable) account of the peace movement's success would emphasize the importance of drawing preexisting groups (Christian but also feminist, socialist, and other types) into its camp and drawing on *their* identities, solidarities, social norms, and networks to eventually forge the collective actor "peace movement" (see Kriesi and van Praag 1987).

By a detour, this brings us back to Olson. To recapitulate, his main point is that large groups will not be able to mobilize merely because all members of the (potential or latent) group share a common interest or aim. To overcome the dilemma of collective action that necessarily arises within such groups, selective incentives are needed that make participation attractive (or passivity unattractive) *for some other reason than that of contributing to the group's realization of its interest, but only attainable by way of such participation.* Thus, in the peace movement example, living up to one's Christian duties and values was the selective incentive that brought Christian activists into the movement's camp, just as feminists were mobilized by a (selective) frame emphasizing war-making as one of the main pillars of patriarchy.[5] To be perfectly clear: the claim here is not that these Christian and feminist activists were unconcerned about the peace issue and interested only in expressing their Christian and feminist identities. The point I want to make is that no matter how concerned about peace they might have been from the outset, they would not have been mobilized if there had been no appeal to their particular identity arguing why they, as Christians or feminists, had a special responsibility to stand up for peace.

This approach to the resolution of collective action problems allows us to establish a link to an important aspect of the framing approach as developed by Snow and his collaborators (Snow et al. 1986). Movement organizers not only have to convince potential followers of the necessity and possibility of change through collective action, they (usually) also want to address a wide constituency. The wider a constituency, the more heterogeneous it will be, and thus successful framing efforts must try to cater to many different tastes. Snow and his co-authors have called this process by which a movement's interpretive frame is extended, differentiated, or altered to incorporate new constituencies "frame bridging." The peace movement example given above illustrates this process: by defining the campaign for peace as a Christian value *par excellence* and opposition to nuclear weapons as a struggle against patriarchy, two important constituencies could be incorporated into the peace movement's platform.[6] Our argument here is that such frame bridging is crucial to the success of mobilization efforts, not just for the reason given by Snow and colleagues, namely, to broaden a movement's constituency, but especially because such frame bridging allows the incorporation of *selective* motivations to participate that will help to overcome the dilemma of collective action and to turn people passive to the movement's aims into active participants.

Thus, what characterizes successful framing efforts is not so much one integrated and overarching "master frame" (Snow and Benford 1992) that addresses as wide a public as possible, but much rather a series of *selective frames* geared to linking different preexisting social networks and collective actors to the emergent movement's cause. Of course, some level of integration of these different selective frames will be necessary to serve as a common focus. But contrary to the view which predominates in the framing literature, such overarching interpretive schemata (or *general frames*) serve mobilization success best when they are vague and general, rather than elaborate and specific. Any focused attribution of blame or responsibility, any clear identification of problem causes, or any fixation on particular solutions on this level will risk alienating certain subgroups in the movement's constituency and would therefore be detrimental to successful mobilization.[7] The example opening this chapter provides a good example: the constitutional principle that "human dignity is unassailable" could be endorsed by a range of actors from the Post-Communist Party of Democratic Socialism to the conservative federal Chancellor Helmut Kohl. Any specification of the causes of xenophobic violence or of the measures to be taken to combat it would have immediately turned these actors into staunch opponents. At the same time, as we shall see below, such specifications were a necessary ingredient of the selective frames that brought all these different groups to demonstrations such as the one in Berlin.

It is important to emphasize that such frame bridging by way of selective frames does not necessarily proceed in a top-down fashion, in which central movement entrepreneurs construct a series of cunning selective frames appealing to a variety of potential constituencies. Especially if the movement in question has already reached a certain level of visibility, resonance, and legitimacy,[8] the process may also proceed in a bottom-up direction. Constituencies originally outside the movement may then find it attractive to ride the crest of the mobilization wave and to construct frames that link the group's own interests and values to that of the wider movement. Lacking a strong organizational structure but at the same time enjoying large public visibility and legitimacy, antiracist mobilization in Germany in the 1990s to a large extent arose out of such bottom-up processes, rather than from centralized mobilization and framing. For our theoretical argument, however, it does not matter whether the expansion of social movements by way of selective framing proceeds top-down or bottom-up. In both cases, the argument states that collective mobilization efforts will only be able to expand to new constituencies through selective frames linking these constituencies' specific interests and values to the wider aims of the movement—regardless of where the initiative for such frame bridging originates.

Before we turn to an empirical test of this argument, it is necessary to ask whether these considerations have any special relevance for collective action for altruistic aims. The argument about the need for selective frames developed so far applies to mobilization efforts regardless of the nature of their aims. However, the argument is of particular relevance to altruistic collective action. The dilemma of collective action in the case of mobilization efforts for collective goods, in which constituency and potential beneficiary coincide (or at least overlap), is that even though every member of the group would benefit from collective action, in the absence of some selective motivation mobilization will not occur. Collective action for altruistic aims, however, confronts a double dilemma: even if collective action does come about, no participant will benefit, because the collective good will accrue to a group that is different from the one that has mobilized. As discussed above, the answer is often sought in the claim that participants in altruistic collective action derive personal satisfaction and fulfillment from their sacrifice for the cause of others. This is undoubtedly true, but, as Olson has rightly pointed out in the text fragment quoted at length above, this is no more than a restatement of the problem. Unless we see altruism as a form of sado-masochism, we may well believe that people acting in altruistic ways feel better by acting in these ways, but this does not amount to much of an explanation. Again, we need an explanation that examines factors outside the mobilization process that one seeks to explain.

As in the case of non-altruistic mobilization, the solution may lie in selective framing, which, however, now has a double function. Not only should the selective frame serve to link the emergent movement's aims to the concerns, identities, values and norms of already mobilized collective actors, it must also bridge the gap between the altruistic common aim and the particular interests of constituent groups. In other words, the frame must convince potential participants that "their struggle" is also "our struggle," to paraphrase the well-known rallying cry of solidarity movements in the field of Third World liberation. There are two basic devices by which this may be achieved. The "diagnostic" variant of such frames will point out that those who are responsible for the beneficiary's situation are also those who oppose the group's particular interests (e.g., metropolitan capitalism). The "prognostic" variant will emphasize ways of overcoming the beneficiary's situation, which are also part of the mobilizing group's own set of demands (e.g., socialization of the means of production). Once more, the point has to be made emphatically that this does not imply that participants in altruistic collective action are selfish egoists in hypocritical disguise. The concern for other people's fate may be very real and sincere—just as in the standard dilemma of collective action there is no need to assume that individuals do not care about the fate of the larger group to which they belong. However, the argument is that without some selective motivation, potential participants may deeply deplore the state of affairs of the wretched of the earth, but are unlikely to move into action.

It is not difficult to find examples of such passivity in the face of widespread suffering (despite widespread concern for that suffering). Ubiquitous as altruistic collective action may be, most of the time the suffering suffer alone. Bloody civil wars in Somalia or Sudan; brutal oppression in North Korea or Myanmar; ethnic cleansing in Bosnia or Rwanda—none of this has given rise to significant mass mobilization in the West. In the absence of some signification or meaning that relates to our own situation and concerns, we have stood by and watched, and perhaps cursed ourselves for it. We then say we feel "powerless," although most of the time we would well be able to do something but cannot bring ourselves to do it, trapped as we are in a double dilemma of collective action.

Selective Framing of Racist Violence and the Extreme Right: Evidence from Germany, 1990-1997

We shall now test the preceding argument by looking at claims-making against racist violence, xenophobia, and the extreme right in Germany between 1990 and 1997. In this period, Germany not only saw an unprecedented wave of violence against ethnic minorities, most notably against asylum seekers, but also successes of extreme-right parties in several regional and local elections. Following the above argument, the fact that this wave of xenophobic mobilization provoked a series of impressive counterdemonstrations and public outcries from a wide spectrum of political and civil society, is in no way self-evident. If our argument is correct, this countermobilization cannot be explained just by the fact that the different actors involved in antiracist activities shared a rejection of the brutal violence that struck ethnic minorities. For mobilization to occur on such a massive scale and with such a wide scope, the different actors involved should have been able to insert into their antiracist claims-making other concerns that appealed to their particular group interests, values, and identities.

To test this hypothesis, I use data based on a content analysis of claims-making against racism and the extreme right derived from the coverage by national newspapers.[9] These data are drawn from a larger project on

"Mobilization on Ethnic Relations, Citizenship, and Immigration" (MERCI) that not only includes antiracist claims-making, but any claims-making related to immigration and the integration of ethnic minorities. Apart from Germany, this project also includes studies of Britain, the Netherlands, France, and Switzerland.[10] For the period 1990-97, a total of 2,580 instances of claims-making against racism or the extreme right were coded for the German case. Claims-making here refers not only to forms of protest mobilization (demonstrations, vigils, etc., which constituted about 20 percent of all claims), but also includes public verbal statements by collective actors (about 80 percent of claims). The latter category was included not only because of its quantitative importance as a form of antiracist claims-making,[11] but also because the discursive information contained in these verbal statements was usually richer than for many demonstrations, of which often little more was mentioned than that they were "against xenophobia." Such detailed information on discursive content is, of course, highly important if we want to investigate the ways in which racism and the extreme right were framed by different collective actors.

From our theoretical argument, we derive the following two hypotheses:

(1) Because of the double dilemma of collective action it has to surmount, altruistic claims-making in an undiluted form is unlikely to occur on a massive scale. We may therefore expect most instances of antiracist claims to be framed in such a way that links are established to other aims, values, and concerns that are not themselves purely altruistic in nature.
(2) To be effective, such links must in addition have the character of selective frames, i.e., they must have a particular attractiveness to specific subgroups in the movement's constituency. Therefore we expect that, rather than one single, all-encompassing master frame that appeals to the movement's entire constituency, we find a series of selective frames, each of which is disproportionally advanced by a specific constituency and substantially linked to this constituency's particular interests and values.

These hypotheses are contrasted with the zero hypothesis of undiluted altruism, which we regard as confirmed if our evidence shows that most instances of antiracist claims-making either do not refer to other aims, values, and concerns at all, or do so in (nonselective) ways that cannot be convincingly linked to the particular interests and values of the claimants.[12]

Table 6.1 shows the distribution of all claims against racism and the extreme right, and demonstrates the wide spectrum of actors that were involved in such claims-making. As the table makes clear, claims-making against racism and the extreme right was certainly not limited to the migrants and minorities that were themselves directly affected by xenophobia (8.8 percent) or by organizations within the German population that are, so to speak, "specialized" in antiracism and pro-minority and human rights advocacy (6.7

TABLE 6.1
Distribution of Claims-Making against Racism and the Extreme Right across Different Collective Actors

State and party actors: Christian Democrats	12.6
State and party actors: Liberals	5.2
State and party actors: Social Democrats	12.1
State and party actors: Greens	4.5
State and party actors: other parties/combinations of parties/party affiliation unknown	11.9
Police and judiciary	9.5
Labor unions	3.8
Employers	1.1
Churches	3.5
Science, education, and cultural professionals	4.7
Jewish and Roma organizations	5.7
Other migrant and minority organizations	3.1
Antiracist, pro-minority, and human rights groups	6.7
Other organizations and groups	8.3
Unknown actor	7.5
Total	100.0%
N	2580

percent). Among the minority actors one should note the large share of Jewish and Roma (gypsy) groups, a share disproportionally high compared to that of other minorities, both considering their numbers and their rate of victimization by racist violence. We will discuss the reasons for this high level of mobilization of Jewish and Roma groups below. In contrast, the migrant group that was by far the most affected by right-wing violence, namely asylum seekers, was hardly involved in antiracist claims-making at all. In only three smaller demonstrations (0.1 percent), involving not more than a few dozen people each, did this most-directly-affected group speak up against racist violence. Of course, there are many reasons for this low level of mobilization of asylum seekers, including their precarious legal status, limited resources, geographical dispersion, and high degree of heterogeneity. In conjunction with these factors, it is not hard to imagine that collective action problems of the type described by Olson played an important role in preventing this "latent group" to mobilize in spite of the fact that it was so strongly affected by the problem of racist violence. Lacking any preexisting sense of collective identity or solidarity, the collective actor "asylum seekers" was not able to emerge. Many individuals in this group might have wanted to do something to improve their situation, but none of them was prepared to face the—for this group, non-negligible—costs and risks of mounting collective action in the face of a high level of uncertainty about whether other members of the group would join the effort.

As table 6.1 makes clear, state and party actors were the most important claimants against racism. This included representatives of all of the major parties, to an extent more or less proportional to their electoral importance. Apart from the predictable involvement of the Green party, which has antiracism and multiculturalism as standard elements of its political program, claims against xenophobia were even more frequently made by the Social Democrats (SPD), as well as by representatives of the governing Liberals (FDP) and Christian Democrats (CDU/CSU). In fact, the latter party, which usually favors restrictive immigration and minority policies, was the most important claims-maker of all against xenophobia. The large number of claims by the police and judiciary, not normally groups strongly involved in political claims-making, is also striking. The same can be said of employers associations and private firms, which joined the chorus of antiracist claims-making although normally these actors tend to speak out mainly when socio-economic issues are involved. If we add the involvement of labor unions, churches, professionals in the educational and cultural sector, as well as a wide variety of other groups, it becomes clear that mobilization against racism and the extreme right embraced almost every segment of German politics and society.

According to the argument developed above, the fact that all these groups shared a rejection of violence against immigrants and ethnic minorities is in itself not a sufficient explanation for this broad scope of antiracist claims-making. In order to investigate whether, in addition to this shared stance against xenophobia, selective motivations played a role that might help to explain the involvement of such widely different groups, a detailed investigation of the internal discursive structure of the claims was undertaken. For each of the instances of claims-making, up to four different discursive elements were coded. Apart from the simple rejection of xenophobia, racist violence, or the extreme right, these elements could include identification of the causes (e.g., unemployment, too much immigration, the declining role of the family) or consequences (e.g., damage to Germany's image abroad, withdrawal of foreign investments) of xenophobia and the rise of the extreme right, as well as concrete policy proposals to combat racism and xenophobia (e.g., strengthening the legal position of foreign immigrants, introducing tougher legislation against racist statements and violence, enlarging the competencies and resources of the police, keeping alive the memory of World War II). Such identification of concrete causes, consequences, and solutions allows us to reconstruct the interpretive frames which the different actors transported with their rejection of xenophobia into the public sphere.

Table 6.2 shows that in 47.5 percent of all instances of claims-making no such interpretive frame could be identified. Thus, with regard to our first hypothesis, the evidence does not allow a clear-cut judgment: in only somewhat more than half of the cases did the claims go beyond the mere rejection of racism and evoke aims, values, and concerns outside the field of

TABLE 6.2
Distribution across Different Interpretive Frames in Claims-Making against
Racism and the Extreme Right

No frame identifiable	47.5
Public order frame	14.9
Pro-immigrant rights frame	12.1
Anti-immigration frame	3.6
Remembering the past frame	3.3
Education and youth work frame	2.5
Work, welfare, equality frame	2.4
Germany's image abroad frame	2.0
Other frames	10.7
Total	100.0%
N	2580

antiracism itself. However, to an important extent this may be a result of missing information in the source—daily newspapers—that has been used. In many cases, the newspaper did not report more than the fact that a demonstration "against racism" had taken place somewhere, or that some politician had "called on all citizens to stand up against xenophobia." Such an undifferentiated discursive structure resulted most probably less often because the actors involved really had nothing more to say about the issue, than from the limited size of the space available, which especially during periods of massive antiracist contention forced newspapers to restrict coverage of the large number of claims.

The inconclusiveness of the data with regard to the first hypothesis implies that the weight of evidence will have to rest on those cases (52.5 percent) for which it was possible to identify the interpretive schemata by which actors gave meaning to their involvement against racist violence and xenophobia.[13] A large number of such frames could be identified, not all of which occurred in sufficient numbers to allow further analysis. These less frequent frames were assigned to the "other frames" category in the table (10.7 percent of all instances of antiracist claims-making), and included the blaming of the communist regime of the former German Democratic Republic; the reaffirmation of traditional family and religious values as a means to combat the extreme right; and the depoliticization of racist violence by describing the perpetrators as "isolated criminals" or blaming the problem on excessive alcohol consumption. Seven types of framing, however, occurred with greater frequency (at least 50 cases):

Public order frame (385 cases):
Identification of the causes of racist mobilization in too high a degree of legal tolerance and liberalism, or in shortcomings in the organization or

intervention of the police; depiction of racist violence as a threat to the rule of law and the state's monopoly on violence; solutions emphasizing harsher sentences, tougher criminal legislation, the creation of special police or internal security branches to deal with the extreme right, or bans on racist and extreme-right organizations, demonstrations, and publications; other forms of increased repression and surveillance.

Pro-immigrant rights frame (312 cases):
Identification of the causes of racist mobilization in the stigmatizing effect created by official immigration policies and by the framing of immigration as a social problem in political discourse, or in the vulnerability of immigrants as scapegoats as a result of their weak legal status; solutions emphasizing the need for more liberal immigration politics and expanding the rights of immigrants.

Anti-immigration frame (94 cases):
Identification of the causes of racist mobilization in the overburdening of the population by too high levels of immigration, in the high crime rate of foreign immigrants, political violence between immigrant groups, misuse of the right to asylum, the high costs of immigration for the taxpayer; solutions emphasizing the need to restrict immigration, to take harsher measures against criminal and extremist foreigners.

Remembering the past frame (84 cases):[14]
Identification of the causes of racist mobilization in insufficient remembrance of, taking responsibility for, and learning lessons from the horrors of the Nazi past; solutions emphasizing the need to reinforce such efforts, especially with regard to young people.

Education and youth work frame (65 cases):[15]
Identification of the causes of racist mobilization in shortcomings in existing youth and education policies; solutions emphasizing the need for improvements in, and more resources for, this policy domain.

Work, welfare, equality frame (61 cases):
Identification of the causes of racist mobilization in unemployment, the dismantlement of the welfare state, a too high degree of social inequality; solutions stressing the need to combat such inequality and to reinstate more "social" socio-economic policies.

Germany's image abroad frame (51 cases):
Identification of the consequences of racist mobilization in damage to Germany's image abroad and the threat of withdrawal of foreign inves-

tors, particularly from the territory of the former GDR,[16] where such investments are badly needed.

Each of these frames offers a completely different interpretation of the problem of racist violence and extreme-right mobilization, its causes and consequences, and possible ways to resolve it. While some of these frames may complement each other (e.g., *work, welfare, equality* and *education and youth work*), and others may coexist without contradicting each other (e.g., *remembering the past* and *Germany's image abroad*), some stand diametrically opposed to each other (*pro-immigrant rights* and *anti-immigration*). The existence of these differing views of antiracism and its causes and solutions in itself does not yet prove our argument. If, as stated in hypothesis 2, our argument is correct, these interpretive linkages should have enabled different actors to insert their own concerns and interests into antiracist claims-making and we should find a concentration of particular frames in the discursive repertoire of specific collective actors, related to the specific interests and concerns of these actors.

To investigate this hypothesis, table 6.3 shows the contributions of the different collective actors distinguished in table 6.1[17] to claims-making within each of the seven interpretive frames. As a standard of comparison, the final column shows the percentage share of the different actors in all instances of claims-making that contained an interpretive frame (including the "other frames" category of table 6.2). Thus, the table allows us to see whether actors disproportionally promoted certain interpretive frames in their claims-making in the public sphere. Figures are displayed in bold type where such overrepresentation was particularly strong (more than 50 percent higher than the actor's share in all framing). The results make clear that in many cases, actors' involvement in claims-making for the sake of protecting minorities from xenophobia and racist violence was far from selfless. By selectively framing xenophobia, links were often established to issues that particularly concerned the interests and political viewpoints of the claimants.

Looking first at the public order frame, we see that the single most important promoters of this frame were the police and judiciary, who obviously had a stake in increased repression and more skills and resources for their institutions. The somewhat less pronounced overrepresentation of the conservative Christian Democrats, whose political program has always had a strong law-and-order component, also fits the picture. Generally, the public order frame is relatively strong among the state and party actors, with the exception of the Greens, who on this issue have always been the clearest opponents of the Christian Democrats' law-and-order policies. Civil society actors are generally underrepresented among claimants advancing the public order frame, with the exception of employers, which should come as no surprise in the light of the business community's well-known interest in political stability.

TABLE 6.3
Association between Actors and Frames: Percentage Share of Actors by Type of Frame

	Public order	Pro-immigrant	Anti-immigration	Remembering the past	Education and youth work	Work, welfare, equality	Germany's image	All frames
CDU/CSU	19.5	6.1	**36.2**	10.7	9.2	11.5	21.6	15.4
FDP	5.7	8.3	6.4	4.8	1.5	—	**19.6**	6.1
SPD	12.5	11.2	16.0	6.0	16.9	**26.2**	7.8	12.3
Greens	2.1	**8.7**	2.1	1.2	4.6	**8.2**	—	4.7
Police and judiciary	**23.9**	2.6	3.2	4.8	3.1	3.3	9.8	10.7
Labor unions	2.9	3.8	3.2	—	**6.2**	**9.8**	—	3.5
Employers	2.3	0.3	—	—	1.5	1.6	**17.6**	1.6
Churches	0.5	5.1	**6.4**	3.6	1.5	**8.2**	2.0	3.5
Science, education, and cultural professionals	2.1	6.1	3.2	7.1	**15.4**	**13.1**	3.9	6.1
Jews and Roma	3.9	6.1	1.1	**23.8**	4.6	—	7.8	6.4
Other immigrants	1.0	**8.0**	—	1.2	1.5	—	—	3.2
Antiracist etc. groups	2.9	**13.8**	4.3	**11.9**	6.2	8.2	2.0	6.7
Other/unknown groups	17.7	16.7	13.9	22.6	23.0	9.8	5.9	17.2
Total	100.0%	100.0%	100.0%	100.0%	100.0%	100.0%	100.0%	100.0%
N	385	31	94	84	65	61	51	1354

Bold figures indicate that the actor's share in claims-making referring to the respective frame is 50 percent (1.5 times) or more above the actor's share in all frames.

The pro-immigrant rights frame is advanced by an entirely different coalition of actors. Here we find those antiracist and human rights groups that specialize in pro-minority and pro-immigrant advocacy in a leading position, as well as, unsurprisingly, a disproportional involvement of immigrants themselves. Within the political system, this frame receives particularly strong support from the Greens, and to some extent also from the Liberal FDP, both of which are traditional supporters of extending citizenship rights to immigrants and their descendants.

The Christian Democrats, by contrast, are the most important proponents of the anti-immigrant frame, a particularly inventive form of altruism that seeks to protect immigrants from violence by curtailing their numbers and rights. The Social Democrats, however, also disproportionally advance this frame, although not nearly as frequent as the CDU/CSU. While the latter party's position on the link between combating xenophobia and immigration and minority politics is relatively clear-cut, the pro-minority rights frame is advanced by only a small minority of the party's spokespersons (most prominently federal President von Weizsäcker). The SPD as well as the FDP, however, appear strongly divided on this point, with pro-minority and anti-minority frames represented among their spokespersons about evenly. Indeed, both parties experienced deep internal conflicts in the period under study on the issue of restricting the constitutional right to asylum—a Christian Democrat demand that was ultimately passed by parliament, with SPD and FDP support, in May 1993 (see Koopmans 1996). Counterintuitive, however, is the overrepresentation of the churches among claimants advancing the anti-immigrant frame. However, in three of the six cases we are dealing with here, the assignment of the churches to this frame resulted from their demand to avoid marginalizing perpetrators of racist violence and to open a dialogue with them, which seems a borderline type of frame that does not necessarily imply an anti-immigrant stance.

If we turn next to the frame that emphasizes the need to continue dealing with the Nazi past, we again see a clear association with particular claimants. By far the most frequent promoters of this frame are Jewish and Roma and Sinti groups (gypsies), main victims of the Holocaust, who have occupied a position as "Germany's conscience" in the public debate. The overrepresentation of antiracist groups is largely due to similar groups: five of the eight claims under consideration came from organizations of former members of the Resistance or of survivors of the Nazi concentration camps.[18]

Another differently composed coalition of actors lies behind the education and youth work frame. In absolute terms, the Social Democrats are the most important proponents of this frame, which is in line with this party's traditional preoccupation with education issues. This Social Democratic tradition is also reflected in the labor unions' disproportional involvement in promoting this frame. By far the greatest overrepresentation occurs, however, among the organizations of professionals in science, education, and culture (which include teachers' associations, social workers, universities and research institutes, and writers' associations). It does not need to be argued that this group would stand to profit the most from an allocation of resources (material and symbolic) to the educational sector.

The same group of organizations of professionals is, for similar reasons, also overrepresented among those who advance the work, welfare, and equality frame. That we find such a strong representation of socio-cultural professionals among claimants who advocate solutions that entail an extension of welfare state provisions (which, of course, these professionals provide) confirms so-called "new class" theories, which have pointed to this factor in explaining the prominent role of these professionals in a large variety of advocacy movements (Brint 1984; Kriesi 1989). Given the fact that "work, welfare, equality" goes a long way in describing the Social Democrats' *raison d'être*, it should come as no surprise that they are particularly prominent among the promoters of this frame. Again, we find the labor unions by their side, this time also joined by the Greens and the churches.

Finally, Germany's image abroad and the possible consequences for foreign investments are, for obvious reasons, of particular concern to employers associations and other business representatives, who concentrate almost all of their claims-making against xenophobia on this frame. Also heavily overrepresented among claimants promoting this frame is the liberal FDP, the most clear-cut representative of business interests among the German political parties. In absolute numbers, however, both these collective actors are surpassed by the Christian Democrats. However, while employers representatives refer in all cases directly to potential damage to the German economy, all Christian Democrat claims within this frame refer broadly to "damage to Germany's image abroad," without specifying the particular damage. (The FDP presents a mixture of these two variants.)

In conclusion, then, we find strong evidence for our second hypothesis. Behind the apparent consensus suggested by the common rejection of racist violence and the extreme right, as well as by the participation of a wide range of actors in demonstrations such as the one in Berlin, a wide variety of interpretations of the problem of xenophobia competed for public attention. These interpretive schemata established links to a wide variety of other policy areas (education, social welfare and employment, dealing with the heritage of the Nazi past, law and order, immigration and minority rights, etc.), which, unlike the rejection of xenophobia, were issues highly contested in German politics and allowed claimants to link antiracism to their own interests and values.

Conclusions

Neither rational choice theorists, nor their opponents who emphasize the role of collective identity and solidarity, have been able to give convincing explanations for the widespread phenomenon of altruistic collective action. Adherents of the rational choice model have either, like Olson himself, defined altruism as a (not very relevant) form of behavior to which their theories do not apply, or have, like many resource mobilization theorists, stretched the notion of "selective incentives" beyond recognition to include anything that gives participants personal satisfaction when participating. While the competing "identity" approach at least has the advantage of being compatible with the ubiquity of altruistic collective action, its explanation is in the end not less tautological, referring as it does, too, to the moral satisfaction, sense of identity, and feelings of solidarity that people derive from sacrifice for the cause of others. The problem with such "explanations" is that ultimately they tell us little more than that people engage in altruistic action simply because they are altruists and feel good about it.

The approach chosen in this chapter has been to see altruism neither as a form of egoism in disguise, nor as a self-explanatory phenomenon. Instead, the argument advanced takes seriously that many people are concerned with the fate of other people, but states that they will only transform this concern into mobilization if there is in place a selective frame that establishes a bridge between the fate of the beneficiary group and the interests and values of the constituency of mobilization. Such selective frames are based on (combinations of) at least three argumentative strategies. They may (a) point to causes of the beneficiary's situation that already concerned the constituency for other reasons; (b) point at consequences of the beneficiary's problem that would affect the constituency; or (c) formulate solutions to improve the beneficiary's situation that were already favored by the constituency for other reasons.

Our data on antiracist claims-making in Germany in the 1990s have largely confirmed this idea. Different categories of claimants tended to promote different assessments of the causes and consequences of, and solutions to, the problem of racism and xenophobic violence, and each of them did so in ways that referred to causes opposed, consequences feared, and solutions favored already for reasons other than the group's rejection of racism. Thus, the police and judiciary called for stricter laws and more resources for law enforcement; the Social Democrats pointed to the need to combat unemployment and preserve the welfare state; employers pointed to the risks of disinvestment and damage to Germany's image abroad; Jewish groups emphasized the need to keep the memory of the Holocaust alive; and the conservatives called for limitations on immigration and harsher measures against immigrant crime.

Once again, it should be stressed that this is not the same as saying that altruism is just egoism in disguise. There is no need to suppose that the rejection of racism and the concern for the fate of its victims was not real among any of the groups just mentioned, nor can it be credibly explained by some sort of personal "feel good" factor. However, while altruism is not reducible to self-interest, neither is it thinkable—at least in its public and collective form—without a healthy dose of it. To be sure, this implies that undiluted altruism is politically unviable, but, then again, probably so is undiluted self-interest. Just as a shot of self-interest is necessary as a catalyst for altruistic collective action, so it is nowadays almost impossible for self-interested collective action to achieve public legitimacy without some credible reference to the common good.

Notes

1. Recall that Olson's main empirical evidence refers to labor unions (as an example of a "large or latent group") and employers associations (an example of a "small or privileged group").
2. The large concession that Olson here seems to make to the generality of his theory is limited by his claim that the phenomena to which it does not apply are relatively rare and insignificant. Thus the reference to "mass movements" is immediately followed by: "which, incidentally, are usually not very massive" (162).
3. This distinction is similar to, though not identical with, Klandermans' (1988) distinction between "consensus mobilization" and "action mobilization."
4. This possibility has, in fact, been taken into account by Olson, although he downplays its empirical importance. According to Olson, large groups may succeed in overcoming the dilemma of collective action by way of "social incentives" if the group consists of smaller groups "each of which has a reason to join with the others to form a federation representing the large group as a whole" (Olson 1971, 62-3).
5. Note that this argument rests on the assumption that these subgroups of the peace movement are already mobilized as collective actors, which themselves have already overcome—at least to an important extent—the dilemma of collective action. Peace movement efforts to link its demands to the interests of another latent group (say, the unemployed) would, in this view, be futile, for they would only relocate, not resolve, the collective action problem.
6. For other examples, see Gerhards and Rucht (1992).
7. For a similar argument and supportive data relating to the German anti-nuclear energy movement, see Kliment (1998).
8. For a further discussion of these three elements of a movement's discursive success, see Koopmans and Statham (2000).
9. For the present analysis, these data were drawn from every second issue (Monday, Wednesday, Friday) of the *Frankfurter Rundschau* between 1990 and 1997. Smaller samples were selected and coded from other newspapers, local as well as national, to check for possible biases in this main source. These checks did not reveal any differences that could have significantly affected the analysis presented here.

Information on these comparisons among different media sources, as well as on external validations with nonmedia sources and intercoder reliability, are available from the author upon request. For a further discussion of this methodology, see Koopmans and Statham (1999a).

10. The British case study is undertaken by Paul Statham at the University of Leeds; Thom Duyvené de Wit at the University of Amsterdam studies the Dutch case; Marco Giugni and Florence Passy at the University of Geneva are responsible for France and Switzerland.

11. For a critique of the tendency in studies of social movements and political contention to focus exclusively on "unconventional" or "disruptive" forms of claims-making, see Koopmans and Statham (1999a).

12. It might be argued that because of the inclusion of verbal claims as a particularly low-risk and low-cost form of mobilization, our data do not allow a valid test of our argument. However, the bias introduced by including low-cost forms of action will run against the hypotheses advanced here, rather than favoring their unwarranted confirmation. Perhaps selective frames (and selective incentives in general) will not be a necessary precondition for low-cost and low-risk claims-making precisely because the costs and risks are so low. However, if we find selective frames to be relevant even in the case of low-cost and low-risk action forms, then we may be reasonably confident that they will be at least as—and probably more—important for more costly forms of collective action.

13. In a small number of cases, several frames were present in a single instance of claims-making. In such cases, the claim was assigned to the least frequent of the constituent elements (as long as it did not belong to the "other frames" category). For example, if an actor referred to both the public order frame and the anti-immigration frame, the claim was assigned to the latter frame.

14. "Remembrance of the past" somewhat clumsily translates the German term *Vergangenheitsbewältigung*, which refers to the need to learn from the errors of German history, i.e., Nazism, World War II, and the Holocaust.

15. It is important to point out here that a large majority of acts of racist violence were committed by young people in their teens and early twenties (see Willems, Eckert, Würtz, and Steinmetz 1993).

16. Racist violence was disproportionally concentrated in the five "new federal states."

17. The table excludes those instances of claims-making for which no interpretive frame could be identified

18. Insofar as such organizations did not specifically represent Jewish or Roma survivors.

7

Political Opportunities for Altruism?

The Role of State Policies in Influencing Claims-Making by British Antiracist and Pro-Migrant Movements

Paul Statham

Introduction

Traditionally the concept of political altruism carries a heavy load of normative baggage. There is a strong bias in the concept of an altruistic movement for conflating the definition of the movement with the reasons for what it does and why it does it. Randall Collins (1992) once warned social movement researchers of the dangers of romanticism, claiming that they over-researched the revolutionary moments at the expense of more "normal" conditions, and that the urge to uncover the next revolutionary movement had become too strongly ingrained in the analytic approach to the subject. In the case of altruistic movements, the consequences of such limitations are even higher, as the explanation for the movement may be predetermined by the normative criteria which were used for defining and selecting it. At worst, the analysis of altruistic movements may become simply a tautology, in which alternative explanations are precluded, and empirical analysis is reduced to seeking "altruism" or "goodness" in the individuals or psychological makeup of the movement's constituents or activists.

Of course, at the individual level we may be dealing with "good" people who are motivated to help others and contribute to a collective public good more than their individual self-interest dictates—thus solving Olson's (1965) classical "free-rider" dilemma of how to explain collective action for public goods with non-excludable benefits. Such cases of "pure" altruistic sentiments may even be considered a psychological phenomenon that is "normal" at the individual level in certain social settings. However, social movements are phenomena that are both *collective* and *political*; they are where people come together with the explicit aim of making a political challenge that is more powerful than the aggregate sum of their individual attributes. Analytically, we are therefore not really interested *per se* in people who transgress the normal limits of altruistic sentiments—i.e., the pathologies of individual cases—but in how "altruism" is constructed and serves as a strategic basis for collective mobilization against state authority in specific political settings. Rather than focusing on the motivations of individuals, this chapter looks at how and why altruistic movements mobilize in relation to the sets of political opportunities which confront them in a specific political issue field. Following the specifications laid down by the editors, who were keen to encourage country and thematic variability across the contributions, the chapter studies political altruism in British immigration and ethnic relations politics.

Inspired by Martin Luther King Jr.'s visit to London in December 1964, the first broad, independent movement, Campaign Against Racial Discrimination (CARD), mobilized against the British state's politics of immigration and ethnic relations. Initially, this movement had some success lobbying for amendments in the 1965 Race Relations Bill and proposing antidiscrimination measures. Amid co-optation of leading activists by the government's National Committee for Commonwealth Immigrants (NCCI) and the Labour party, however, tensions emerged between moderate and radical campaigners and CARD was a spent force within a few years (Shukra 1998). In the intervening years, most British attempts to form a broad, church-affiliated, antiracist and pro-migrant movement have collapsed like a "house of cards." At times British activists have been tempted to look with envy across the Channel at the size and public visibility of solidarity movements, such as SOS Racisme in France (see discussion in Mactaggart and Phillips 1995). Nonetheless, despite the absence of a mass mobilized solidarity movement, the British state's institutional framework for combating racism and discrimination is today more robust than France's, which indicates substantive gains for some of the movement's goals. This apparent paradox underlines a point that is central to the contribution here: that it is necessary to look at the context of power relationships in the contested political field, and in particular the policy approach of the state, when assessing the actual strength of solidarity movements. The political influence of solidarity movements does not necessarily reflect the visible "size" of organizations, demonstrations, or protests in the public domain. Under conditions of state policy responsiveness, mobilizing moral discourses of exhortation and public displays of solidarity may be a relatively ineffective use of resources. "Solidarity" may be adequately performed by small, specialist organizations targeting insider publics in the policy arena.

It is not coincidental that the decline of CARD, as a broad issue movement, occurred at the same time as the decision by the British political elite to inaugurate new immigration and ethnic relations policies. Discussions of such impacts of state co-optative and preemptive responses to challenges by social movements are commonplace in the literature (see, especially, Gamson 1990). However, less attention has been paid to the relationship between state responses to social movements that are making political demands for other constituencies rather than themselves. In Britain, the marginal political position and relatively small size of the foreign migrant and minority populations mean that support from national and ethnic majorities will be an important factor in achieving gains for these beneficiaries. In addition, as *state intervention* constitutes a political authority for defining and providing a public good—thus providing a common way for societies to overcome Olson's "free-rider" dilemmas—it is the relationship of the state to the beneficiary group that will be challenged by altruistic movements. In this contribution, I apply a political opportunity approach and study the British state's policy intervention into immigration and ethnic relations, in relation to the nature of the challenges by altruistic mobilization in that contentious field of politics. Defining altruistic mobilization as claims-making in which the beneficiary of the political goal differs from the constituency group that makes it, our two movements for enquiry are: firstly, antiracist mobilization by the ethnic majority against the inequality caused by racism and discrimination for ethnic minorities; and secondly, pro-migrant mobilization by British nationals on behalf of groups without national or equivalent citizenship status, such as asylum seekers, foreigners, and refugees.

Although British state policies distinguish sharply between race relations and immigration, this is a nationally specific political construction. In addition to co-opting the challenge of CARD, it was the policy decision taken by the British state in the late 1960s to prevent future immigration from the New Commonwealth and Pakistan, but at the same time to "integrate" ethnic minorities who were already resident, that has had a long-term political effect. It has produced a set of rights different for Britain's resident Commonwealth subjects than for the ones living away from the motherland. This process was completed by the 1971 Immigration Act and 1981 British Nationality Act in which the state effectively severed the rights of nonresident Commonwealth subjects. In the meantime, race relations legislation built an institutional framework for preventing racial discrimination and upholding ethnic minorities' rights within Britain. This split between "foreign migrants" and "national ethnic minorities" still underlies the idiosyncratic British politics of immigration and race relations. Objectively, they are not really separate political issue fields, but strongly related with overlapping constituencies. By comparing antiracist and pro-migrant movements, it is possible to see what effects the different approaches of state intervention—one pro- and one anti-beneficiary—have in shaping the field of political contention and opportunities that are available for mobilization on behalf of these similar groups.

In the next section, I develop this conceptual approach to altruistic mobilization. I then give brief details on the "migrant" and "minority" beneficiaries in the context of British immigration and ethnic relations politics. After setting the scene, the remainder of the chapter is a detailed comparison of the political issue fields in which the altruistic movements operate, their organizations, action forms, targets, and framing strategies. Finally, in the conclusion, an attempt is made to bring together the particular characteristics and determinants of this type of movement that are highlighted by the British experience.

Altruistic Mobilization: Framing Beneficiary Interests within Broader Concerns

When direct forms of institutional access to the polity are blocked, challenges for extending a beneficiary's rights require a more indirect strategy for changing state policies (Tarrow 1998). As it occurs when beneficiaries are too weak to make autonomous demands on the state, altruistic mobilization has a specialized function that is strongly based in discursive strategies and public constituency building. The principal task is introducing a definitional change within a political discourse so that the interests of the beneficiary are defined as part of the common public good, and are no longer seen as something that can be provided for by the pursuit of individual interests—a market logic, which leads to "free-riding." Ultimately, movements intend this redefinition of the public good to become the legitimating basis for state policies. Thus altruistic mobilization attempts to push the state to define racism and discrimination as detrimental to the whole of society, not just as a problem for individuals of ethnic minority origin, and immigration as beneficial to the whole of society, and not just as the self-interest of the asylum seeker or foreign migrant, or potential employer. Introducing such changes into the way that a national political community defines itself is clearly no easy task. Public perceptions are notoriously intransigent, not least because they are embedded in a resilient national culture and legitimated through the existing institutionalized political practices of the nation-state.

Faced by the difficult task of attempting to link the interests of a beneficiary to the perceived interests of other actors, the first task of altruistic mobilization is mobilizing a consensus (Klandermans 1988), so that sufficient visibility is given to the problem in the public domain. Campaign strategies for attempting to introduce new definitions and perceptions of political problems into the public domain, to galvanize the interests of a broad constituency of public actors, or to mobilize increased support, have been discussed as "frame alignment processes" (Snow et al. 1986). Snow and his collaborators use the concept of "frame alignment processes" for studying the ways in which individuals link their interpretative orientations of interests, values, and beliefs (individual frames), to the set of interpretative orientations represented by the activities, goals, and ideology of a movement organization (movement frames). Although their own research focuses on the participation of individuals, they also point out that "frame alignment processes" can take place at the organizational level, either between two movement organizations or between movements and other organizations (467). Importantly, this means that movements may use strategies to produce "frame alignment processes" within the interpretative frameworks of other public actors. This framing approach—which links movement frames to the dominant representations of the political environment, and points out that discontent, resources, and opportunities have to be cognitively defined and constructed, i.e. "framed," for collective mobilization to take place—is now commonplace (see, especially, Gamson 1988; Gamson and Modigliani 1989; Snow and Benford 1988; Eder 1996). It emphasizes that movement activists have to define issues as problematic collective concerns, identify causes, present solutions, and make the actors and institutions that are supposed to implement them both accountable and visible in the public domain. They do this not only to convince their constituents that mobilization is necessary, but to be more convincing than other actors, such as counter-movements, civil society actors, and public authorities, who promote alternative definitions of the situation and policy proposals. The public domain is thus a competitive field, and movement activists must make their demands appear more convincing than their opponents, otherwise they have little chance of mobilizing support, or provoking reactions, that may lead to political change and state responses.

In the past, the framing approach has been criticized for not being determinant in specifying why some framing attempts are more successful than others, and for falling back on post hoc explanations (Koopmans and Duyvendak 1995; Diani 1996; Koopmans and Statham 1999a, 1999b). Obviously, not all framing attempts are likely to be equally successful in mobilizing support. Political issue-fields have a structure that influences the potential of the framing attempts by movements to be effective (Gamson 1988). Moreover, this structure of political issue fields and the potential for an issue to become contentious is largely dependent on the institutional structures and power configurations that have been the traditional focus of political opportunity approaches (see, especially, Tarrow 1989, 1998). Much recent work has led to the discursive dimension of contentious issue-fields being related more systematically to the institutional dimension in defining the political context into which claims are mobilized (e.g., McAdam, McCarthy, and Zald 1996b; Gamson and Meyer 1996; Statham 1998). Starting from this premise, political discourse may be seen as a set of *discursive opportunities* that determines which of the strategic framing attempts by movements are more likely to achieve visibility, resonance, and legitimacy in the public domain (Koopmans and Statham 2000).

From this perspective, discursive opportunities are the public-sphere dimension of "institutional" political opportunities, and include access to legitimating discourses, potential alliance networks, and public support that may be disseminated through the news media. There are at least three conditions that need to be met for movements to introduce effective "frame alignment processes" into politics, and which will be particularly important for altruistic movements. First, unless a movement organization possesses sufficient resources to make itself *visible* in public by having its actions and aims reported by the media, it will have few chances for reaching potential adherents. Second, unless it mobilizes demands that provoke reactions from other public actors, that is, it *resonates* in the public domain, it will have few chances of carrying the contention to a broader public. Third, regardless of how visible and resonant a contention becomes, the movement organization will only have the chance to become successful when its demands are perceived as *legitimate* by a constituency sufficiently large to create a general perception that a political response is necessary.

Turning to the possible outcomes, the first ones concern the movement. If an altruistic movement succeeds in mobilizing highly visible and resonant demands, that are perceived as legitimate by a sufficiently large public constituency, then at some stage the state is likely to make some form of political response. Of course, elites may choose to ignore or repress movements. However, another possible type of state response is that the political elite will co-opt or preempt the movement's demands, which is likely to open up institutional channels of access to the political challenge (Gamson 1990). Under these circumstances the discursive strategies of challengers are likely to be replaced by more direct forms of institutional involvement in the political process. For altruistic movements, this successful outcome carries a paradox. Once political elites start responding to the framing efforts of altruistic mobilization, the task of the altruistic movement—making the goal visible and redefining the relationship between the general public good and the beneficiary group—has been largely achieved. Altruistic mobilization thus tends to play a sort of "midwife" role in the life of a successful campaign movement and is rather ephemeral on the public stage, unless the state chooses to resist. In the long term, altruistic movements are only likely to be sustained as a large public movement if they are relatively unsuccessful in achieving a political response to their demands. When a substantial political response occurs their altruism withers away, though in real power terms the challenge may be stronger as it is reinforced through the institutional framework of the nation-state.

A second consequence of successful altruistic mobilization is its effect on the nature of the contested issue-field. When political elites start to sponsor the issue by including beneficiary interests within the common public good, even in a watered-down form, then this opens up channels of institutional access to a whole range of intermediary actors, who suddenly have a self-interest in adopting a compliant position. New collective actors may enter the field in the scramble for state patronage and resources, and the movement may be marginalized, as the whole nature of the contentious political field is transformed. For example, if a state policy is promulgated stating that racism and discrimination require redress, this political act restructures the set of political opportunities—both institutional and discursive—facing collective actors and provides incentives for actions which fall into line with official policy. Such material, status, solidarity, and moral inducements—in this case provided by the state—were seen by Olson (1965) as "selective incentives" that offer a way of explaining collective mobilization by actors for public goods with indivisible benefits (on "selective incentives" for movements, see also Fireman and Gamson 1979; Snow and Benford 1988; Koopmans, in this volume). The aim of this contribution is to demonstrate how the availability of such "selective incentives" is shaped as a set of political opportunities by the state's policy stance toward the beneficiary group.

To study the public dimension of conflicts in immigration and race politics, and compare altruistic mobilization in the two fields, a set of data is used for political claims-making on ethnic relations, citizenship, and immigration in Britain in the period 1990-96.[1] Political claims-making takes the form of public statements, interviews, press conferences or other speech acts, but also includes protest forms such as demonstrations or violence. The data set is derived from a content analysis of instances of political claims-making—by all kinds of actors, not just movements and civil society actors—which were reported in the national media. In addition, the findings from the data set were interpreted with reference to in-depth semi-structured interviews with antiracist and pro-migrant activists.[2]

In the next section, background details are given on the relationship of the movements' beneficiaries to British politics, before moving on to the empirical analysis.

The Beneficiaries: Minorities and Migrants in Britain

Race and immigration are similar issue-fields in that they define the relationship of a specific beneficiary group—ethnic minorities and migrants—to the national political community. Ethnic minorities and new migrants have similar characteristics in their racial and ethnic difference from the majority population, but the main difference between them lies in their access to rights of national citizenship and the political system.

Ethnic minorities, which in Britain account for about 5 percent of the population, are a group which has faced high barriers against becoming an autonomous force in politics. Britain's African-Caribbean and Asian populations have made some inroads in the political system. There are a handful of black members of parliament and trade union leaders, and ethnic minorities play an important role in the local politics of areas of high minority concentration. However, British ethnic minorities remain a relatively small minority of the population who suffer disproportionately high disadvantages—because of the effects of discrimination—according to virtually all social indicators (see, e.g.,

Mason 1995; Modood et al. 1997). Although significant steps have been taken through race relations and antidiscrimination policies to combat the inequality and discrimination faced by minorities (Lester 1998), the political opportunities facing them are not sufficiently favorable to make autonomous mobilization superfluous (Statham 1999).

Another group with even less material and symbolic resources to mobilize an autonomous presence in British politics are migrant noncitizens. Foreign migrants, asylum seekers, refugees, and illegal immigrants, who lack access to British or European Union (EU) citizenship rights, are by definition excluded from the national process of political participation. Unlike ethnic minorities, who in most cases possess full formal social and political rights, either by being a Commonwealth subject on entry or by birth, contemporary non-EU migrants to Britain face extremely high barriers to receiving official rights to residence, let alone citizenship. Britain has been depicted as a "would-be country of zero immigration," and policies have resisted immigration even when this might have brought economic benefits (see, e.g., Layton-Henry 1994). Current inflows of migrants are asylum seekers fleeing political unrest or persecution, but nonetheless the British elite pathology for resisting new migration at all costs remains intact, not least because of fears that it may upset the balance of existing "race relations." Although bound by international and human rights conventions—for example, Geneva Convention, United Nations—to uphold minimum rights of access for migrants, Britain routinely admits fewer potential refugees per head of population than most other EU countries. In addition, asylum seekers are strongly stigmatized in British political discourse as "bogus" and "welfare scroungers," which once more reinforces the symbolic boundary markers to excluding them from the national community.

The Political Issue-fields of Race and Immigration

In assessing the potential for antiracist and pro-migrant challenges to achieve framing successes—that is, binding the interests of their beneficiary within a common public good—it is important to know the overall political context and discursive opportunities which confront them. Table 7.1 represents the discursive political space in which the two challengers operate. It gives a distribution of the political claims-making by all actors in the issue-fields of immigration (column 1) and race (column 3), and an average "valence" score to show the position of each actor in the issue-fields (columns 2 and 4), ranging from -1 for an anti-beneficiary position to a +1 pro-beneficiary position. Thematically, "immigration" covers all political claims-making that refers to the relationship between foreign migrants and the British national political community, including border control, policies, social provision, and migrants' rights. "Race" politics is the issue-field of claims concerning the

TABLE 7.1
Claims-Making by Actors in Immigration and Race Fields, 1990-1996
(Percentages and with Average Valence Scores)

	Immigration		Race	
	Actors (%)	Valence (1 to -1)	Actors (%)	Valence (1 to -1)
Supranational/foreign government	2.7	0.25	1.1	n/a
Central and local government	29.0	-0.51	6.3	0.36
Central and local legislative	19.5	0.52	14.6	0.48
Judiciary (national)	9.9	0.65	5.6	0.59
Security agencies (police/immigration)	2.3	-0.55	7.5	0.09
State institutions (health, education, social services, etc.)	1.2	0.33	1.6	0.67
Total institutional	**64.6**	**0.02**	**36.7**	**0.42**
State sponsored bodies for minorities/migrants (e.g., CRE, RECs)	1.2	1.00	6.1	0.91
Central/local political party organizations	1.2	0	1.7	0.30
Unions and professional organizations	1.4	0.86	4.6	0.88
Employers and business organizations	1.9	0.11	1.1	0.50
Churches	2.3	0.82	1.1	0.67
Media	1.2	0.67	3.0	0.18
Research, education, cultural, and arts organizations	0.4	n/a	7.0	0.90
Civil society organizations/groups (other)	0.4	n/a	1.1	0.83
General welfare and human/civil rights organizations	4.1	1.00	1.8	1.00
Beneficiary-specific [a] welfare and rights organizations	11.2	1.00	1.3	1.00
Antiracist organizations and groups	0.2	n/a	6.7	0.87
Beneficiary organizations and groups	6.8	0.91	18.4	0.90
Minority organizations non-beneficiary (only asylum/immigration)	2.1	1.00	—	—
Racist and extreme-right organizations and groups	0	n/a	6.8	-0.87
Public actors	0.8	n/a	2.6	0
Unknown actors	0	n/a	0.2	n/a
Total civil society	**35.4**	**0.85**	**63.3**	**0.61**
Total	100.0		100.0	
N	483		570	
Overall average valence		**0.31**		**0.54**

Subcategories do not add up precisely to 100% due to rounding errors.

For valence score to be attributed: N > 5.

[a] Migrant-specific for immigration; minority-specific for race.

relationship between the ethnic majority and minorities with full access to citizenship in Britain. It covers institutional policies, implementation, and outcomes, including claims that the state is a source of discrimination, and acts of societal racism, prejudices among the majority public, and extreme-right mobilization.[3] For "valences," each claims-making act was coded as to whether it was anti-migrant or anti-minority/racist (-1), pro-migrant or pro-minority/antiracist (1), or neutral or ambivalent (0). Average valence scores thus position an actor, or an issue-field, on an axis between pro-beneficiary (1) and anti-beneficiary (-1).

A first general point is that the race issue-field is more pro-beneficiary (0.54) than immigration (0.31). This shows that actors are more likely to take positions that are favorable to ethnic minorities than they are toward migrants, and that political contentions over race take place on an axis which is more pro-beneficiary than those over foreign migrants. Another general difference concerns the split between institutional and civil society actors. Immigration controversies are dominated by institutional actors who account for two-thirds of claims-making (64.6 percent) with an overall anti-beneficiary position (0.02, compared to mean 0.31). In contrast, almost two-thirds of "race" claims-making (63.3 percent) is by civil society actors. Race is thus predominantly a conflict within civil society, whereas the state's institutional actors play a dominant role in immigration conflicts. Regarding the split between state institutional and civil society actors, there is much less polarization between institutional actors (0.42) and civil society actors (0.61) in race politics than immigration (institutional actors 0.02; civil society actors 0.85). Importantly, this shorter discursive distance between civil society and institutional actors in race politics indicates a much more favorable set of discursive opportunities and a greater potential for framing attempts to travel from the public domain to political decision-makers.

These general differences between race and immigration politics can be traced back to the position of the British state on minorities and migrants. The state defines ethnic minorities' interests as part of the common public good, by officially recognizing that racism and discrimination are detrimental to the whole of British society. Under the 1976 Race Relations Act, and the advice of the Commission for Racial Equality, the state upholds the principle of "racial equality," and undertakes to redress any inequality caused by direct and indirect discrimination against individuals on the basis of "race, color, or national origins." In contrast, since the 1971 Immigration and 1981 British Nationality Acts, foreign migrants' interests are defined externally to the national common good, and defended by the British state principally by requirements of international and human rights conventions. These differences in the British state's definition for extending rights and obligations to migrants and minorities strongly influence the opportunities available for pro-beneficiary claims-making. Whereas opposition to the inequality brought by racism and discrimination is formally embedded in state legislation and political practices, extending rights and recognition to minorities within British politics, foreign migrants have heavy restrictions placed on their rights of access, and are defined as "outsiders" to the national political community. In general, then, it is much easier for actors to support minorities than migrants, as the institutionally embedded stance of the state provides greater "selective incentives" of material and symbolic resources for claims-making on behalf of a beneficiary whose well-being is officially part of the common good.

Turning to the different positions among the state institutional actors, these are important indicators of the discursive opportunities available for entering politics and finding powerful institutional allies. With the exception of the police (7.5 percent; 0.09 valence score), the antiracist movement faces a relatively favorable and consensual political institutional setting, though it is more likely to gain backing from the judiciary and state bodies than legislative and government bodies. In immigration politics there are clearly strong divisions among institutional actors, in particular between the government which has a very strong anti-migrant position (29.0 percent; -0.51) and the legislative (19.5 percent; 0.52 valence) and judiciary (9.9 percent; 0.65) which have strong pro-migrant stances. These conflicts between government and parliament over immigration, and with a pro-migrant judiciary, clearly offer opportunities for the pro-migrant movement to find powerful institutional allies despite the overall hostility of the political environment.

Another important way that challenges can be mediated between state institutional politics and civil society is through party politics. Although not shown in table 7.1, it is possible from the data to aggregate the different types of actors—for example, members of parliament, prime minister, local councilor—by their party political identity. In immigration politics there is a strongly polarized position. The governing Conservative party takes a strong anti-migrant stance (33.1 percent; -0.50), and the Labour opposition party a strongly pro-migrant position (10.6 percent; 0.80). On race the main political parties are more consensual, although once more the Labour party (9.3 percent; 0.66) takes a more pro-beneficiary stance than the Conservatives (7.2 percent; 0.29). This left-right party polarization of race and immigration fits with the Labour party tradition for promoting minority interests—having several members of parliament of minority ethnic origin—and the Conservative tradition for one-nation nationalism. After inserting the caveat that the Labour constituted the political opposition for the period of the data, and that it is easier for parties in opposition to be more positive than governments, there are nonetheless clear opportunities for antiracist and pro-migrant movements to find discursive allies and institutional backing through targeting claims toward the Labour party.

After briefly outlining some of the differences and similarities in the institutional politics of race and immigration, highlighted by the data, we now turn to table 7.1 and compare the alliance networks within antiracist and promigrant challenges in civil society, before examining the nature of these challenges more closely in the remainder of the empirical section. A first point concerns the share of claims-making by beneficiaries. In race politics, ethnic minorities are the single most prominent actor, accounting for just less than a fifth (18.4 percent) of all claims-making. In comparison, foreign migrants account for less than a fourteenth (6.8 percent) of immigration claims. Minorities are able to draw on sufficient material and symbolic resources—as a beneficiary defined by the state within the general interests of the political community—to importantly shape the politics which is *about* them. Migrants, as a group that lacks legitimacy in state politics, are more reliant on other actors to challenge on their behalf.

A second point is that state sponsorship of minorities actually stimulates a broad network of supporters for the antiracist challenge. This occurs directly through the state's race quangos—that is, quasi-autonomous nongovernmental organizations—(6.1 percent; 0.91), such as the Commission for Racial Equality, and indirectly through the availability of "selective incentives" of material and symbolic resources of state patronage to civil society actors. Thus research, education, cultural and arts organizations (7.0 percent; 0.9), and trade unions (4.6 percent; 0.88) find "incentives" for making antiracist demands, for example, by advocating good race relations practices, holding cultural events which ritualize the nation-state's antiracism, or producing knowledge that legitimates it. There might even be high costs for not taking a public antiracist stance when the state upholds such principles as part of national citizenship. However, these mainstream civil society actors have far less to say about immigration. In the relative absence of state patronage, it is the church (2.3 percent; 0.82) and resident minorities (2.1 percent; 1.0) which take up the pro-migrant challenge by drawing on non-state "incentives" of shared faith and kin with the beneficiary. The pro-migrant challenge is dominated by the solidarity sector of migrant welfare and rights organizations (11.2 percent; 1.0), and general welfare and rights organizations (4.1 percent; 1.0). These draw on material "incentives" for servicing the state's welfare obligations to migrants, and moral and solidarity "incentives" defined in international civil and human rights discourses.

Overall the nature of the race and immigration fields are strongly shaped by the different positions of the state toward the beneficiaries. The contentious field of immigration resembles a classical state-challenger dichotomy in which migrants and welfare organizations mobilize against the government, attempting to frame foreign migrants within the national public good. In the context of state intervention, race politics is more like a multi-organizational field, in which a range of state and civil society actors, and the beneficiary, take up positions defining disputes within a broad antiracist consensus. The clear opponent to this broad consensus is the extreme-right British National Party and racist organizations (6.8 percent; -0.87). They seek to reverse the state's commitment to include minorities within the national public good, and take up a highly anti-minority position that is a discursive gulf away from all

other civil society and state actors. The small number of antiracist organizations in the race field form a mirror-image to the racists in valence and size
(6.7 percent; 0.87), which indicates movement and counter-movement dynamics between the two actors explicitly engaged in pushing the normative
limits of the state's antiracism. It is possible to bring out more specific details
of these differences between race and immigration by looking more closely at
the type of organizations which make up the pro-migrant and antiracist challenges in civil society, as well as the action forms which they use to mobilize,
and the institutional and civil society actors whom they target with demands
(addressees).

Pro-Migrant and Antiracist Activism: Organizations, Action Forms, and Addressees

In table 7.2 only the civil society actors making pro-beneficiary demands are
included.[4] These actors are subdivided into four categories along an axis
ranging from beneficiary to state-sponsored organizations which co-opt their
goals. Between the poles of "beneficiary" and "official" advocacy, we find
altruistic mobilization. "Core" altruistic claims-making is conducted by organizations that have identities that define the sole purpose of their activism
in defending the interests of the beneficiary. In contrast, "general" altruistic
claims-making is by organizations which act for more general constituencies
than either "national minorities" or "foreign migrants." Table 7.2 also gives
the distribution of action forms used by of these actors. "Conventional" are
those such as public statements and press conferences; "demonstrative" are
symbolic non-confrontational protests, such as peaceful demonstrations and
vigils; "confrontational" protests include strikes, hunger strikes, and boycotts;
and finally, "violent" protests are illegal acts, causing damage to people or
property.

The types of organizations and distribution of action forms indicate important differences in the movements. Although accounting for only an eighth
(12.1 percent) of the challenge, core antiracism has a highly protest-oriented
(39.7 percent) and even violent (21.2 percent) action repertoire. This radical
core comprises of a large number of small organizations. They include protest campaigns such as Anti-Racist Alliance, Anti-Nazi League, Youth
Against Racism in Europe, Searchlight, Campaign for Racial Justice; local
and single-issue groups such as Tower Hamlets Anti-Racist Committee,
Hackney Community Defence Committee, and Quaddus Ali Committee; and
even a militant clandestine group, Anti-Fascist Action. In contrast, core pro-
migrant activism has a larger share in claims-making (35.3 percent), but more
than nine-tenths (92.6 percent) used conventional action forms. Core pro-
migrant activism was dominated by two organizations which provide welfare
support and advice to migrants (81.5 percent), the Joint Council for the Wel-

TABLE 7.2
Action Forms of Pro-Beneficiary Actors in Civil Society, 1990-1996 (Percentages)

	Antiracist beneficiary	Antiracist core	Antiracist general	Antiracist official	Antiracist civil society [a]	Pro-migrant beneficiary	Pro-migrant core	Pro-migrant general	Pro-migrant civil society [b]
Conventional actions	81.3	60.6	95.5	90.6	**88.1**	62.1	92.6	85.9	**89.5**
Demonstrative protest	7.3	15.2	2.7	9.4	**6.3**	0	7.4	12.5	**9.7**
Confrontational protest	3.1	3.0	0.9	0	**1.1**	37.9	0	1.6	**0.8**
Violent protest	8.3	21.2	0.9	0	**4.5**	0	0	0	**0**
Total	100.0	100.0	100.0	100.0	**100.0**	100.0	100.0	100.0	**100.0**
% of all pro-beneficiary claims by civil society actors	35.3	12.1	40.8	11.8	**64.7**	19.0	35.3	41.8	**81.0**
N	96	33	111	32	**176**	29	54	64	**124**

[a] All civil society demands, excluding beneficiary claims-making.
[b] Includes six cases of "official" pro-migrant (which are not subcategorized due to small size).

fare of Immigrants and the Refugee Council, whereas protest campaigns such
as Asylum Rights Campaign and the Campaign to Close Campsfield are less
prominent.

Turning from the core to the general movement sectors, the antiracist challenge is composed less of campaigning nongovernmental organizations (13.5
percent) than its pro-migrant counterpart (37.5 percent). Whereas antiracism
is carried by a whole range of mainstream civil society actors, almost two-
fifths of the general pro-migrant challenge was carried by campaign organizations. These encompass human and civil rights organizations such as Amnesty International, Charter 87, International Red Cross, Liberty, Citizens'
Advice Bureau; welfare campaigns such as Medical Foundation for the Care
of Victims of Torture, Alert, Homeless Families' Campaign; and, to a lesser
extent, minority organizations like Council of British Pakistanis, Black Female Prisoners' Scheme; and the antiracist organization Youth Against Racism in Europe.

For the antiracist movement, it appears that frame alignment at the organizational level has advanced to such an extent that the challenge is normal-
ized and carried by mainstream civil society institutions. This has polarized
core antiracism into a small, radical set of movement organizations.
Antiracism carries such resources of legitimacy in British society that a considerable proportion of the radical core (21.2 percent) even consider themselves justified in undertaking violent and illegal actions. In contrast, frame
alignment processes in the pro-migrant challenge move between the core
organizations and a set of more general human and civil rights campaign
organizations. Facing a more restrictive political context, the constituency-
building of core pro-migrant claims aims at tying in other campaign organizations, and thus attempting to generalize the beneficiary-specific claims as
visible political demands.

Table 7.3 develops the picture further by showing the state institutions and
civil society organizations addressed by pro-beneficiary claims. A general
striking difference is that three-quarters (74.4 percent) of pro-migrant claims
directly target government and legislative state actors, whereas the antiracist
challenge targets a broader range: a quarter (26.2 percent) address other civil
society organizations, another quarter (24.8 percent) the extreme-right/racist
groups, and only a quarter (24.1 percent) the government and legislative.
Once more this is best explained by the different opportunities facing the
movements. The pro-migrant movement needs to target the state with demands and force a political change so that the state recognizes migrants
within its definition for the common public good. In contrast, in race politics
in which the state gives a special recognition to defending minorities, the
antiracist challenge makes sure the state enforces this commitment, challenges other civil society actors to uphold these principles of racial equality,
and combats those who refuse to accept minorities within the political community. Whereas the pro-migrant challenge attempts the difficult task of

TABLE 7.3
Addressees of Pro-Beneficiary Actors in Civil Society, 1990-1996 (Percentages)

	Antiracist beneficiary	Antiracist core	Antiracist general	Antiracist official	Antiracist civil society [a]	Pro-migrant beneficiary	Pro-migrant core	Pro-migrant general	Pro-migrant civil society [b]
Supranational and foreign government	0	0	0	0	0	4.3	5.0	2.4	5.7
Central and local government and legislative	10.5	8.3	25.5	34.8	24.1	60.9	82.5	66.7	72.7
Judiciary	7.1	4.2	8.2	13.0	8.3	13.0	5.0	2.4	3.4
Police and security agencies	43.5	16.7	12.2	4.3	11.7	13.0	5.0	9.5	6.8
State institutions (other)	2.4	0	5.1	8.7	4.8	0	0	0	0
Civil society organizations	24.7	4.2	30.6	30.4	26.2	8.7	2.5	19.0	11.4
Extreme-right and racist organizations/groups	11.8	66.7	18.4	8.7	24.8	0	0	0	0
Total	100.0	100.1	100.0	99.9	99.9	99.9	100.0	100.0	100.0
% with addressee	88.5	72.7	68.5	71.8	82.4	79.3	74.1	65.6	71.0
N	85	24	98	23	145	23	40	42	88

Self-references are excluded.
[a] All civil society demands, excluding beneficiary.
[b] Includes six cases of "official" pro-migrant.

introducing frame alignment processes into a hostile institutional political environment, the antiracist challenge has the legitimacy of state support to extend frame alignment processes into the public domain.

The general differences are brought out more clearly by differences between the core and general movement sectors. The core pro-migrant sector directly challenges the nation-state (82.5 percent), and even makes demands on supranational and foreign governmental institutions (5.0 percent) to change British immigration politics. Core antiracism also has a targeting function, but mobilizes principally (66.7 percent) against extreme-right and racist organizations. Considering its violent action repertoire this emphasizes the counter-movement function of core antiracism. In contrast, the general movement sectors of both antiracism (30.6 percent claims addressing civil society organizations compared to 4.2 percent) and pro-migrant claims (19.0 percent compared to 2.5 percent) have a more constituency-building function within civil society than their respective cores.

Having studied the issue-fields, organizations, action forms, and targets, I now turn to types of frames and language that antiracist and pro-migrant groups use in the attempt to make their demands visible, resonant, and legitimate.

Framing in Antiracist and Pro-Migrant Challenges

The type of frame which collective actors use is an important indicator for the way that they attempt to make their claims resonant and legitimate in broader public discourses—introducing general frame alignment processes. In their important research, Snow and Benford (1988, 200-204) distinguish three types of framing: diagnostic, prognostic, and motivational. Diagnostic framing occurs when claims identify and define a problem or attribute blame or causality. Prognostic framing goes a step beyond problem specification or blaming to define strategies, tactics, and targets concerning "what is to be done." Both diagnostic and prognostic framing use "factual" reasoning. Diagnostic framing points out "causes and effects" and culprits, whereas prognostic framing sets out how to do something about these identified "causes and effects" and responsible culprits by acting. Lastly, motivational framing goes beyond both diagnostic and prognostic and constitutes a "call to arms" and rationale for action that is strongly normative. Motivational framing adds a moralizing dimension to the specification of problems, culprits, and strategies, and produces cognitively "hot" arguments that demand collective action to redress perceived injustices.[5]

Moving from diagnostic and prognostic to motivational framing involves a shift from factual to normative based reasoning, and from invoking a responsive to pro-active stance in the target public. Regarding the potential for introducing frame alignment processes into the perceptions of other actors, motivational framing is particularly important, as it not only seeks to build consensus for specific problem definitions, but it actually gives a justification for people to join in and do something about them. Motivational framing comes closest to demanding a general pro-active frame alignment in an issue-field, by mobilizing a set of counter-norms into the political discourse by defining a perceived injustice.

Table 7.4 gives the distribution of the framing in claims made by pro-beneficiary actors in the race and immigration issue-fields.[6] To Snow and Benford's three framing types, I have added moral appeals. Moral appeals are parallel to diagnostic framing in that they function to define a problem. Instead of specifying problems through references to "causes and effects" and culprits, moral appeals construct a normative image of the beneficiary by referring to values, such as depictions of asylum seekers as "victims," or minorities as "good people." Unlike motivational framing, a moral appeal is without a "hot" cognition or a call to arms; it simply states the problem in a value-laden setting. A first general finding relates to the type of framing by altruistic movements in race and immigration politics. Pro-migrant demands use an equal amount of normative framing types (45.2 percent moral appeals and motivational) and factual framing types (47.6 percent diagnostic and prognostic), whereas the ratio of factual to normative framing types in antiracist demands is 3:1 (62.5 percent diagnostic and prognostic compared to 22.8 percent moral appeals and motivational). The higher use of moralizing frames by the pro-migrant challenge can be explained by the discursive opportunities facing the two organizations. Facing few channels of access to state institutions and a hostile political environment, pro-migrant claims-makers undertake consensus mobilization strategies—by making moral appeals to society's values, or invoking a "hot" normative reasoning so that an injustice suffered by the beneficiary is highlighted as of sufficient general concern to provoke response *within* British politics. In contrast, antiracist claims-makers are able to align their demands in a political discourse in which the state already acknowledges the legitimacy of the beneficiary's grievances and the need to address its problems. First, this makes it easier for antiracists to cross the first hurdle of gaining visibility for their demands, and second, it means their demands lock directly into factual policy debates for specifying the causes of and solutions to the problem. Clearly, the factual types of antiracist framing which directly target policy debates are more likely to be effective politically than moralizing strategies aimed at public constituency building.

Looking at framing within the pro-migrant and antiracism challenges, once more differences are apparent in the function of the core and general movement sectors. In both cases, the core activists used more motivational framing than the general sector (antiracist: 27.3 percent core, 11.7 percent general; pro-migrant: 42.6 percent core, 25.0 percent general). This shows that the core sectors mobilize to push the normative limits of the challenge and at-

TABLE 7.4

Framing in Pro-Beneficiary Demands by Actors in Civil Society, 1990-1996 (Percentages)

	Antiracist beneficiary	Antiracist core	Antiracist general	Antiracist official	Antiracist civil society [a]	Pro-migrant beneficiary	Pro-migrant core	Pro-migrant general	Pro-migrant civil society [b]
Moral appeals	7.3	9.0	5.4	6.3	**6.3**	13.8	14.8	12.5	**12.9**
Diagnostic	31.3	18.2	41.4	28.1	**34.7**	17.2	14.8	25.0	**20.2**
Prognostic	24.0	12.1	30.6	34.4	**27.8**	—	27.8	23.4	**27.4**
Motivational	17.7	27.3	11.7	21.9	**16.5**	5.3	42.6	25.0	**32.3**
Frame absent	19.8	33.3	10.8	9.4	**14.8**	65.5	—	14.1	**7.3**
Total	100.1	99.9	99.9	100.1	**100.1**	100.0	100.0	100.0	**100.1**
N	96	33	111	32	**176**	29	54	64	**124**

[a] All civil society demands, excluding beneficiary.
[b] Includes six cases of "official" pro-migrant.

tempt to make proactive political responses appear legitimate in the public domain. In race politics, the general movement sector is strongly characterized by diagnostic and prognostic framing (72.0 percent) as compared to the core (33.3 percent). This shows that general activists are better able to mobilize frames relating factually to the political problem, whereas the core carries the normative challenge. Such differences are less pronounced between the core (42.6 percent) and general (48.4 percent) sectors of the pro-migrant movement, which mobilize similar proportions of diagnostic and prognostic framing strategies.

Lastly, it is worth studying the actual language used in some of the claims, to see how the movements attempt to frame the beneficiary's interests in relation to broader constituencies. Here the focus is on motivational framing. This is the process in which movements explicitly aim to push the normative limits of a problem definition in the public domain, and attempt to invoke favorable responses of active political support. Following Snow et al. (1986), who identify four dimensions of "frame alignment processes"—frame bridging, amplification, extension, and transformation[7]—I analyze the alignment properties that are evident in the language of antiracist and pro-migrant claims.

The motivational framing by "core" antiracists focused principally on issues in which injustices were defined as relating to racial attacks, the ineffectiveness of state attempts to prosecute perpetrators of racial attacks, and extreme-right activism:

> The black community has a right to defend itself and will do so in the face of such violence (Anti-Racist Alliance, 9 September 1993).

> There is something rotten at the heart of the Crown Prosecution Service when it deals with racist murders (Anti-Racist Alliance, 29 July 1993).

What is interesting in the language of these claims is that they attempt to bring a general frame alignment process into the official legitimating concept of "racial equality." By bridging antiracism with general injustices perceived in the workings of the British justice system, and amplifying the special rights of black people faced by racial violence, the core activists attempt to introduce a general frame transformation by pushing the limits of the official concept of "racial equality" to a more proactive variant.

In contrast, motivational framing by the general antiracist movement focuses on issues that are related to perceived injustices in the existing race relations framework, and the state's and public actors' obligations to implement and uphold "racial equality":

> Black and Asian staff, large numbers of whom work in the Department of Social Services agencies, are already cynical about their employers' commitment to racial equality. This will make them more cynical (trade union, 28 April 1996).

The council has become apparently out of control, flying in the face of its commitment to good race relations practice, unwilling or unable to honour a cardinal policy pledge (college, 14 March 1993).

The Church of England is a racist organization. People there constantly act in a racist way towards ethnic minorities (public, 3 December 1992).

This resettlement scheme could give legitimacy to racists seeking to expel black people. It would set back the fight for black people to be accepted as belonging to this country. This is a Pandora's box which should be resisted by anyone with a sense of decency (Joint Council for the Welfare of Immigrants, 7 October 1993).

Here, rather than pushing for the recognition of a new set of "racial equality" rights, activists attempt to legitimate their demands by amplifying their reference to the existing rights for minorities that are defined within race relations politics. They push the limits by seeking a frame alignment which justifies a more general proactive implementation of existing measures by state bodies and civil society organizations.

In sum, the core claims attempt to transform the beneficiary's interests within the public constituency, so that greater recognition is given to the injustices of racism and greater special group rights of protection extended to ethnic minorities, and to frame this as part of the common public good. In contrast, the general claims draw on the existing definition of the beneficiary's interests within the public constituency that is laid out in race politics, and amplify this obligation within the common good.

Turning to the pro-migrant "core," motivational frames mobilized here focused on issues relating to perceived injustices in legislative proposals for immigration and asylum, and the administrative implementation of state policies for foreign migrants:

The new clauses are a slap in the face for black people who experience all too often the refusal of visa for family occasions (Joint Council for the Welfare of Immigrants, 1 August 1994).

It was a total humiliation for black people. We will be challenging the fact that they have no right of appeal (Joint Council for the Welfare of Immigrants, 22 October 1992).

The only goal British immigration policy has ever had was to keep certain people out. That was never morally sufficient, and now it is not even a pragmatic solution (Joint Council for the Welfare of Immigrants, 26 December 1993).

The proposed visa list was clearly directed at black people and would divide the Commonwealth along race lines (Joint Council for the Welfare of Immigrants, 30 October 1990).

The interesting feature of these demands is that they attempt to legitimate the position of migrants in British society by bridging and extending immigration issues into the legitimating discourses on race relations. By referring to race, black people, and the Commonwealth, activists aim to transform the legitimating basis of the political discourse on immigration. These demands "racialize" immigration and asylum politics and aim for a general frame alignment, so that the state's actions toward migrants appear as part of its special obligations to ethnic minorities laid out in the commitment to "racial equality." Although the state now treats them as separate policy fields, immigration and race relations policies historically have been strongly related in British politics (Layton-Henry 1994). The motivational framing of pro-migrant "core" attempts to bridge these fields by reaching into the legitimating discourses of antiracism.

Finally, the motivational framing by general pro-migrant claims-makers focused on the same set of issues as that of the core:

The blatantly unjust way in which this country has dealt with these people is widely condemned throughout the world . . . . The government should release all detainees unless the Home Office is prepared to provide clear proof (Liberty, 7 March 1991).

Torture victims are the most vulnerable people in the world and most of those who applied for asylum came from countries which had historical ties of empire to Britain. The motive behind Mr Howard's bill is to introduce a harsh regime (media actor, 23 April 1996).

Not only does the "safe third countries rule" have no basis in international law but the Home Office's failure to ensure that the asylum seekers concerned will be admitted to the third country has led to some people being returned to the country of persecution (Amnesty International, 25 July 1993).

The portrayal of those failing the test as foreign benefit "spongers" is a travesty of the truth . . . . The majority of cases are British citizens returning from abroad for quite legitimate reasons, who are being denied the right to live here (Citizens' Advice Bureau, 29 January 1995).

In contrast to the core, the general pro-migrant activists do not aim explicitly to "racialize" the obligation of the British state to migrants. Instead, the general motivational frames aim more to amplify the international obligations of the British state, by bridging concerns for migrants to legitimating discourses on human rights and the special rights of citizens former British colonies. Here the attempt is to introduce a general frame alignment by moralizing the rights of migrants to be present in British society.

Regarding pro-migrant claims, these frame the beneficiary's interest within the public constituency, by bridging and extending migrants' rights into the special recognition that ethnic minorities already receive, or alternatively by amplifying the international, historical, and human rights obligations of the British state.

Conclusion

This study of altruistic mobilization began with a dilemma similar to Olson's (1965): How can such movements mobilize and define a beneficiary's interests as part of the common public good, when public goods invite "free-riding" and are notoriously difficult to provide by a market logic for pursuing individual interests? After comparing the different political contexts faced by the antiracist and pro-migrant challenges in relation to their various action forms, addressees, and framing, it is clear that the important factor is the intervening role of the state in contentious politics. Despite similar characteristics in racial and ethnic difference of the beneficiary groups, the comparison of antiracist and pro-migrant challenges reveals significant differences that can be traced to the differential level of political sponsorship by the state. From this I deduce that the availability of political opportunities—and, in particular, the role of the state in defining "selective incentives" for pro-beneficiary positions—is a better explanation for the forms, addressees, and framing strategies of altruistic movements than those based on assessments of the overall levels of individual altruistic sentiments. As state intervention provides common public goods that market forces and individual self-interest will not, and is a way that societies overcome "free-rider" dilemmas, it should perhaps not surprise us that a state's political approach toward the beneficiary has central importance in shaping altruistic mobilization. However, the moral discourses of altruistic movements have sometimes deflected the attention of researchers away from such contextual political explanations, although they are commonplace for other types of social movements.

In the case of antiracism, the state has assumed an official duty to redress racism and discrimination against its ethnic minority citizens, and a whole range of "selective incentives" are structured into the political opportunities facing other actors to actively support antiracist positions. Trade unions and the Labour party court ethnic members and voters, whereas the interests of research and cultural institutions are supported by grants for antiracist advocacy activities. Actually there would be high costs for these institutions if they did not publicly support antiracist positions. When the state extends special group rights to its minority citizens, this becomes part of the public common good, embedded in the reflexive legitimating discourses of the national political community. Discourses upholding "racial equality" become a basis for citizenship and part of the national identity, embedded in the public perceptions of civil society actors. As a consequence, frame alignment processes which are sponsored by antiracist challengers have a relatively short distance to travel to convince political decision-makers, and are unlikely to provoke outright opposition in the public domain. Many civil society actors face opportunities to help themselves by helping ethnic minorities, and compete to position themselves for state patronage. Conversely, taking up a racist position bears the high costs of challenging the dominant legitimating discourse and may lead to being outcast from the political community—the fate of the extreme right.

Operating in this generally favorable political context, core antiracist activism has specialized into a set of small organizations. These organizations still primarily direct their campaign efforts to the public domain, but as their beneficiary is officially recognized as a special member of the national community, their function has moved beyond constituency-building among the general public. Instead, these groups aim to push the limits of a state's recognition of its special obligations to uphold racial equality still farther, and enforce compliance with such principles by other public actors. Their discursive strategies target specialist publics of the "insiders" in the policy community, and their confrontational actions target the political "outsiders" of the racist extreme right. For example, Searchlight has the status of an educational trust, producing a monthly magazine of original research and providing information services and lecture tours. Searchlight has a very small core team of six people and six volunteers, but has access to strong contacts and relationships with investigative journalists and television documentary teams. In an interview, Gerry Gable, editor of the magazine, told us that Searchlight "holds the moral high ground and can criticize anyone" and attempts to "bring people news and analysis they will not get anywhere else." The communication strategy of this discursive wing of the core movement sector makes sure that the public duty of "altruism" toward minorities remains visible, and its moralizing presence is designed to ensure that the state and civil society "specialists" in the field do not forget to implement their political obligations.

In contrast to antiracism, the pro-migrant challenge finds strong opposition and its main opponent in the nation-state. British governments take an anti-immigration position, and intervene in assisting migrants only to the extent that they are required by international law and human rights norms. New foreign migrants are officially defined as undermining the common public good, a position reflected in the discourses on national identity and belonging which construct the "otherness" of foreigners. Official state sponsorship of the non-legitimacy of foreign migrants—or at least those without EU citizenship—is embedded in the national conception of citizenship, and the public perceptions of national identity reflecting the British "island mentality." Confronted by this hostile discursive and institutional political context, pro-migrant challengers face the difficult task of mobilizing frame alignment processes into the very conception of the national political community. Without state sponsorship, other public actors have few incentives for lending support. Only the church and resident ethnic minorities were significant allies pursuing the non-state "selective incentives" of common faith and kin. Relatively isolated in the public domain, the pro-migrant movement does draw some support from other campaign movements which broadly address human and civil rights.

Despite these high barriers, the pro-migrant movement is still able to mobilize sufficient resources to mount a visible public challenge to the authority of the British state. Pro-migrant activists appeal for including migrants in the national community on the basis of the special post-colonial or human rights obligations of the British state. Relatively lacking in direct channels of access to British politics, the claims of the pro-migrant movement target the public domain and have a strong moralizing dimension in their constituency-building strategy. Core activists seek to make migrants' interests appear part of a common good, or shared common grievance, or injustice. At the grass roots, mobilizing public support relies on a difficult strategy of bringing people into contact with the beneficiaries, and appealing to universal principles of justice and fairness. Suke Wolton of the Campaign to Free Campsfield[8] told us that it was the detention of asylum seekers that proved the turning point in galvanizing public support:

> People who would have been very doubtful about Britain accepting immigrants and very . . . quite racist basically . . . have been transformed by the idea that people lose their liberty on the basis of nothing, and particularly, it's extraordinary in Oxford to meet lots of . . . how do I put this lightly? . . . little old ladies who are completely radicalized by the experience of visiting detainees. . . . They come out much more political and active about the whole issue.

The sharp distinction made between migrants and ethnic minorities is a political construct, and to some extent a national peculiarity of Britain. It is, however, a political construct that has a basis in British citizenship rights, and is strongly embedded into public perceptions, even shaping minority political action (Statham 1999). Confronted by this differential set of political opportunities, it is unlikely that the antiracist and pro-migrant challenges will combine in a broad church movement again. Antiracists no longer need to attempt to change attitudes by exhortation. They can work and campaign within an institutional framework for neutralizing racial discrimination. Subsequently, the supporters of the new migrants are left even more isolated in the public domain, and their beneficiary even more remote from access to rights. However, pro-migrant activists' motivation for a more internationalist Britain, one that is more attentive to upholding human and civil rights, provides sufficient incentives to carry the campaign forward and at least make it visible in the public domain.

Notes

1. The present data are based on every second issue (Monday, Wednesday, Friday) of the *Guardian* for Britain 1990-96. The reliability and validity of these sources were checked and confirmed by comparisons with several other national newspapers. This

data base has been collected as part of a large international project on mobilization on ethnic relations, citizenship, and immigration (MERCI) that covers Britain (current author), Germany (Ruud Koopmans of WZB Berlin), France, Switzerland (Marco Giugni and Florence Passy of the University of Geneva) and the Netherlands (Thom Duyvene de Wit of the University of Amsterdam). The British data collection was funded with a grant award from the Economic and Social Research Council (R000236558) held by the current author. Further details on the method, based on an extension of protest event analysis, are given in Koopmans and Statham (1999a).

2. Activists were interviewed from the following movement organizations between November 1998 and January 1999: National Assembly Against Racism, Operation Justice, Churches Commission for Racial Justice, Hit Racism for Six, Anti-Nazi League, Searchlight, Campaign to Close Campsfield, and National Coalition of Anti-Deportation Campaigns. These interviews were made possible by a grant award from the Economic and Social Research Council (R000236558), and I thank Windsor Holden for his assistance in conducting them.

3. Excluded from this "race" field are issues relating to demands by minorities for "homeland politics," and cultural demands for group rights and recognition that occur outside of the relationship of minorities to the nation-state.

4. Each act by a civil society actor in which the claim scored a +1 valence, i.e. in which pro-migrant in the immigration field, and pro-minority/antiracist in the race field.

5. Gamson (1992) also emphasizes the importance of "injustice" in successful collective action frames.

6. The frames were coded from the actual use of language in the claim (direct and reported speech) that appeared in the newspaper source.

7. *Frame bridging* occurs when two or more different types of frames are linked together by a movement on a particular issue or problem. *Frame amplification* is a strategy for invigorating an interpretative frame for a particular issue, problem or set of events, so it has greater appeal to public constituencies. *Frame extension* takes place when a movement amplifies specific frame elements in order to encompass interests or points of view that are incidental to its primary objectives but of considerable importance to potential adherents. Lastly, *frame transformation* occurs when a movement redefines its primary interpretative frame, by defining new causes and effects of the problem, or blaming a new set of opponents for the perceived injustice.

8. Campsfield House is a former youth detention center near Oxford which was "converted" for housing asylum seekers amid controversy.

Part III

Transnational Dynamics

8

Situational Effects on Political Altruism

The Student Divestment Movement in the United States

Sarah A. Soule

Introduction

The chapters in this volume examine various aspects of a common phenomenon we call *political altruism*. By this, we mean social movements with an altruistic orientation in which participants mobilize to defend the interests and rights of others. We assume that participants in such movements do not benefit directly from their actions, an assumption that runs counter to Olson's (1965) assertion that individuals will only act collectively if there is a possibility of attaining selective benefits. We assume that activism, sometimes even very high risk activism, is often motivated by moral, rather than selfish, concerns. In fact, our use of the term *political altruism* is somewhat akin to Hannah Arendt's (1961) assertion that political action is motivated by "principles," not merely by individuals' self-interest.

To be sure, ideas about the existence of altruism in social movements and political activism are not new. Two decades ago, McCarthy and Zald (1977) wrote of "conscience constituents," a term borrowed from Harrington (1968), and Gamson (1975) wrote of "universalistic movements." An early example of empirical work in this area is Rosenhan's (1970) study of highly committed activists in the civil rights movement whom he terms "autonomous altruists." But only recently have social movements scholars revisited this earlier work. One example of this more recent work is Rucht's (1995) concept of "distant issue movements," or movements in which no improvement is expected in activists' own conditions; instead, participants act purely on behalf of others whom they will probably never meet. Smith's (1996) exceptional book on the U.S. Central American peace movement is a prime example of a scholarly account of a "distant issue" or altruistic movement. Teske's (1997) analysis of U.S. activists' accounts of involvement clearly demonstrates that not all political participation is motivated solely by external rewards.

In addition to the growing interest in altruistic behavior by scholars of social movements, social scientists outside of this subfield have begun to reconsider the concept of altruism. Scholars in two excellent edited volumes by Mansbridge (1990) and Powell and Clemens (1998) have offered an alternative to the notion that individuals are motivated exclusively by self-interest. Many of the authors represented in these two volumes offer an alternative to rational choice explanations for human action by arguing that, in many instances, moral concerns *do*, in fact, motivate human action.[1] Simply put, many of these authors believe that "principled concerns somehow carry the actor beyond considerations of simply what is good for the actor" (Teske 1997, 24).

This growing body of work has been indispensable as we as social scientists attempt to understand altruistic behavior. But missing from these recent treatments is a serious discussion of the voluminous body of research by psychologists and social psychologists. In particular, it may be useful to examine the long tradition of field and experimental research on *situational factors* found to influence altruistic behavior.[2] In this chapter, I explore how some of these situational factors may have influenced one case of political altruism in the United States: the student divestment movement between 1978 and 1990. I have chosen, for the purposes of this chapter, to focus on two of the situational factors which seem especially useful to the study of political altruism: the modeling of altruism and the observation of wrongdoing.[3]

First, psychologists and social psychologists have found that altruistic behavior is very likely to occur when the potential actor witnesses others engaged in altruistic behavior. Rather consistently, research has shown that altruistic responses may be induced by behavioral examples. In other words, altruistic behavior is often imitated or copied by other actors. This seems especially relevant to the social movement discussed in this chapter. In the 1980s, U.S. college campuses came alive with student protest aimed at encouraging universities to divest of their holdings in securities related to South Africa. The quintessential protest tactic used during this student movement, the "shantytown," rapidly diffused or spread across campuses (Soule 1995, 1997).[4] I argue here that part of the reason for the spread of this tactic is that altruistic behavior, more generally, has been shown to diffuse through processes of imitation or modeling. In essence, models provide information on the costs, benefits, and possible outcomes of some behavior; when advantageous, others imitate that behavior, leading to its diffusion.

A second situational factor found by psychologists and social psychologists to influence altruism is the observation of harm-doing. According to this research, if a potential actor witnesses the wrong done to a victim, he or she is far more likely to act on that victim's behalf. This also seems quite relevant to the case of the student divestment movement in the United States, as students were able to witness the effects of apartheid on black South Africans through the international news media coverage of events in that country, which grew to unprecedented levels in the 1980s. On top of this, students at campuses where activists had constructed shanties were provided with a symbolic demonstration of the harm-doing in South Africa. In short, it was not easy to ignore the plight of black South Africans under the system of apartheid. Observing the wrongdoing via the mass media and the construction of the shanties may have led U.S. students to act altruistically on behalf of individuals in that country.

It is important to note at the outset that these two factors have been found by social psychologists and psychologists to influence altruistic behavior at the *individual* level. Part of the task of this chapter, then, is to suggest that these might also operate at the *collective* level in the case of a social movement such as the student divestment movement. To this end, I will attempt to illuminate the collective parallels to some of the underlying psychological mechanisms hypothesized by these researchers. Following a brief history of the movement in the United States, I will describe each of these two situational factors influencing altruistic behavior in greater depth and attempt to show how they may have come into play between 1978 and 1990 during the student divestment movement. To do this, I will discuss how altruistic behavior is imitated and diffuses, and how this may have fostered the diffusion of the shantytown protest tactic used during the divestment movement on college campuses. Following this, I will discuss how the observation of harm-doing increases altruistic behavior, and I will argue that both media attention to South Africa and the shantytown tactic itself may have induced potential participants to act altruistically.

The Student Divestment Movement in the United States

Beginning in 1948, the South African system of apartheid was formally installed, making South Africa the "most ethnically stratified society of the modern world" (Aguirre and Turner 1998, 275). Essentially, apartheid refers to the state-sanctioned segregation of the entire population according to skin color. Apartheid's racial laws determined all aspects of South African citizens' lives, from where they lived and went to school, to whether or not they were allowed to own land or marry a neighbor (IDAF 1983). The system of apartheid made it possible for the numerical minority (white) to completely dominate and subjugate the numerical majority (black). By controlling the land, the governing body, the media, and access to economic resources, white South Africans were able to maintain apartheid for over four decades (IDAF 1983). Apartheid made it possible for over 80 percent of the nation's resources to be allocated to less than 20 percent of the population (Obasanjo 1977). The intent of apartheid was well articulated in 1971 by Prime Minister H. F. Verwoerd when he said: "We want to keep South Africa white. . . . [K]eeping it white can only mean one thing, namely, white domination . . . not leadership, not guidance, but control, supremacy" (quoted in Williams-Slope 1971, 16).[5]

One of the best examples of a politically altruistic movement in the recent history of the United States is the student divestment movement that took place in the 1970s and 1980s. It is important to note, however, that the divestment movement had its origins in its broader predecessor: the student antiapartheid movement (Soule 1995). The origins of the student antiapartheid movement may be traced to the Sharpeville Massacre of 1960 in which sixty-nine peaceful black protesters were slain by police in South Africa. This event was followed by the United Nations African-Asian block boycott of South Africa, which helped fuel the fires of activism on campuses in the United States (Jackson 1992). Following these events, the immorality of the South African system of apartheid concerned activists in the United States, but the level of this concern fluctuated in the 1960s and 1970s, as indicated by the cyclical nature of such student activism (Soule 1995; Jackson 1992; Vellela 1988).

In the late 1970s and 1980s, though, students narrowed their goals from the broader goal of ending apartheid to the more narrow call for divestment by their own universities. In 1976 and 1977, a group called Catalyst began sponsoring speakers on divestment at colleges and universities (Vellela 1988). These speakers brought to the attention of students the fact that college portfolios routinely held stock in companies entrenched in South Africa, a fact which galvanized support amongst students (Vellela 1988). The first college to divest was Hampshire College, after an organized student movement on that campus. Within a year, students at the University of Kansas were actively involved in a campaign to force university divestment. By 1982, student activists at Columbia University were pushing for divestment with frequent student protests (Soule 1995). In short, divestment had become "The Big Issue" (Williams et al. 1985).

This narrowing of the movement's primary goal from concerns about human rights violations under apartheid to university divestment was consequential. At the same time as this was happening, the racial situation in South Africa was worsening, drawing a great deal of media attention to the country. In 1985, the South African government declared a state of emergency, triggered by political activism by black South Africans. More than five thousand people in South Africa had been killed as a result of the increasing levels of political violence, a number that would rise to eleven thousand five years later (Soule 1995). The deteriorating situation in South Africa prompted organized labor, the clergy, and politicians to call for divestment by U.S. companies (Soule 1995). This call did not fall upon deaf ears at colleges and universities; rather, students pressed forth with their call for university divestment.

In the remainder of this chapter, I shall describe the two situational factors that affect altruistic behavior and discuss how these may have influenced the student divestment movement in the United States and the diffusion of a protest tactic. First, I shall describe how the modeling of altruistic behavior may be an important mechanism which helps explain the diffusion of the shantytown tactic. Second, I shall describe how media attention to South Africa and the symbolic meaning of the shantytown tactic itself may have allowed activists the opportunity to observe the harm done by apartheid, and thus may have increased the propensity to act altruistically on behalf of the victims of apartheid.

The Modeling of Altruistic Behavior

According to psychologists and social psychologists, the observation of models induces individuals to imitate behavior (Krebs 1970; Bandura and Walters 1963). In the case of altruistic behavior, this has been found to occur under experimental conditions in both the laboratory and the field. For example, Rosenbaum and Blake (1955) and Rosenbaum (1956) demonstrated that volunteering behavior on the part of a model induced others to volunteer. Bryan and Test (1967) and MacCauley and Berkowitz (1970) showed that individuals are more likely to donate money to the Salvation Army kettles when they have just witnessed a model donating money.[6] Rosenhan and White (1967) and Hartup and Coates (1967) both show that children act altruistically by donating their own gifts and gift certificates won in a game when they have watched a model making such donations.[7] In studies more relevant to the field of social movements, a model's willingness to sign a petition increased on-lookers' willingness to do so (Blake, Mouton, and Hain 1956; Helson, Mouton, and Blake 1958); leaders of the abolitionist movement reported that they had been influenced by altruistic others (Tomkins 1965); and committed civil rights activists reported influences from altruistic parents (Rosenhan 1970).

Social psychologists and psychologists have attempted to uncover the underlying psychological mechanisms for the tendency of altruistic behavior to generate imitation. In general, most agree that the model helps individuals to define and choose appropriate behavior by helping to clarify the potential costs and rewards of altruistic behavior (Berkowitz 1972; Bar-Tal 1976).

I wish to suggest in this chapter that this *individual* level mechanism for the diffusion of altruistic behavior may also operate at the *collective* level. In the subsequent section, I will argue that the careful, and collective, monitoring of other campuses during this movement provided information about the costs, benefits, and perceived outcomes of the shantytown tactic. I argue below that students and the media alike regarded shanties as successful at encouraging universities to divest; thus this altruistic activism spread rapidly across campuses.

The Evolution and Diffusion of a Protest Tactic

The hypothesis that altruistic behavior will be copied or imitated by others is important to the study of social movements, especially to the study of diffusion within social movements. There has been a recent increase in interest about diffusion within social movements (see Strang and Soule 1998 for a review). Thus understanding how altruistic behavior may diffuse is important to the study of social movements, especially politically altruistic movements.

Few scholars would disagree with the contention that at any particular point in time, there is a relatively limited set of different forms of collective action employed by social movement organizations. How is it that disparate social movement organizations seem to converge on a similar set of tactics? Tilly (1978) argues that social movement organizations often employ flexible repertoires of contention which permit the observation and imitation of other groups' tactics. By mimicking tactics utilized by other groups, a social movement organization may increase its effectiveness—especially if the tactics copied are successful. Activists "do not have to reinvent the wheel at each place and in each conflict. Rather, they often find inspiration elsewhere in the ideas and tactics espoused and practiced by other activists" (McAdam and Rucht 1993, 58).[8]

In the mid-1980s, activists all over the United States began protesting, demonstrating, signing petitions, building blockades, staging sit-ins to encourage U.S. companies to sell off their South Africa-related securities. As part of this movement, students began to build shantytowns at their colleges and universities to encourage such divestment, and this innovative tactic of protest diffused rapidly across college and university campuses as activists sought new tactics perceived as successful (Soule 1997; Postal 1985).

Was student divestment activism altruistic? Certainly by the definition employed in this volume, it was. Activists believed that they were the "moral conscience" of the university (Landau 1987), that they had a "moral imperative" to act on behalf of South Africans (Weiner 1986), and that they had as much "moral advantage" as the abolitionists to fight apartheid (Williams et al. 1985). Activists were called to action on behalf of people in distant lands whom they would probably never meet.

How did the shantytown tactic come to be employed by students? At Columbia University in March 1985, students met to call for divestment of South Africa-related stocks and bonds (Vellela 1988). Pro-divestment sentiment among the students was so strong that the building in which the meeting was scheduled was too small to accommodate their growing numbers. Student leaders at Columbia, determined not to discourage activism, turned this meeting into a "sit-out" where at least three hundred students quite literally sat outside and conducted their peaceful protest meeting on the steps of the building. The protest scene was described as "covered with sitting, sprawling, hunkering students, maybe two hundred of them, debating, laughing, reading, conferring, and establishing a presence. Armchairs and sofas dragged out from a nearby dormitory offered some comfort. Tarps were rigged up to provide shelter; blankets covered some who slept" (Vellela 1988, 24). The blockade lasted almost two weeks, culminating in a speech by the Reverend Jesse Jackson which drew over five thousand people (Loeb 1994).

Unknown to them, by moving this meeting outdoors, the students had started a trend. Princeton University activists staged a "camp-out" quite similar to the Columbia event, followed by another "camp-out" at the University of California at Santa Cruz (Vellela 1988). Students at Harvard University held a "sleep-in" at the library. At the University of Iowa, over one hundred students camped outside the administration building, which they renamed "Biko Hall" after a well-known South-African leader (Lacey 1985). The "sit-outs," "camp-outs," and "sleep-ins" marked the beginning of the evolution of a new protest tactic: the shantytown.

The first shantytown appeared at Cornell University in the spring of 1985. Students collected scraps of wood, tar paper, and plastic, and built a small, makeshift structure in front of the administrative offices at the university. Their shack was the first in what later became known as a shantytown (Vellela 1988). Students called their shack the "Karl Marx House" and the structure provided a meeting place for activists. Embarrassed by the unattractive shack and the connotations of its name, the Cornell administration demanded its removal. After several attempts at dismantling the structure, which were followed by its repair and rebuilding, the administration finally acquiesced; the Karl Marx House was allowed to remain standing. Students and some sympathetic faculty members celebrated their small victory.

Media attention to the Cornell students' success encouraged students at other universities to experiment with the building of such structures. Late in the spring of 1985, a one-day shanty appeared at the University of Washington (Vellela 1988). By the fall of 1985, students at the University of Vermont had erected a shantytown and, by this time, the structures which had appeared on scattered campuses across the country had become symbolic of the poor living conditions of black South Africans (Vellela 1988). The Vermont shantytown was emblazoned with slogans of the pro-divestment group, the Apartheid Negation Council (ANC). The University of Vermont activists claimed success when the board of trustees voted in November 1985 to divest the university's South African securities.

The evolution of the shantytown from the initial "sit-out" at Columbia to the first shanty at Cornell was consequential to the diffusion of a protest tactic. The tactic had its roots in the existing student repertoire, but evolved into an innovative tactic that resonated with conditions in South Africa. Thus the tactic not only disrupted the landscape of the college campus, but it also served as an ugly reminder of the racial situation in South Africa.

It is abundantly clear that students engaged in a careful monitoring of other activists for clues on what to do about the divestment issue. For example, a University of Utah activist, Connie Spencer, bemoaned the fact that the tiny divestment movement at her university could not get off the ground. She remarked: "Then the three of us read about Dartmouth and how the shanties galvanized things there. We said, 'We'll do the same thing.' So, we put up two shanties over the weekend" (quoted in Weiner 1986, 338). Similarly, a student activist at Boston College remarked, "A year ago, two years ago, well, it was 'we'll do our thing on our campus,' but now they're really looking outward to other campuses to see what they can learn, and see how they can help" (Vellela 1988, 30).

In the case of the divestment movement, it seems clear that altruistic behavior in the form of an innovative protest tactic did, indeed, diffuse. The monitoring of activists by others in different locations, coupled with the imitation or modeling of tactics, led to the diffusion patterns described in this chapter and in Soule (1995, 1997). In particular, the shantytown protest tactic diffused among colleges and universities of the same type (for example, research, liberal arts, and so forth), and among colleges of similar prestige and endowment levels (Soule 1995, 1997).

But *why* did this altruistic tactic diffuse? As mentioned earlier, one of the reasons identified by psychologists and social psychologists for the diffusion of altruistic behavior is that the model provides information on the costs and potential rewards of altruistic action (Bar-Tal 1976).[9] Implicit to the study of diffusion of tactics is the notion that tactics perceived as effective or successful are more likely to be imitated (Tilly 1978; Soule 1997; Strang and Soule 1998). In the case of the divestment movement, the perceived likelihood of success, or the activists' sense of efficacy, helped to translate the moral outrage into altruistic activism. In interviews with student activists, this was often very explicitly stated, and it is clear that they believed that their actions would indeed lead to university divestment. Protesters linked university portfolios to a larger social issue for which it was easy to gain support (Williams et al. 1985). In sum, students felt that when compared to other foreign policy objectives, "university divestment was an obtainable goal by college students" (activist Jon Klavens, quoted in Williams et al. 1985). In an article in *The Nation*, Todd Gitlin (1985, 586) nicely summarizes this point: "Why South Africa? Apartheid is morally unambiguous and is sufficiently far away to be a safe target for moral outrage. It is also sufficiently close to provide a point of leverage: university investments, to which faculty and staff contribute directly, help shore up the apparatus of apartheid."

An activist at Harvard, Evan Grossman, echoed Gitlin's point when he remarked, "It's stupid for me to protest U.S. involvement in Central America because what can [the university] do?" (quoted in Williams et al. 1985, 62). Grossman's implicit comparison between the student divestment movement and the movement against U.S. involvement in Central America shows that he believed that protesting divestment might actually bring results. He, like other student activists, believed in the efficacy of the movement.

Loeb (1994) also found that the students he interviewed believed that by "putting pressure on their administration, their campus, their board of trustees" they would "steer history in a direction more humane and just" (174). Loeb (1994) unequivocally accepts the notion that the student divestment movement brought "quick and visible results" (398).

Furthermore, the student divestment activists believed that the shantytown tactic *in particular* was successful in encouraging the university to divest. Loeb (1994) makes the explicit link between protest shanties and some form of divestment at one hundred fifty schools. Student activists believed that divestment was an "obtainable goal" and that the shantytown tactic was a good way to encourage changes in university policy (Williams et al. 1985, 62). An article in the *Harvard Crimson* reported that nearly 60 percent of five hundred randomly selected Harvard students believed that this tactic of protest was an effective mechanism to force university divestment (Kramnick 1985). In the words of activist Eric Arnesen, "The shanties worked" (quoted in Weiner 1986).

Perhaps this was a safe assumption to make. Everywhere students looked, the link between protest and divestment was made. In a *New York Times* article, the connection between activism and success was made when the author remarked that protests and shanty-construction were increasing at colleges and universities because they were "buoyed by the success" of other campus divestment movements (Williams 1986). The article went on to link divestment at "dozens of colleges" to the student divestment movement and shantytowns. The divestment strategies of the University of Wyoming, Bryn Mawr, and Bucknell were all linked to shantytowns at these universities in a media report on the efficacy of shantytowns (Weiner 1986).[10]

Thus it seems that in the case of the student divestment movement, altruistic models provided information about the costs and potential outcomes of the altruistic action. Activists widely perceived the tactic to be successful, in part because of the media construction of this as fact. Hence, student activists imitated the so-called models, leading to the diffusion of the shantytown tactic.

The Observation of Wrongdoing

Several studies by psychologists and social psychologists have shown that the willingness to act altruistically is increased when an individual witnesses an event of harm-doing. For example, Konecni (1972) showed that when a potential altruistic actor witnessed someone bumping into another person, causing him or her to drop some belongings, the potential helper was far more likely to help him or her than when the person dropped his or her belongings without being bumped. Another study by Rawlings (1968) found that when subjects in laboratory experiments witnessed a person administering an electric shock to another, they were likely to act altruistically toward the person being shocked. When it was the subject's turn to shock the person, they did so at only low levels with short duration, despite instructions to keep shock levels constant. Other studies have shown that both *minor* (for example, knocking over a box of index cards) and *major* (for example, ruining experimental equipment) incidents of wrongdoing seem to elicit helping behavior on the part of observers (Bar-Tal 1976; Cialdini, Darby, and Vincent 1973).

Psychologists and social psychologists have attempted to understand the underlying individual-level reasons why observing wrongdoing increases the propensity to act altruistically. There seem to be three related psychological mechanisms identified in the literature. First, harm-doing creates aversive feelings, so individuals attempt to make themselves feel better by helping others (Cialdini et al. 1973; Bar-Tal 1976). Second, harm-doing highlights the existence of injustice, motivating people to act to eliminate injustice (Regan 1971; Bar-Tal 1976). Finally, harm-doing arouses sympathy by highlighting the sensitivity to others' suffering (Bar-Tal 1976; Rawlings 1970).

I wish to suggest here that, like the modeling of altruistic behavior, these *individual* level mechanisms may also operate at the *collective* level. In particular, the second of these three mechanisms seems especially important to the student divestment movement. The United States (and certainly other nations) was inundated with news coverage of South Africa which, as I elaborate upon below, mushroomed during the 1980s. However, students were also presented with a vivid display of the harm done by apartheid when activists built shantytowns. Shanties came to be symbolic of the circumstances for black South Africans under apartheid, not only because of their physical presence and appearance, but because of the repressive response they sometimes elicited (Soule 1995). Thus shanties themselves (in addition to being an innovative tactic which diffused) were galvanizing entities, helping induce potential participants to act altruistically.

It is relatively easy to see why, in the case of the student divestment movement, witnessing the harm done to black South Africans under apartheid might elicit altruistic activism. Below, I will argue that the increasing media attention to South Africa, coupled with the symbolic display of living conditions offered by the shanties, helped activists and potential activists to get a clear sense of the harm done by apartheid.

Media Attention to South Africa

From the research on the observation of harm-doing described above, it is possible to extrapolate the general claim that part of the reason for altruistic behavior by student activists during the divestment movement was their exposure to the events in South Africa through the increasing news coverage of that country. News reports from South Africa flooded the United States, publicizing violations of the rights of black citizens under the system of apartheid. Video-tapes of mass demonstrations at funeral processions of black South Africans killed in events of political unrest and photographs of segregated public facilities served as painful reminders of conditions in the United States in the not-so-distant past. It seems quite plausible that witnessing the situation in South Africa through international news coverage may have spurred student activism in the United States (and other countries, for that matter). In fact, this was shown to be the case in Rosenhan's (1970) work on the civil rights movement. This author found that "newspaper stories of very moving or tragic . . . events" seemed to elicit monetary contributions from activists (Rosenhan 1970, 259).

The sheer scale of media coverage of South Africa was at unprecedented levels in the mid-1980s, helping to broadcast the situation abroad. A simple count of articles indexed in the *Reader's Guide to Periodic Literature* shows that in the 1985 volume alone, there were 333 articles on "Race Relations in South Africa." In the two volumes covering the earlier, nearly two-year period from March 1978 through February 1980, there were only 75 articles on the "Race Question in South Africa." Even earlier, around the time of the Sharpeville Massacre in 1960, there were 80 articles in the volume spanning March 1959 through February 1961. Clearly, race relations in South Africa captured the media's attention in the mid-1980s, more so even than during the Sharpeville Massacre.

Table 8.1 shows the yearly counts of articles indexed in the *Reader's Guide to Periodic Literature* covering *any* topic having to do with South Africa. Clearly, the number of articles on South Africa rose to unprecedented highs in 1985 and 1986, with 349 appearing in 1985 and 447 in 1986. The table also shows that prior to 1984 there were fewer than 100 articles indexed each year in the *Guide*. It seems clear from this data that during the mid-1980s, news coverage of South Africa increased greatly.

Another way to gauge the media attention to South Africa is to look at the *Television News Index and Abstracts*. In 1985, there were 307 network news segments broadcast on "apartheid/discrimination in South Africa," 431 on "unrest/race riots in South Africa," and 46 on the "state of emergency in South Africa." Thus, the number of news segments for 1985 totaled 784. In 1979, by contrast, there were only 5 network news segments on "discrimination" and only 4 on "unrest" in that country (a total of 9 news segments on discrimination and unrest in South Africa).[11]

TABLE 8.1
Number of Articles on South Africa in
Reader's Guide to Periodic Literature, 1975-1990

1975	22
1976	58
1977	67
1978	71
1979	51
1980	65
1981	83
1982	49
1983	88
1984	111
1985	349
1986	447
1987	236
1988	155
1989	129
1990	187
Total	2,580

Shantytowns as Evidence of Harm Done under Apartheid

In addition to the role of the media attention, it is worth noting again that the shantytowns themselves also helped to display the harm done by apartheid. Symbolic of the living conditions of black South Africans, the shantytowns provided a graphic representation of the evils of apartheid, and thus helped to mobilize potential participants to act on behalf of people in a very distant land. Constructed from cardboard, tar paper, newspaper, scraps of wood, and tin, and emblazoned with antiapartheid and pro-divestment slogans, the shanties were difficult to overlook on college campuses. Shanties were often named after notable individuals in South Africa—"Biko Hall," "Biko Memorial Hall," and "Mandela Hall," to name just a few. An activist, Joshua Nessen, remarked that the shanties, "symbolized the lives and conditions of black South Africa" (quoted in Vellela 1988, 34). Another activist argued that the shanties symbolized "the viciousness of apartheid and the oppression of South Africa's blacks" (quoted in Weiner 1986, 337). A third activist told a *Newsweek* reporter that the shanties "make a statement to the University of Washington that this is what living conditions are like in South Africa for blacks and people of color" (quoted in Williams et al. 1985, 61). Loeb (1994) argues that they were so effective because they "made distant wounds immediate and salient" to ordinary students (174).

It should also be noted that the repressive response that many of the shanty-town protests encountered seemed to underscore the symbolic nature of this tactic. At Yale, an alumnus burned down the shantytown; at Johns Hopkins, a shanty was firebombed; at Harvard, conservative students built an "anti-shanty"; and at Dartmouth, the "Committee to Beautify the Green" took sledgehammers to the shantytown at that campus. These extra-institutional attempts to disrupt the divestment movement were not the only form of repression. The shanties were met with official response as well. At the University of Wisconsin, University of California-Berkeley, and Cornell, and numerous other campuses, the admini-stration forcibly dismantled the shantytowns. Repression of both types, in effect, fed the flames of the divestment movement, as the activists were able to draw striking parallels between the repression of the American and South African demonstrations. In essence, then, the shantytowns and the repression they engendered, presented students with a symbolic representation of the human rights violations in South Africa under apartheid.

If the hypothesis that the observation of wrongdoing increases altruistic be-havior is accurate, then it certainly seems plausible that the media attention to the worsening conditions in South Africa, coupled with the representation of these by the shantytown tactic, may have increased student activism. In 1985 and 1986, when media coverage of South Africa peaked, divestment activity in the United States reached all-time highs (Soule 1995, 1997; Vellela 1988; Jackson 1992). Once this movement was underway and shanties were being built all over the country, other potential activists were called to action in part because the shantytown tactic so resonated with their collective understanding of the human rights violations under apartheid.[12]

Discussion

In the past few years, social scientists have revisited the notion of altruism and, accordingly, a number of fine treatments have appeared in journals and edited volumes on this general topic. At the outset of this chapter I noted that, despite this refreshing revisitation, social scientists have scarcely mentioned the work of psychologists and social psychologists on the determinants of altruistic behavior. In this chapter, I have examined how two of the many empirical findings presented in that literature may help to explain both the diffusion of a protest tactic within a social movement and the mobilization of participants to a social movement. I suggest that the psychological mechanisms offered to explain these two empirical findings may operate at the collective level in the case of the student divestment movement in the United States.

I have noted in this chapter that it has been shown by social psychologists and psychologists that altruistic behavior diffuses. This is due, at least in part, to the fact that behavioral models provide information about the positive and negative outcomes of behavior. It stands to reason that if an innovative model is expected to be beneficial and achieve a desired outcome, then others will adopt it, leading to the spread or diffusion of the innovation. I provided examples of how this was the case during the student divestment movement. A new protest tactic, the shantytown, was believed to be especially efficacious in forcing universities to divest themselves of their South African investment holdings. Because it was assumed to be effective, and because it was, by definition, a politically altruistic response, it diffused across campuses during this period.

I also noted in this chapter that the social psychologists and psychologists have shown that witnessing wrongdoing is likely to induce altruistic behavior. This is due, in part, to the fact that witnessing harm-doing reminds individuals of injustices and motivates people to act. I provided examples of how this may have come into play during the divestment movement. First, I showed that media attention to South Africa and apartheid reached unprecedented levels. This may have led individuals to act on behalf of others by reminding them of the injustices and inducing them to act on their moral concerns or moral outrage. Second, I also argued that the shantytown itself (and the repression of it), as a symbol of the human rights violations under apartheid, provided another graphic reminder of the need to act altruistically. Because it resonated with Americans' understanding of the living conditions in South Africa, it was especially successful in mobilizing potential participants.

The discussion in this chapter raises an interesting question for future research in this area. Specifically, it raises a question about whether or not politically altruistic activism diffuses more easily or readily than other types of activism that are *not* purely altruistic. In other words, can the two situational factors that influence altruistic behavior (modeling and witnessing harm done) be applied more generally to other social movements? For example, it may be argued that most actions taken by activists associated with the environmental movement are not purely altruistic. While it is clear that all people benefit from these activists' gains (for example, cleaner air and water), the activists *themselves* also benefit from these gains. Thus, it would be interesting to ascertain whether or not tactics used by environmentalists diffuse and, if so, whether or not the situational factors described in this paper may account for the diffusion of these tactics.

In sum, this chapter has illuminated some of the many contributions by social psychologists and psychologists to the study of altruistic behavior. This literature has, in large part, been overlooked as social scientists revisit the issue of altruism and I wish to suggest that we look more closely at this tradition.

Notes

1. In particular, see Jencks (1990), Elster (1990), Mansbridge (1998), and Wolfe (1998).
2. Altruistic behavior is often referred to in this literature as "helping" or "prosocial" behavior.
3. See Bar-Tal (1976), Krebs (1970), and Berkowitz (1972) for thorough reviews of the other situational factors found to influence altruistic behavior.
4. The "shanties" were small, makeshift shacks, constructed on campuses to protest university investment in South Africa-related stocks and bonds. At some universities, a single shanty was built, at others "shantytowns" were constructed. At many universities, students lived in the shanties, causing great distress to their administrations.
5. Apartheid began to unravel in 1990 when F. W. DeKlerk, the then-South African prime minister, freed Nelson Mandela, a leader of the African National Congress. Additionally, DeKlerk reinstated banned black organizations, and in 1991 signed a peace accord with other African leaders. In 1994, South African voters elected Mandela president in the first national election in which all citizens could vote.
6. Blake, Rosenbaum, and Duryea (1955) find that the amount of money donated to a charity is also modeled by observers.
7. See Krebs (1970), Berkowitz (1972), and Bar-Tal (1976) for more examples of this research.
8. This process, of course, resembles DiMaggio and Powell's (1983) discussion of "mimetic isomorphism" among organizations. They argue that under conditions of uncertainty, organizations may be especially prone to imitating other organizations. By adopting innovations successfully tried by others, an organization may increase its chances for survival and/or increase its effectiveness (DiMaggio and Powell 1983; Tolbert and Zucker 1983; Zhou 1993; Soule 1995).
9. Bandura (1977) and other social learning theorists note that in ambiguous situations, information attained by witnessing the outcomes of behavior is especially useful in influencing behavior. This is especially true when the observer defines himself or herself as similar to the model (Hornstein 1970, 30). Bikhchandani, Hirshleifer, and Welch (1998) argue that imitation is an evolutionary adaptation whereby people survive by imitating others who have already gathered critical information about a particular decision.
10. However, the media constructed the success of the shantytowns without ever ascertaining if they did indeed cause university divestment. A careful analysis (Soule 1995, forthcoming) shows that shantytowns did *not* increase rates of divestment. However, as mentioned earlier, this is largely irrelevant because students believed that it was a successful tactic, sure to bring divestment.
11. In addition to print and television coverage of South Africa, popular rock and roll songs graced the airwaves, deploring the killing and imprisonment of political activists in South Africa. For example, the Specials AKA song entitled "Free Nelson Mandela" and the Peter Gabriel song entitled "Biko" were both widely played on college and other radio stations in the mid-1980s. Additionally, Alan Paton's 1948 novel, *Cry the Beloved Country*, was reprinted in 1986, relating the heart-wrenching story of a Zulu pastor and his son under the oppressive policies of apartheid.
12. Readers will note that this portion of my argument is somewhat similar to

predictions from the framing perspective. In essence, proponents of that perspective might argue that the social construction of the shanties as symbolic of the living conditions and human rights violations in South Africa is part of the protest frame. Because it resonated with impressions of South Africa, the shantytown helped to mobilize participants to action. Thus one might argue that the framing of the shantytown in this manner was quite successful.

9

Mobilizing for International Solidarity
Mega-Events and Moral Crusades

Christian Lahusen

Introduction

Social movements have made use of an endless variety of activities and events in order to raise awareness and funds for their cause and recruit members for their activism. Rallies, pickets, sit-ins, marches, petitions, leafleting sessions, torchlight vigils, information stands are among those most commonly associated with political protest. However, activists have employed almost any kind of activity of everyday life for their own aims: buffets, festivals and civic receptions, music concerts, art exhibitions and theater performances, disco benefits, public screening and fashion shows, football tournaments, sponsored bicycle rides or hikes, to name but a few examples. Indeed, social movements are also characterized by the fact that their protest actions are "unconventional," that is, not standardized nor bound by fixed routines, social conventions, or formal protocols. Consequently, it becomes almost impossible to do justice to the variety of protest activities and the related creativity of movement activists.

While considerable progress has been made in the study of those mobilization strategies and structures closely associated with the "core" action repertoire of social movements, we will extend the scope in this chapter in order to grasp at least part of the broader arsenal of public activities and related mobilizing structures. This will be done primarily by analyzing a number of events that used popular music, celebrity endorsement, and (more generally speaking) art as a medium and means of mobilizing. For this purpose we shall deal with a few organizations from the solidarity movement, for example, the Anti-Apartheid Movement, Amnesty International, and various Tibetan solidarity groups, all of which employed these event and campaign formats as part of their wider activism. More specifically, we shall focus on some of the *mega-events* of the so-called "rock-for-a-cause" era of the 1980s and 1990s, in particular the trend-setting Live-Aid of 1985, the concert tours organized by and on behalf of Amnesty International (the Conspiracy of Hope USA tour of 1986, the Human Rights Now! world tour of 1988), the Nelson Mandela tributes organized in collaboration with the British Anti-Apartheid Movement in 1988 and 1990, the Tibetan Freedom Concerts of the Milarepa-Fund in 1996, 1998, and 1999, the activism of Artists for a Free Tibet, and the EarthDance events in 1997 and 1998 in aid of Tibet.

These mega-events, as well as many other smaller activities on the national or local levels, seem to pertain specifically to the solidarity movement. Indeed, while charity concerts and gigs have been staged for a variety of causes, it is not by chance that the most important mega-events (that is, the above-mentioned concerts) addressed issues of the solidarity movement. In fact, the latter seems to be particularly akin to this kind of mobilization. For this reason, the events analyzed will allow us to shed more light on important aspects and changes within the structure and logic of political mobilization (McAdam et al. 1996b). Let us briefly sketch these aspects before entering into the case studies themselves.

First, solidarity movements combine political advocacy for social change and a philanthropic or charitable concern for the weak and suppressed (Baringhorst 1998). While the latter is primarily oriented toward ameliorating grievances, the former is geared to address the causes of these grievances themselves. Both orientations belong together, although they also embody different intentions and commitments. The philanthropic and humanitarian wing of the solidarity movement, in particular, has allowed for an expansion of the action repertoire toward mainstream audiences in general, toward (mainstream) pop music in particular, through its primary concern for love and friendship, mutual care and understanding (Street 1986). In doing so, the humanitarian and charitable strand within the solidarity movement is strengthening, to the detriment of a more overtly political commitment, as we will see.

Second, these events are organized to mobilize a wider audience of people who are but loosely coupled to the movement and/or have not yet committed to the cause. In this sense these activities do not supplant but rather complement the standard action repertoire of the solidarity movement. The events aim to bring the solidarity issues closer to new audiences by using the media, the celebrities, the narratives and standard themes which these people like or are used to. Moreover, they diminish the costs of participation (Olson 1968) in that people attend or watch the events because they are interested in the show itself. In this regard, altruism, as a primary feature of solidaristic commitment, does not necessarily imply that one does not benefit directly from action. Rather, in the cases under analysis, altruism and political advocacy are exposed to a process of "aesthetization" and "entertainization," which has much to do with changes in the structure of the movement's audiences and mobilizing networks.

Third, this points to the fact that the "societal environment" of social movements is composed of different groups, communities or (sub)cultures which have their own arsenal of narratives, identities, and daily-life practices. That means that mobilization efforts have to be in tune with the imagery and discourse of the diverse audiences and groups being addressed and have to strike the proper chords. Here, indeed, the correct approach and style of communicating and acting in public becomes important (Gamson 1988; Melucci 1985). However, as sociological studies show, society is exposed to an ever-increasing process of individualization that frees the individual from "inherited," fixed group memberships by the very multiplication and differentiation of social groups and circles to which the individual belongs (Simmel 1971). This process makes participation and membership more elective, and makes solidarity bonds within and between groups more "organic" (Durkheim 1964). This means that communities and networks remain an important channel and means of mobilization. However, mobilization cannot tap ready-made communities (religious, ethnic, professional, age groups, among others), which are then activated en bloc. Activists increasingly have to convince the individual to turn up and get involved, providing him or her with an opportunity to express his or her personal preferences, commitments and identities, but also as a means of reaffirming his or her membership in a community he or she chose to be a part of. Indeed, our cases reveal that people use these events as a means of gathering and socializing, of expressing and reaffirming their collectivity (for example, a youth subculture). Hence, movement organizations have to meet the challenge of the individualization process by building up proper mobilizing networks, that is, by linking to and molding the many groups, communities, and (sub-)cultures they are addressing.

Fourth, this process increasingly has adopted a transnational outlook. This has to do, as we shall demonstrate, with the so-called globalization processes, particularly with the international integration of national market economies, accompanied by the concentration of mass media and increases in intercultural communication, among other factors (Robertson 1992). This has allowed for the establishment of transnational (pop music) "taste-cultures" and (sub-)cultures. In this regard, transnationalization and individualization are complementary processes, in that individual actors often choose to interrelate or identify more with other fellow members of transnational groups, subcultures, or social networks. Therefore, the mass media, the music business, and audiences open to social movements a small window to the wide world. It is a small window, because these media and communities differentiate and specialize increasingly according to issues and activities, to the interests and backgrounds of the participating individuals. It is a window to the wide world, because these transnational audiences and cultures increase the scope and outcome of political mobilization. The cases under review will provide empirical evidence for these various elements of the mobilizing structures and networks of the solidarity movement. It is hoped that this chapter will contribute to the current and intensifying research on transnational movement organizations and their mobilizing structures and strategies (Smith 1998; Smith et al. 1998) by pointing to the surrounding mobilizing networks that become a guiding and stabilizing force in the transnationalization of social movements.

Social Movements and Popular Music

Social movements and popular music exhibit a long tradition of intimate interrelations. Unfortunately, though, social movement research has paid little attention to this phenomenon, while many (popular) music studies address these relations between politics and music on a more general level (e.g., Cloonan and Street 1997; Orman 1984; Pratt 1990). The available literature will, nevertheless, enable us to portray the broad outlines of the topic and lay a foundation for the case study that follows.

The Rhythm of Social Change

The history of social movements and political conflicts could be easily reconstructed from an analysis of (popular) music songs and artists' involvement. Indeed, social movements of any kind have inspired musicians in their artistic work, as much as music has moved masses to support a diversity of issues. Many popular protest songs were even written for specific historic events and societal problems: "[t]he assassination of President John F. Kennedy in 1963, the burgeoning American military involvement in Southeast Asia after 1965, the continuing struggle for black civil rights and economic equity for women and minorities throughout the 1960s and 1970s, and the political cynicism generated by the Nixon presidency prompted increasing numbers of chart-topping anthems" (Cooper 1988, 53-4). These include, for example, *the Unknown Soldier* by the Doors, *War Song* by Neil Young and Graham Nash, *Power* by the Temptations, which call for love, peace, brotherhood, social and political change and had a repercussion often far beyond the United States. Indeed, some of these songs became anthems of political commitment and protest in general, as in the case of Bob Dylan's *Blowin' in the Wind* or the gospel song *We Shall Overcome*. Similar alliances between protest and music appeared in other countries as well, although in a less pronounced manner. In Great Britain and Germany, for instance, political issues such as the Vietnam War, military rearmament, nuclear power plants, right-wing racism, or environmental degradation became the object of song-writing and a general commitment of musicians (Eisel 1990, 134-58; Frith and Street 1992). Popular music has become a particularly important arena and a subtle means of protest in all those countries in which institutional opportunities for expressing and organizing political protest are restricted, as, for example, in China, formerly socialist Hungary, Spain and Argentina under military dictatorships (see Brace and Friedlander 1992; Szemere 1992; Lahusen 1991; Vila 1992). In these countries the total and centralized control of culture had the effect of politicizing artistic production and reception, both by motivating a political "reading" of unpolitical music and by instigating a subtle political rhetoric within the arts.

Hence, popular music has taken up worries and concerns of larger social movements, and in doing so it has become an important means of capturing "the hearts and minds" of the people, as the power of music is recurrently described. This impact is due, on the one hand, to the fact that music is an emotional means of communication that strikes the feelings of its audience, creating a sensitivity and concern for the themes and issues addressed. Music composition and performance are, in a certain sense, about the "management of the emotions" in that they aim to maximize the emotional impact of the message. On the other hand, music is also a cognitive communication medium both in regard to the lyrics and the music. Popular music recurrently wishes to capture and portray fundamental human worries and desires, grievances and conflicts, often also addressing questions of common fortunes and collective identities. Indeed, popular music seems to play a prominent role when issues of collective identities are at stake, as in the case of nationalist minorities or ethnic communities (Zook 1992; Lipsitz 1992; Lahusen 1991), or in the case of the young generation's search for self-awareness and self-realization (Eyerman and Jamison 1995, 453; Street 1986).

This relationship has led to a certain parallelism in the development of both the musical and social spheres. Reebee Garofalo (1992a) has shown this in regard to the relation between the civil rights movement and "black" popular music: the importance of church gospels and rhythm and blues in the 1950s; the upbeat black pop of early Motown releases acceptable to white audiences in the "integrationist" 1960s; the connection to African roots and black pride during the decade of Black Power beginning in the 1970s; and the "soft soul" during the 1980s. In this case, as in many others as well, these manifold interrelations between popular music and social movements made them ever more interdependent. "The [Civil Rights] Movement provided the folk singers with more than an audience, it provided content and a sense of mission over and above the commercial. In fact, it helped justify an anti-commercial attitude and foster a sense of authenticity, as well as life-style" (Eyerman and Jamison 1995, 458). At the same time, popular music lent its voice to the movement, sublimating and aesthetizing their issues, claims, and values, and thus reaching a broader audience.

This intimate relationship should not make us forget, however, that politics and art are two distinct spheres of action, and that this historically grown differentiation has brought about a clear "division of labor," with each side having its distinct professional roles, identities, and rationales. Indeed, while politics might be a source of inspiration for artists, they make clear at all times that they are, above all, *artists*, and thus primarily concerned about the aesthetic value, the authenticity, and (due to the strong industrialization of popular music) the commercial value of their artistic work (Frith 1987; Booth and Kuhn 1990). Hence, even if "political" songs can meet these criteria of "good" popular music, and even if artists and musical styles are absorbed into social movements, still the validity of the two spheres' rationale and logic is not dissolved but merely coupled momentarily. This differentiation becomes more apparent once tensions emerge among politics, aesthetics, and mar-kets—tensions that have accompanied popular music over the years. In fact, politically committed music has been repeatedly criticized as "bad" music, in the sense of degrading music to the level of propaganda and of perverting the necessary autonomy, creativity, and authenticity of music. Proponents of social and political commitment, instead, have argued for the deeper truth and authenticity of their aesthetic mission against the artistic degradation of commercial music. In fact, the development of popular music has seen oscil-lations between consecutive trends of "commercial" and socially concerned music. This had happened to the civil rights movement by the end of the 1960s, because the "singer, who earlier had often been a songwriter, per-former, producer and activist all rolled into one, became an 'artist' projecting a personal vision rather than a collectively political one," leaving the collec-tive group in order to follow a far more commercial and individual path (Ey-erman and Jamison 1995, 451).

Mega-Events and Mass Movements

The interrelation between social movements and popular music has thus undergone important changes. In the 1960s and before, "music generally served as a cultural frame for what were more or less developed political movements. The civil rights and anti-war movements engaged millions of people in the politics of direct action primarily on the strength of the issues themselves" (Garofalo 1992b, 17). These social movements strongly influ-enced the themes and styles of popular music, fostering a cultural transfor-mation and change within popular culture at large (Eyerman and Jamison 1995). Since the 1980s, however, "music . . . has taken the lead in the relative absence of such movements. With the decline of mass participation in grass-roots political movements, popular music itself has come to serve as a cata-lyst for raising issues and organizing masses of people" (Garofalo 1992b, 17). In fact, since the 1980s many "mega-events" (Garofalo 1992c, 8) have been produced and staged in the aftermath of the Live-Aid concert of 1985.

This concert addressed humanitarian and political causes and had a strong impact in terms of the funds raised, the media coverage produced, and the members recruited for the affiliated organizations and groups (Ullestad 1992). However, while this observation is correct, the explanation needs more precision. It was not necessarily the weakness of social movements but the stronger differentiation between both spheres of action that led to the advent of mega-events. The increasing industrialization and commercialization does strengthen the ability of popular music to invent and stage ever-new music pieces and performances (Lopes 1992), and the international integration of the music business allows producers to "think big" when conceiving of products (Negus 1993; Wallis 1990). Yet the primary claim of *popular music*—its authenticity—is not guaranteed by the market alone but rather demands a communicative reconstruction of popular music's basic roots and founding myths (for example, youth rebellion, personal autonomy and self-realization, the black soul) and a reinvention of its mission (for example, compassion and love, brotherhood and social justice), for which social and political concerns remain an essential point of reference and medium, as Eyerman and Jamison (1995) argued for in the 1960s.

Therefore, the differentiation of social movements and popular music does not annul the intimate relations, but rather transforms them into short-term "joint ventures," thus restricting and magnifying the potential effects of this alliance. It restricts this interrelation because these songs and events are time-bound consumer products which compete with many others and are ousted by new songs, styles, or trends. It magnifies the outcomes of these "joint-ventures" because the musicians mobilize the entire skills, workforce, and power of the market, its industries, and mass media. This can be seen clearly in the cases under analysis. In 1986, the U.S. section of Amnesty International organized a "Conspiracy of Hope" tour in collaboration with concert promoter Bill Graham, traveling to several American cities to celebrate the twenty-fifth anniversary of Amnesty International. The shows featured performers U2, Peter Gabriel, Sting, Bryan Adams, Lou Reed, Joan Baez, and the Neville Brothers. According to Amnesty International, the tour raised about $2.5 million and recruited about one hundred thousand new members. These concerts provided Amnesty many contacts and much respect in the music industry, thus encouraging the staff to organize the "Human Rights Now" world tour in 1988 to commemorate the fortieth anniversary of the Universal Declaration of Human Rights and bolster the development work of Amnesty in countries with smaller memberships. The $20 million tour, sponsored by the Reebok Foundation, included Peter Gabriel, Sting, Tracy Chapman, Youssou N'Dour, and Bruce Springsteen, besides a number of local acts at various venues. The tour traveled to eighteen countries (Great Britain, Hungary, Canada, United States, Japan, India, Zimbabwe, Brazil, and Argentina, among others) and reached an audience of about one million spectators. Moreover, a billion television viewers in sixty-two countries watched a documentary program on the tour. Many smaller branches of Amnesty International doubled their memberships (for example, Greece, Spain, Japan, and Italy, which had between two thousand five hundred and six thousand members initially), and the entire campaign was able to collect about 1.2 billion signatures in support of the Universal Declaration.

The first Nelson Mandela tribute was organized by concert promoter Tony Hollingsworth, the British Anti-Apartheid Movement, and Artists Against Apartheid, and took place at Wembley Stadium on 11 June 1988. This eleven-hour show assembled many internationally renowned musicians (including Stevie Wonder, Whitney Houston, George Michael, Sting, UB40, the Eurythmics, Simple Minds, Dire Straits, and Eric Clapton), but also "world music" and rappers (such as Amampondo, Mahamatini and Mahotena Queens, Salt N Pepa, the Fat Boys), as well as a number of film stars (among them Richard Attenborough, Richard Gere, Whoopi Goldberg, Denzil Washington). The concert raised about $3.6 million through ticket sales, broadcasting rights, and donations, and was broadcast to seventy-two countries, reaching a potential audience of 200 million viewers. With the release of Mandela from prison in February 1990, a second tribute concert with a comparable set of acts was organized in London to welcome him and provide him a forum to address the world. This concert was part of an international campaign to rededicate the international community to maintaining its pressure on the government of South Africa to abandon apartheid and instigate a process of democratization.

Finally, the Milarepa Fund has produced a number of Tibetan Freedom Concerts since 1996 to raise awareness of human rights issues in Tibet. The first Tibetan Freedom Concert was staged 15 and 16 June 1996 at Golden Gate Park in San Francisco with the Beastie Boys, Smashing Pumpkins, Red Hot Chili Peppers, Rage Against the Machine, Sonic Youth, and Yoko Ono, among many others. More than one hundred thousand attended the concerts and approximately $800,000 were raised. Students for a Free Tibet chapters increased from approximately eighty to over three hundred nationwide within only three months after the concert. Similar concerts with a variety of musicians and music styles were held in June 1997 and 1998 in New York and Washington, D.C., raising $1.2 million and $1.3 million, respectively, for the Milarepa fund, while also contributing several new members for the students' network. On 13 June 1999, four concerts were staged simultaneously in Chicago, Amsterdam, Tokyo, and Sydney. These events featured forty-seven bands (including Blur, Beastie Boys, Rage against the Machine, Alanis Morrissette, Neil Finn, Buffalo Daughter, Live, and the Cult), attracted approximately fifty thousand concertgoers, and raised an estimated $150,000.

Indeed, mega-events allow "thinking big" about fund-raising by capitalizing on popular music's international markets, industries, and circuits of business professionals. Charities and social movements can tap this business for fund-raising purposes by persuading artists, corporations, and/or professionals to work for free and/or waive their royalties and revenues. Whenever individuals buy a charity record, a ticket for a benefit concert, or the related merchandise; whenever radio or television stations broadcast a song dedicated to a good cause; whenever the mass media pay for the broadcasting rights to a benefit event, then the associated charity or social movement organization receives hard cash—not counting the donations collected at the venues or elicited by broadcasts. At the same time, popular music's star system and the intricate interrelationship between the music industry and the media can be instrumentalized for public awareness and membership recruitment, if celebrities speak or act on behalf of social movements. While fund-raising and media coverage were a quasi-direct output of the business' normal operations, this is not necessarily true for the success in membership drives because the ability to recruit constituents en bloc is much more attributable to the logic of the public events themselves, as will be pointed out later in this chapter.

A New Repertoire of Transnational Activism?

By the early 1990s, business professionals and artists were quite certain that this era of charity concerts was coming to an end. As Jack Healey, president of Amnesty International USA, argued: "I think there is charity-concert fatigue in the West, particularly in the U.S. and U.K. . . . We may be getting to the end of this type of concert" (*New York Times*, 1 September 1998, C19). However, the international solidarity campaign on behalf of Tibet is demonstrating that "politically" committed songs and concerts are here to stay. This is true in the case of the local level and smaller initiatives. Local gigs, disco benefits, festivals, and the like have become an integral part of the conventional protest repertoire of advocacy groups, particularly when appealing to youth. But also on the national and international level, mega-events are becoming a "normal" form of mobilization. Artists and musicians will continue to come up with initiatives and/or accept the calls of advocacy groups. The "business" will not oppose and sometimes it will even support these ideas. This is the case because, as John Costello, vice president of Pepsi, put it (in Garofalo 1992b, 27): "Live Aid demonstrates that you can quickly develop marketing events that are good for companies, artists, and the cause." Indeed, these "joint-ventures" demonstrate that mega-events do not necessarily follow the logic of zero-sum games, wherein the gains of the one side are the losses of the others. Participants engage in (re-)defining these events as non-zero-sum games. As the case of the first Nelson Mandela tribute of 1988 exemplifies, each side attempts to capitalize on the event for its own interests and goals. The artists' managers used the performance as a means of public relations and image-building; the production company saw the opportunity to enter into the business of producing international media events; the advocacy group constructed an entire campaign to capitalize on the momentum created by the concert for its long-term activism (Lahusen 1996, 100-31).

The consolidation of this mobilization form has two important aspects. On the one hand, it seems as if the continuing success of mega-events in terms of fund-raising, public attention, and membership, and the experiences and skills acquired is creating an industry and a separate group of social movement organizations (SMOs) specializing in this kind of events. That is, the strong differentiation between popular music and social movements is creating an intermediate infrastructure of groups regularizing and stabilizing this new form of cooperation between both spheres of action. This is the case with the Milarepa Fund, which specialized in this form of events as a part of the wider Tibetan solidarity movement (for instance, its concerts and events also mobilize members for other groups, particularly the Students for a Free Tibet). This is also the case when the artistic communities organize themselves around a specific issue or movement, for example, the apartheid system in South Africa (the former Artists Against Apartheid in Great Britain or the Artists United Against Apartheid in the United States) or the Chinese occupation of Tibet (the World Artists for a Free Tibet).

On the other hand, these mega-events have formed a gateway to the transnationalization of social movements. This is true for Amnesty International's Human Rights Now! world tour, which was explicitly conceived as a means of propelling the development work of its smaller branches. It also applies to the Mandela tributes, their aim being to raise awareness for the antiapartheid issue worldwide, specifically mobilizing support for the African National Congress, the British antiapartheid movement, and other national groups, capitalizing on the broadcast and international media coverage. In all these cases, artists had committed themselves to support specific movement organization or alliances. In some cases, artists had taken the lead in mobilizing and organizing the artist communities or specific youth cultures. In these instances they were no longer a mere medium and channel for the transnationalization of established SMOs, but became themselves a mobilizing actor (loosely) coupled to a network of solidarity groups and organizations. For instance, World Artists for a Free Tibet initiated and coordinated thousands of local actions worldwide in the summer of 1998 to raise awareness for the Tibetan issue. The same can be said for a smaller event, the EarthDance of 1997 and 1998, which linked a series of local parties into one global dance floor to focus the attention of this rave and house-music culture and trigger support for Tibetan solidarity groups. Both cases coordinated a series of events cross-nationally on the basis of a common issue, time, symbol, or core activity, while each local show had its own actions and was associated with a local solidarity group. The umbrella organizations and activists therefore provided merely a minimal program with core issues, demands or contacts, and a series of informational services to help consolidate and diffuse this network of events across space and time.

The Imagery and Discourse of "Popular" Events

So far we have argued that popular music and social movements maintain changing but intense relations because both have something valuable to offer each other. Social movements struggle for causes and concerns, which helps popular music to reinvent or reaffirm its beliefs, identities, and missions (using the plural notion of identities and missions, because this aesthetic and political debate is prone to conflict, given the different genres, communities, and artists involved). Popular music, for its part, lends social movements a voice to express and convey issues and claims (using the singular notion of "a" voice because the solidarity movement is also composed of a variety of different voices, many activists being wary about popular music's role and function altogether). However, the imagery and discourse of these "popular" events capture and mirror one branch of the movement and help illustrate important developments within the movement. These developments largely concern the increasing aesthetization and sublimation of solidarity and altruism. These trends might take quite different directions. However, in the case of popular music, this sublimation increasingly moralizes and "spiritualizes" the discourse, while at the same time intensifying the hedonist entertainment value of political activism.

Politics, Morals, and Spirituality

[The World Artists for a Free Tibet]'s vision is to use the power of artistic expression to bring attention to a major struggle facing us today, human rights violations. The focus of this project is the situation in Tibet. We believe that if people around the world were informed about the Tibetan plight, there would be a world-wide response of compassion which would lead to the alleviation of the suffering of the Tibetans, and therefore our suffering. It is time, as we come to the start of the new millenium, that we accept and embrace our interdependence and interconnection with each other, and all living things. Artist around the world can express our diverse cultural beauty as we unite around our true essence (http://www.art4tibet1998.org).

This statement gives a first impression of the discourse we are dealing with. It is spoken of "discourse" here because a closer look into the inner life of these events and their surrounding campaigns will soon disclose that they do not present a monolithic message, but unfold a number of different, sometimes conflicting statements and arguments, hence, a proper discourse about the issue at stake and the proper manner of solving it. However, as a first step into the analysis of this discourse we wish to highlight a leitmotif of the events' discourse that is touched in the above quotation: the notion of the moral and spiritual essence of political conflicts. In a sense this is the result of the campaigners' attempt to find an uncontroversial basis of reaching, persuading, and mobilizing a worldwide mass audience. This is done by supposing an inherent solidarity among all humans, and by assuming that the case of human rights violations in Tibet is obviously an injury to this planetary community of all living things in general, of this multicultural family of humankind in particular. More public information is needed to activate this inherent but "sleeping" solidarity. It is implicitly argued that this international solidarity has to be constructed as well, both in regard to the rational recognition of humankind's unity within cultural diversity and in regard to empathy and the compassion for others' suffering. Hence, international solidarity is something not at all inherently given, but communicatively constructed or made (Rorty 1989).

Celebrities repeatedly underemphasize their power to influence the public, and prefer to see themselves as a source of information which individuals may use at their own choice. This focus on information and free personal will has, however, a deeply rooted moral aspect: the individual has to choose freely to act in solidarity with the oppressed. This approach leads us to a sort of voluntarist solidarism which structures the discourse decisively. First of all, solidarity requires "the ability to think of people wildly different from ourselves as included in the range of 'us'" (Rorty 1989, 192). Hence, voluntarist solidarism implies that a community of belongingness is communicatively constructed, uniting "them" and "us." In the mega-events under analysis this was done in two ways. On the one hand, music and art were used as a persuasive and sensational means of bridging cultures and arguing for their belongingness. In the Mandela tributes, black music served as a bridge between (white) Anglo-Saxon music and African culture into a transculturated space of mutual influences and traditions. On the other hand, these events and campaigns propagated a "joyful" and "beautiful" multiculturalism that staged the cultural diversity of the autochthonous artistic community. The first Mandela tribute, for instance, included a wide array of acts to represent the big family of popular music (for example, Whitney Houston, Stevie Wonder, Joe Cocker, George Michael, UB40, Simple Minds, Salt N Pepa, Huge Masekela, Miriam Makeba). While explicitly defending the dignity and intrinsic value of each culture (thus highlighting the *differences* between the people), this multiculturalism explicitly relativizes each single culture by arguing that all humans are *equal* in sharing feelings and sensations, worries, and desires. Ultimately it is emotions and empathy which intimately link "them" and "us."

Second, due to the voluntarist solidarism, political struggles are recurrently reframed as moral and spiritual crusades. Political power and violence, inequalities and injustices are signs of moral decay, of a lack of compassion, love and brotherhood. Ultimately, the imagery of the "popular events" constructed two antagonistic forces: political power as domination, and moral or spiritual power as empowerment and togetherness. Actress Whoopi Goldberg expressed this view in the first Mandela tribute when she claimed that oppressors aim to repress the quest for freedom by creating fears and blocking the spiritual contagion of compassion, altruism, and love. But, she added, "oppressors tend to forget that the spirit cannot be held" (in Lahusen 1996, 230). The struggle and its missions are therefore about faith—"faith that we can change what is going on in this world through changing the way we as individuals live, and that if we continue to insist on truth we begin to possess a sort of power that in the end is stronger than any violence we will come up against" (the Milarepa Fund). Leaders such as Mandela are, in this sense, moral and spiritual leaders who teach us about what "the power of the individual, who is motivated by kindness and compassion and altruism, . . . what effect that has on the whole planet," as actor Richard Gere put it at the Mandela concert of 1988 (in Lahusen 1996, 229). Ultimately this discourse takes up an important topic of mainstream pop and rock: "Pop's exploitation of the imagination enables it to propagate the liberal idea that everything is possible, that the world is what we choose to make it" (Street 1986, 168).

Third, voluntarist solidarism has a strong emotional dimension. Indeed, while this discourse does not deny the power of reason and rational scrutiny of issues and claims, it emphasizes that our emotional nature, our ability to suffer and love, will awake us from lethargy and ignorance about the other's sufferings. More than that, empathy gives us a sense of the planetary community of which we are but a part. Rave and house-music, for instance, explicitly trigger this "collective consciousness" (Chris Dekker, in http://www.earthdance.org) beyond individual, rational bonds, through their music performances and dance styles. This non-individualist and anti-rationalist stance mounts to a sort of "neo-tribalism" that "entails relations of tactility, of body to body, and the privileging of collective sentiment as the 'glue' which binds people together" (Gore 1997, 56).

Particularly within charity events, this moral and spiritual orientation might degrade to a "moral minimalism" that empties the "normative nucleus of solidarity" (Baringhorst 1998, 208). Due to the increasing heterogeneity of the moral orientations and beliefs of a (global and amorphous) mass audience, campaign messages and appeals on behalf of international solidarity are in real danger of referring merely to a vague and indeterminate humanitarism. Especially in the case of charities dealing with humanitarian causes (for example, Live-Aid's famine relief) this emotionalist and minimalist moral notion of "basically we are all human beings" tends to strip the individual from all cultural and societal traits and ties, but also from more demanding political entitlements and social rights. Thus solidarity and altruism are reduced to a mere question of securing survival, in the end depoliticizing the issue of famine and reproducing paternalistic relations between those donating and those in need (Baringhorst 1998, 207-214).

This tendency was apparent in the mega-events analyzed, particularly because these concerts involved a number of mainstream pop and rock stars, whose political interests and ambitions were uncertain, in order to make these events commercially viable as a global broadcast show. However, the discourse of these events was in part normatively more demanding and ambitious. On the one hand, voluntarist solidarism was morally the more demanding and challenging, the stronger it argued for common social and political rights of all humans. This was obviously the case within Amnesty International's Human Rights Now! world tour, which used the fortieth anniversary of the Universal Declaration of Human Rights to publicize all social, cultural, and political entitlements, giving the campaign's discourse on international solidarity an even higher normative standard. Still, Amnesty's own focus on individual human rights violations allowed the participating pop and rock musicians to address these issues in terms of individual hardships, cases, and testimonies, drawing on standard topic and foci of the imagery of popular music (Street 1986). In fact, even outspoken songs have raised political issues by focusing on specifics and individuals, like, for instance, *Biko* by Peter Gabriel, *They Dance Alone* by Sting, or *Free Nelson Mandela* by Jerry Dammers.

This concern for human rights became, on the other hand, the more politicized, the stronger it focused on the context of social injustice and discrimination, institutional power and state repression, into which the individual is placed and by which the individual quest for freedom and belongingness is inhibited. Here, the Mandela tribute of 1988 is indicative. While this event included many artists who basically called upon a humanitarian solidarity with an imprisoned, righteous man, some artists politically identified with him as a means of solidarizing with the political struggle against the system of apartheid (Lahusen 1996, 223-33). Indeed, this event, as well as the others, not only included a number of chart-hitting artists and songs (*I Just Called* by Stevie Wonder, *Somebody* by Brian Adams, or *Everybody Wants to Rule the World* by Curt Smith, among others), but a series of political songs as well (Little Steven van Zandt's *Sun City*, ASWAD's *Set Them Free, Mandela Day* by Simple Minds, *Stand Up Get Up* by Bob Marley). Hence, all these events were conceived to "work" both commercially and politically. Understandably, they were no self-evident phenomenon with an obvious message or function, but rather a "contested terrain" (Garofalo 1992c, 8). The general focus and message of each event was heavily debated and negotiated at the production stage (through the choice of acts, speakers, stage design) and embattled even in their realization. In fact, while the media coverage focused almost exclusively on the "entertainment news" (the U.S. broadcast of the Mandela tribute even cutting most of its political elements), movement activists conceived of campaigns that framed and commented on this concert and aimed, in part successfully, to pick up on the momentum of public concern created by these events (Lahusen 1996, 273-83).

Activism and Edutainment

One might think that trying to create this beloved, compassionate community out of all of this violence and suffering would require a hardened disposition, a serious tone, and a heavy heart. But in actuality, we have found that our greatest tool towards this goals is a light heart, laughter and joking around. And so we will continue to combine education, entertainment and activism, and to create environments where people can have fun in a way that is not harmful to others and that infects them with the ideal of compassion (http://www.milarepa.org).

The Milarepa Fund's approach toward political activism illustrates well the second aspect of the aesthetization and sublimation of political mobilization: all these campaign events verbalize elementary, vital questions of humankind, often even discrediting any politically partisan view, yet in an entertaining and hedonistic manner. Ultimately, advocacy work is submitted to entertainment formats and values, as happened with what has come to be called infotainment or edutainment. This "advotainment" is part of the manifold interrelations between social movements and popular music described above. At this point, however, it may be of interest to explore the meaning and function of "advotainment" in regard to political mobilization and solidaristic activism.

First, entertainment is not necessarily alien to social movements, in that mockery and irony have always served as a weapon of political protest and subversion (Babcock 1984). Moreover, joy, laughter, and festivities become a legitimate means of political activism that is fighting frustration, resignation and despair. Finally, in a spiritual struggle for faith, hope, and love, entertainment and joy are a natural ally insofar as they celebrate and elevate the solidaristic community and its struggle. Amnesty's world tour, for instance, celebrated the fortieth anniversary of the Universal Declaration, while the Mandela tributes used his seventieth birthday and release from prison as festive occasions to celebrate this man and rededicate the public to his struggle.

Second, "advotainment" has a specific, instrumental function to accomplish. These entertainment events were to reach and activate a wider public, thus giving potential participants a reason for joining in altruistic action—to the point that the purchase of an entertainment product (a ticket for a concert, a compact disc, merchandise, books) and the indirect funds raised became the very "altruistic" act. Through "advotainment," doing something for others and for oneself become compatible. However, this case does confuse, but not erode, the difference between altruism and utilitarianism. In fact, activists were very conscious about the instrumental function of entertainment. While the entertainment aspect was to serve as an inducement for participation, these events were to raise the awareness, interest, and concern of the audiences addressed, and to instigate, consolidate or reaffirm stable bonds of solidarity and lasting commitments to the cause. In regard to the Tibetan Freedom Concert, for instance, organizers wrote: "While a majority of these concert-goers would have preferred to remain ignorant to the harsh realities that define the Tibetan struggle, the Milarepa Fund subtly assured that nothing of the sort would happen. At every turn concert-goers found reminders of the Tibetan cause, and of the necessity for youth activism." Hence these events were to motivate and initiate the youth into altruistic action in a joyful and entertaining manner.

This latter function suggests a third aspect of "advotainment," namely, the focus on the experiential power of public events. In fact, mega-events like the Tibetan Freedom concerts were designed to give ample room for a personal experience of the issue at stake. For instance, a temporary Tibetan monastery was constructed at the concert site, complete with Tibetan Buddhist paintings and symbols. Concertgoers had the opportunity to watch monks work and meditate; Tibetan food was served at concession stands; a number of monks, nuns, and other speakers gave testimonies of the Tibetan struggle. This experiential dimension is of particular relevance when membership in groups is not compulsory but optional, and when solidarity bonds are not mechanical but organic (Durkheim 1964). Within mass audiences, which are heterogeneous and less structured according to fixed groups and closed communities, the experiential quality of participation and solidarity meets the expressive needs of the individual, who is increasingly freed and forced to construct a personal identity and a sense of social belongingness (Schulze 1994). Consequently, in differentiated and individualized societies increasingly "apolitical associative networks based on affiliation through sentiment and shared interests" emerge, as in the case of rave culture and the dance-floor movement (Gore 1997, 55). These youth cultures use and rely on social concerns and political causes as an expressive means to define and reassert their own mission and meaning, and in doing so they become a medium of political mobilization.

Thus "advotainment" is becoming a relay for interweaving social movements and popular music, social and cultural transformation (Eyerman and Jamison 1995). The smaller EarthDance event is a good case to show how transnational mobilizing networks are used and constructed in the process of mobilization itself. EarthDance was organized in 1997 and 1998 as a "Global Dance Party for Planetary Peace" in aid of Tibet, the first event encompassing twenty-five countries and the second global dance linking sixty-one locations in thirty-six countries from Mexico to Kazakhstan, Hungary to Bolivia. Its aim was to raise awareness and funds on behalf of Tibet within the international dance-floor community. Each party cooperated with a local Tibetan support group (mostly the Dalai Lama's charity fund), and included acts and performances. Yet all events were linked through the Internet ("webcasts" and chat rooms) and unified by a meditation and a specially-created soundtrack on world peace, simultaneously performed at all sites. In this regard it is important to note that although dance-floor or house-music are often represented as "global" or transnational youth (sub)cultures, important local differences remain (Rietveld 1998). Indeed, while EarthDance tapped into a transnational "taste culture" for Tibetan solidarity work, it also required much networking to build the transnational structures leading to this event. At the same time, the success of this global dance made transnational clubbing (commercially) more attractive for disc jockeys, musicians, and party promoters. While in 1997 the organizers had to struggle with lack of support and many initial problems in setting up organizational structures, the experience and the feedback is allowing them to expand the range of the global party and institutionalize it as a yearly event that will, however, shift its issue and beneficiary from year to year.

Finally, EarthDance illustrates the performative and experiential dimension of political mobilization in all its clarity. "United as one . . . we dance" was the motto of EarthDance, and this inclusion and suspension of the individual within a united community represents much of the sense and power of this dance music. "A crowd which dances to house music is bound on a route to pure escape whilst at the same time celebrating a sense of community which has been forged at the moment of interactive consumption" (Rietveld 1998, 189). Dancing can create an ecstatic trance, similar to shamanic or religious experience, which results in a momentum of disappearance of the individual self within the community's ego. A rave party or "a house music event can be a carefree ritual of death and rebirth, that is suited to a contemporary 'global' culture which relies on electronic communication technologies" (Rietveld 1998, 205). EarthDance was all about the idea of using the dance floor's ecstatic and communal dynamic to give a particularly dense and deep, sensational and emotional experience of international solidarity, of the multicultural, human community, into which one was called into action. Indeed, EarthDance was concerned with triggering a "collective consciousness" by linking a series of dance floors across the world "with the same energy happening everywhere" and by enacting a "ritual visualization" of the issue at stake in order to give a focus to this energy (Chris Dekker, in http://www.earthdance.org). While house-music and rave put a particular emphasis on this collective trance and passage, much the same is true for other mega-events in particular and public events in general (Handelman 1990). In fact, the "magic" of these events, and the "energy" of the music, was recurrently attributed to the ability to create common feelings and moments of collective concern. If political mobilization is a social fact or phenomenon *sui generis*, then the cases analyzed provide ample evidence for demonstrating that the mobilization *process* has the ability to alter preferences, generate commitments, and coordinate collective action.

Conclusion

The mega-events under review were successful in raising funds, attracting public attention, and recruiting new (primarily young) members. It was the "magic" of these events that created a momentum of collective concern, laid the foundations for forging solidarity bonds, and opened the door for a stronger commitment to the common struggle. Indeed, the primary concern was to adapt events and activities so as to reach and mobilize a wider audience of bystanders and potential supporters. However, while activists do not see other alternatives to broadening their action repertoire and mobilization strategies, this broadening challenges the established mobilization structures and networks of the solidarity movement—and this can be seen in regard to the arguments raised in the introduction. First, we argued that these events lower the costs of participation, particularly by making collective action an aesthetically appealing and entertaining commercial product. Consumption becomes an important intention and aspect of participation, changing the logic of mobilization itself. In fact, lasting commitments were not always the rule, as the high turnover among the newly recruited membership of the organizing SMOs indicates (Lahusen 1996, 313-18). Again, questions arise as to whether emotional media campaigns, commercial celebrity shows, and edutainment are inconsequential and inconclusive in terms of "serious," profound, and lasting commitments, or whether political struggles and citizens' activism degenerate to mere voyeuristic concern, to a pompously enacted sale of indulgences (Baringhorst 1998, 324-42).

Second, these events demonstrate that SMOs engage in all sorts of acts and activities. Apparently the loosening of fixed constituencies and the competitive struggle for resources seem to push the big SMOs into indiscriminate use of upcoming opportunities, into a trial-and-error of "anything goes." This is all the more important as it decouples political mobilization from the direct control of SMOs, because all these different events have to meet their own conditions of (commercial) success and operate under their own rules, participants, statements, and acts. SMOs are often put into a reactive position that compels them to either capitalize on the outcomes or engage in damage control.

Third, the discourse of philanthropy and humanitarianism raises the danger of degrading altruism and solidarity to a charitable paternalism between donors and recipients. This is the case as long as "they" participate only as an object of "our" solidarity, that is, as long as international solidarity is lacking in reciprocity. Solidarity movements have often been explicit and strong on this argument, because for them it is necessary to conceive of donors and recipients as partners in a common struggle to overcome the structural causes of grievances. Political solidarism asks for a substantial social change of unjust systems both privileging donors and discriminating recipients. However, the need to "think big" led these charity events to go "mainstream" and strengthen charitable commitments to the detriment of political advocacy.

Fourth, this reciprocity is more of a problem when moving to the international arena, where a solidaristic relation between very distant people (a common "we") has to be established, embracing different cultures, religions, or nations. In the case of Amnesty International, for instance, this is done in reference to universal human rights. Accordingly, local solidarity groups from various countries are involved in reciprocal and common action against human rights violations regardless of their origin. Other organizations, such as the World Artists for a Free Tibet, aim to shelter the manifold cultures of this planet, particularly Buddhist spiritualism, melting them into a solidarity based on inner values, moral commitments, and spiritual beliefs in a peaceful and "unpolitical" struggle for worldwide understanding and brotherhood. In both cases, common solidaristic bonds are established by defining a set of general values and ideas that embrace all the particular cultures and people. However, this gradual generalization of a moral and spiritual discourse on international solidarity is possibly only realized at the expense of lowering normative claims, with altruism and solidarity becoming possibly a matter of a minimalist humanitarianism or "happy multiculturalism" (Baringhorst 1998, 238-49). Movement activists were among those articulating all these worries, their primary aim being to politicize these events, broaden the understanding, and deepen commitments. Indeed, the public events under review were an "embattled terrain." In this regard the progress made by the transnationalization of mobilizing structures depends on the ability to infuse this "embattled" discourse on international solidarity with a concern for social and political rights of an individual and collective type.

10

From Altruism to a New Transnationalism?

A Look at Transnational Social Movements

Ivana Eterovic and Jackie Smith

In recent decades, we have witnessed an unprecedented compression of time and space (Giddens 1990) as individuals, groups, and governments increasingly integrate political, economic, and social processes across national boundaries. These changes are paralleled in the social movement sector, where we see a significant increase in the number of transnationally organized social movement organizations (TSMOs). We examine here the question of what impact global integration has had on the character of social movement activism. Specifically, how is political altruism affected by global structural changes that have transformed nation-states? The effects of the relocation of a segment of social movement activity to the transnational level appear to transcend a simple change in the locus or scope of activity. We ask whether transnational social movements represent and reinforce new identities based on an awareness of global interdependence.

Does the political action within the transnational social movement sector flow primarily from the global North toward the global South? Do the contemporary forms of transnational association stem from the altruistic motives of more economically privileged activists working on behalf of their relatively deprived counterparts in other countries? Or do the transnational movement organizations base their activity on notions of more collaborative, interdependent relationships? Viewing TSMOs as an organizational response to economic, cultural, and political integration across national borders, we explore the social processes manifest in globalization as well as those within TSMOs themselves for evidence of how they may be encouraging among their participants a convergence of new values and action frames.

Altruistic patterns of association, in which constituencies do not overlap with the beneficiaries of collective action, presume that relations between more economically privileged areas (for example, the global North) and the later-industrializing, poorer countries of the global South are characterized by one-way dependency.[1] In other words, the North's economic dominance over the South can only be mitigated through assistance that mirrors other patterns of northern domination over the South. If one presumes that the relations between the global North and South are *interdependent*, the altruistic forms of cooperation would not fundamentally challenge the underlying sources of activists' grievances. Intergroup relations characterized by political solidarity, however, would have greater potential to challenge the global structural sources of grievances that are common to activists in both the North and the South (see, e.g., Macdonald 1995).

Observations of contemporary transnational activism suggest that a new form of political action and identity is emerging. Moreover, this transformation—at least its more rapid and broad expansion—appears to be a direct consequence of the intensification of global economic and political integration of the post-Cold War era. One observer noted that coalitions of diverse activists in the debates over the North American Free Trade Agreement (NAFTA) signaled a "promising new phase of internationalism in social movements." He observed that

> [w]hereas recent internationalism[2] in US social movements has been defined by northern nonprofit organizations addressing economic inequities and environmental degradation in the South, the new internationalism is considerably more reciprocal. Based on mutual solidarity between movements in different countries, it seeks to reorient the direction of development in the North as well as the South (Hunter 1995, 6).

Hunter also sees a new expansion of cooperation among different movements such as women, labor, environment, and indigenous peoples, an observation that parallels our own observations and that complements the movement among U.S. peace movement organizations from single-issue to more structural, multiple-issue frames documented by Marullo and his colleagues (Marullo, Pagnucco, and Smith 1996).[3]

The new transnationalism suggests an important difference in the diagnosis of social problems and in the prescription for addressing them, compared to those of more traditional, altruistic action frames. We see this frame transformation as a product of both structural changes in the global system and in the related changes in the social movement sector. In other words, changes in the structure of inter-state political and economic relations have relocated important decisions to inter-state policy arenas. This has required new forms of social movement organization in order to effectively target these arenas. These new organizations, in turn, help generate new forms of social and political interaction that foster transnational dialogues and cooperation and alter traditional social movement frames. In this chapter, we discuss the key ways that changes in the global system have affected the possibilities for transnational mobilization, and we examine the work of a particular transnational social movement organization, EarthAction, to evaluate the extent to which it has been able to overcome national differences and to promote transnational solidarity.

Altruism, Solidarity, and Social Movements

Authors within the social movement literature have illuminated a set of processes associated with the meaning and effects of "political altruism," or participation in political action aimed at benefiting others. In their influential statement of the resource mobilization approach to the study of social movements, McCarthy and Zald (1987) depart from the traditional view that social movements are necessarily based on resources and labor of aggrieved groups. One of the key innovative elements of the resource mobilization approach to the understanding of collective behavior is that social movements "may or may not be based upon the grievances of the presumed beneficiaries" (McCarthy and Zald 1987, 19). In the process of resource mobilization, social movement organizations extend their efforts (often successfully) to individuals and groups that are not potential beneficiaries. McCarthy and Zald refer to these individuals and groups as "conscience adherents" and "conscience constituents." Their participation and support are not based on expectations of direct benefits, but rather on secondary benefits or solidaristic incentives.

Some studies of social movement activity emphasize the key role the support of individuals and organizations outside the aggrieved group can play in determining the success of collective action. In their comparison of two instances of farm workers' insurgency, Jenkins and Perrow (1977), for example, found the support of more-established organizations to be one of the crucial factors determining outcomes of the challenge. In his conceptual scheme of protest activity by marginalized groups, Lipsky (1968) asserts that protest leaders attempt to influence their target organization to accept their group's goals indirectly. They direct their activities toward two "outside" constituencies—mass media and "third parties"—established "elite" groups, and organizations that serve as mediators of their interests. Both the chances of success of relatively powerless groups and the form of their protest activity depend on the process of bargaining, involving the aggrieved group, the target of their political activity, media, and external allies (Lipsky 1968). In the context of inter- and/or transnational social movement activity, the principle of political altruism has been associated with what Rucht (1995) calls "distant-issue movements," or Third

World solidarity movements. In the context of these discussions, "solidarity" refers to actions of altruistic constituencies, actions by "conscience constituents" to promote interests of a different group of beneficiaries.

But intergroup solidarity goes beyond these more transient or superficial alliances toward a framing of one's problems as symptomatic of broader structural ills. Proponents of change may come to see the sources of their own problems as manifested in the experiences of others. Hirsch (1986) describes this as political solidarity, or the transition toward an understanding of the structural sources of grievances and an acceptance of social movement organizing as a vehicle for addressing them. For Hirsch, political solidarity is an important by-product of participation in collective action. Rochon (1998) also views group solidarity as a crucial foundation for social movement mobilization, emphasizing that group solidarity should be understood as a politicized group identity that emerges when members feel discontent regarding group status, when they identify external causes of their situation, and when they view collective action as a means of improving their situation. This notion of solidarity corresponds with what McAdam has called "cognitive liberation," in which grievances are seen as the product of systemic forces that are subject to change through group action (McAdam 1982).

According to analysts mentioned above, as well as to other central work in social movement theory (e.g., Gamson 1990; Tilly 1978), political solidarity helps movement leaders resolve the perennial "free-rider" problem by justifying individual-level motivation for participation in collective action to redress grievances. Some form of group identification is important for sustained collective action, particularly where the change targets seem far removed from one's actual experience. This would be particularly true in many transnational social movement campaigns, which focus on elusive goals of universal human rights or on remote international treaties and institutions such as the World Bank rather than on localized, readily observable targets of change.

It is also important to note that, for all of these analysts, interaction with other group members is crucial to the generation of political solidarity. In other words, "[i]t is not possible for one to feel solidarity with a group with which one does not identify" (Rochon 1998, 79). Thus, social movement organizations that facilitate interaction among group members and across different groups who share similar grievances create conditions that are essential for the formation of political solidarity. Recognizing this, Rochon (1998) emphasizes two key components in the process of solidarity-building. First, to cultivate solidarity there must be interaction among participating groups that helps to create a common, shared experience. Second, there must be a unified frame that allows for shared interpretations of events. Both of these components are more difficult to achieve at the transnational level, characterized by a much broader range of constituencies in a geographic and cultural sense, as well as in terms of traditions of collective action.

The relocation of a segment of social movement activity to the transnational level both reflects a changed political and economic reality and promotes new forms of political solidarity that transcend national boundaries. That solidarity is based on transnationalism as a new and emerging form of political identification and action. Transnational social movement activity is encouraged by increasing levels of awareness of global interdependence, and the social processes embedded within TSMOs themselves encourage a convergence of transnational values and action frames. Below we outline how the changed political context affects transnational mobilizing structures and opportunities, and we examine how a particular TSMO has worked to generate collective action in a diverse range of local and national affiliates.

Transnationalization of Social Movement Organizations

In recent decades, the number of transnational social movement organizations (TSMOs) has increased significantly, from just under two hundred organizations in 1973 to more than six hundred in 1993 (Smith 1997, 47; Sikkink and Smith, forthcoming). The formation of transnational social movement organizations, moreover, parallels the expansion of intergovernmental organization (Meyer, Boli, Thomas, and Ramirez 1997), suggesting that this organizational growth signals a widespread and growing perception of global interdependency (Young 1991) and that the formal organization of the intergovernmental sector requires parallel organizational shifts among social movements.

Global political institutions provide opportunities for TSMOs to target government and international officials, and they also encourage groups to seek geographically diverse representation as a means of amplifying their voices in international forums (Smith, Pagnucco, and Chatfield 1997). Thus, although earlier transnational alliances may have been largely motivated by altruistic purposes, contemporary technology and global political structures appear to encourage more reciprocal global solidarity-building within TSMOs.

Has transnational social movement activism led to the emergence of a new transnationalism that replaces more traditional, dependent forms of altruism? If solidarity inherent in transnationalism is displacing altruism as the basis for transnational association, we should find changes in the geographic location and membership bases of TSMOs as well as in their strategic orientations. We review evidence on transnational social movement activity to determine whether there have been changes in the sector that are consistent with our expectations.

Geography

Transnational social movement organizations are still disproportionately based in the North, and they tend to over-represent constituencies from developed countries (Smith 1997, 49). This is not very surprising, given that international decision-making centers are based predominantly in the global North, where transportation and communication infrastructures are most advanced. Social movements focusing on these institutions can substantially increase their effectiveness and limit their costs by basing their organizations in London, New York, or Brussels (Sassen 1997). The effect of the structural and other forces that favor the interests of northern or core countries is that, even as they might encourage transnational communication, global technological and social infrastructures continue to reflect existing global inequalities. Nevertheless, despite the large and persistent gap between the global North and South in levels of participation in TSMOs, there is evidence that this gap has been closing (however slowly) in recent years. The percentage of TSMOs with members in developing countries was 61 percent in 1993 compared to 46 percent ten years earlier. In that same period, the percentage of TSMOs with organizational headquarters in the South rose from 17 percent to 24 percent (Smith 1997, 49).

The increased level of integration of southern activists in organized transnational social movement activity can be explained by facilitating effects of new communication technologies (Young 1991; Kriesberg 1997). The end of the Cold War has also contributed to greater North-South integration among both governments and societies by expanding the global political agenda (for example, at the United Nations and other global forums) and reducing political obstacles to communication.

From the point of view of transnational social movement collaboration, the most relevant effect of the end of the Cold War has been the expansion of UN-sponsored international conferences during the 1990s. As arenas for global problem-solving, UN conferences have provided forums for intensive interaction and dialogue among governments, corporate representatives, and nongovernmental actors. By focusing the global political agenda on a concrete problem and by providing both opportunities and occasionally new resources for activists to assemble for purposes of networking, planning, and cultivating common perspectives on emerging global problems, global conferences serve as important contributors to greater North-South solidarity. A cursory review of the histories of TSMOs suggests that many groups were formally established as a direct or indirect result of a global conference.[4]

Strategy

A shift from altruistic forms of association to more solidarity-based association should be reflected in the strategies adopted by TSMOs as well as in their geographic makeup. Like geographic distribution, the pattern here seems to mirror prevailing global inequalities. But there is some evidence of transformation in the patterns of North-South association, possibly as a consequence of transnational social movement organization and activity.

Results of a 1996 survey of one hundred fifty transnational human rights organizations show that North-based organizations were more likely treat "promoting or protecting the rights of specific groups" as their main organizational goal. Fifty-eight percent of northern groups listed this as a major goal, compared to 40 percent of South-based organizations (Smith, Pagnucco, and Lopez 1998). This indicates that many northern groups might still see themselves partly as serving conscience adherents and constituents that are not direct beneficiaries of collective action (McCarthy and Zald 1987). This evidence is mixed, however, given the relatively small size of the differences in the responses of northern and southern groups on their main political strategies. Lacking data on prior years, we cannot tell whether the North-South difference is growing or shrinking. However, we have reason to believe that the trend runs toward a narrowing of the North-South gap.

Transnational collaboration is both a response to and a facilitator of a growing sense of global interdependency (Young 1991). More traditional conscience constituencies, such as early Amnesty International advocates for political freedoms or contributors to multinational development aid efforts, have given way to new types of transnational association. This newer form of association involves more direct, two-way communications between activists in the global North and South. Thus, the issues around which transnational activism has been organized have shifted over time from a predominant focus in the 1950s on human rights and development assistance to a broad agenda including women's rights, locally-empowered development, and (since the 1970s) the global environment.

Issues related to environment, human rights, and development based on social justice, to name just a few, are increasingly perceived as global issues that are affected by political decisions beyond the control of any single nation-state and that thus require active transnational organizing. Therefore, the growth of TSMOs and their expansion across the globe might also be indicative of another shift in the collective action on the transnational level—that from activism on behalf of certain individuals and groups to collective action based on the sense of a globally shared fate. The formation of transnational associations, moreover, signals not only a new approach to political mobilization, but it also manifests new interactive processes among groups and individuals across national boundaries. These intra-organizational processes may be based upon more traditional altruism, reinforcing existing dependencies in the world system, or they may reflect and build upon solidary relations among organizational participants.[5]

While global integration has facilitated transnational cooperation, and while global structural changes have required activists to transcend national borders to address the problems they face, global political institutions also create pressures for activists to actively cultivate transnational solidarity. As an organization of all national governments, the United Nations' organizational ethos places a premium on wide international representation. Organizations that request consultative status and routine access to the United Nations and its delegates must demonstrate that their organizational purpose and composition transcend a single nation-state. And the most credible lobbyists and advocates in the halls of the UN are those who can claim to represent citizens from a large number of countries. Thus, the strategic imperative for operating at least in universal supranational forums encourages efforts for greater transnational solidarity.

Globalization and Mobilizing Opportunities

Because national political structures continue to be central to shaping the local experiences of most of the world's people, a key strategy of transnational social movement organizing is the mobilization of transnational pressure to promote national-level changes. In cases in which local or national social movements cannot achieve their goals by targeting directly their national governments, transnational solidary action targeting international institutions provides a new "target" level. Integration into the international system makes national governments vulnerable to an additional set of pressures from other national governments and from international organizations such as the World Bank or United Nations, thus reducing traditional notions of state sovereignty. In the context of increasingly internationalized political processes, social movement activists can draw attention to a government's failure to uphold international norms or appeal to international allies to bring pressure for changes in a government's domestic practices. Keck and Sikkink (1998) refer to such a pattern of influence as a "boomerang effect." Allies can be found in either international bodies or in individual governments, and the links are often made through mediation of transnational social movement networks. Brysk's (1993) study of human rights activism in Argentina demonstrates the boomerang effect by which local activists were able to achieve their goals through the activation of international networks and the subsequent international pressure on the Argentine regime.

It is important to note that the process is not one-directional, but rather reflects certain agency from the apparently "receiving" end. Brysk's analysis shows that the strength of national social movement sectors is crucial to achieving local goals, regardless of the level of international support. This conclusion is reinforced elsewhere. Kidder and McGinn (1995), for instance, argue that transnational workers' alliances to resist the North American Free Trade Agreement (NAFTA) were most effective where strong local organizations were already present. Activists reporting on transnational organizing work in the Chiapas region of Mexico and in Croatia and Bosnia likewise concluded that transnational efforts were most effective when local groups were able to both define and influence the terms of cooperation (International Fellowship of Reconciliation 1999).

Some transnational social movement organizations, organized as "umbrella" organizations, provide the potential for activating international pressure to promote local or national goals. In this case, a rather formalized partnership more clearly indicates at least potential reciprocity, since—in contrast to coalitions that come together to pursue a specific policy goal—such organizations imply an ongoing relationship that extends through multiple campaigns. Support for a local cause is often framed as a defense of a *shared* set of transnational principles (for example, human rights or environmental protection), rather than simply as support for a specific beneficiary constituency (for example, an individual activist jailed for his or her activities).

Processes of solidarity-building in the opposite, "top-down" direction have also been documented. An important strategy of transnational social movements is to generate constituencies for global policies. Through interaction with broad networks of national and local organizations, transnational social movement organizations attempt to harmonize national positions on relevant issues through transnational education and mobilization. TSMOs craft and disseminate action frames that relate citizens' concerns to global institutions and processes. They spread information about how citizens can draw upon international institutions and law to further their social change agendas. Another aim of transnational social movements is to exert direct influence on the formulation of policies at the intergovernmental level. Transnational umbrella organizations and coalitions rely on their local and national membership bases to gather relevant information on the problem they seek to address and to legitimize their claims to represent a broad transnational constituency.[6]

The strengthening of intergovernmental institutions and other forms of global political integration has induced another set of challenges to localized collective action by shifting decision-making away from the locale and even the nation-state and toward remote, supranational institutions. Smaller, locally, or even nationally based social movement organizations lack financial resources to actively participate in political battles at the international level, since doing so often requires some training in international law as well as access to information on global negotiations. Additionally, international bodies are highly bureaucratized structures, and they require social movement actors to adapt their organizational structures and repertoires to such a setting. Through the process of "institutional selectivity" (Wisler and Giugni 1996), large international organizations tend to favor organizational challengers that are more formalized and bureaucratized and that operate in accepted international languages (cf. Clemens 1997). In this sense, TSMOs serve as important mediators between local or national grievances and the global political arena. Political globalization can also present new challenges to social movements. Examining social movement activity within the European Union, both Rucht (1997) and Tarrow (1995) argue that the shift of the locus of political activity to supranational level completely restricts the ability of social movements to effectively promote interests of their constituencies, since they lose some of the disruptive potential of noninstitutionalized protest action. Transnational social movement organizations assist the formation of transnationalism through their strategy of assisting social movements in reframing issues perceived as locality-specific into global issues. Smith (1999) illustrates this linkage of local problems to their global sources by Greenpeace's campaign to end international trade in toxic wastes. Greenpeace used its resources to coordinate a global campaign, but relied heavily on activation of local groups and strategic linking of local struggles with global issues.

We emphasize that social movement work at the transnational level is especially burdened by the dissimilarity of actors' historical, social, and cultural traditions and experiences. The process of "frame alignment" (Snow et. al. 1986) or the resonance of interpretive frameworks of different actors in *national* movement activities is very difficult and not always successful. Thus, we can expect even greater framing difficulties when attempting to develop and support transnational mobilizing frames. Not only do global-level institutional processes lengthen and complicate the "causal chain" (Keck and Sikkink 1998) between a local experience and a policy solution, but they also can affect people from different regions and locales very differently.[7] Gabriel and Macdonald (1994), for instance, illustrate some of the obstacles to transnational frame alignment in their analysis of transnational organizing efforts among Canadian and Mexican women against NAFTA. Differences in social positions of activists both within the Canadian groups and among Canadian and Mexican women made the process of creation and maintenance of collective identity and action frames a complicated one. Similarly, in her analysis of the Indian rights movement, Brysk (1996) points to the conflict between the need for effectiveness on the transnational level and adequate representation of the interests and values of different local communities.

How have organizations responded to the globalization of political institutions and to the challenges of transnational organizing? Structures of the political environment in which TSMOs operate influence the organizational forms they adopt for their mobilizing efforts, as well as patterns of intra-organizational collaboration that emerge in their efforts to influence national or intergovernmental levels of governance. Through its influence on organizational structure of social movements, the context of social movement activity defines the range of strategic choices available to movement actors (Rucht 1996). TSMO members, either individual or organizational, come from different social, cultural, and political contexts and bring with them a range of experiences and traditions of collective action. Young (1991, 13) points out that "international associations must draw together groups of people from different cultures, speaking different languages, perceiving their (presumably) common problems in different ways and intensities and living in countries having different economic capacities, political traditions, and readiness for change." This reality affects strongly the forms and effectiveness of organizational integration.

The process of "frame alignment" (Snow et al. 1986, 467) or the correspondence of interpretative frameworks held by movement participants and the leaders of a TSMO can be complicated by the diversity of backgrounds and experiences of members. How well a TSMO can overcome differences among members is both a function of the extent to which members can draw from a common base of shared experiences as well as how effectively the organization promotes communication. Globalization processes that integrate economic, political, and social institutions across national boundaries provide a structural base for transnational social movement organizing, since problems experienced in many locales (for example, economic dislocation and unemployment) are often caused by the same transnational actor or policy (for example, globalization of trade and expansion of transnational corporations). But we can presume that national differences will continue to challenge efforts to fully integrate transnational associations, particularly those working on contentious political issues.

How effective are TSMOs at overcoming the obstacles to transnational solidarity-building and mobilization? What kinds of organizational structures enable groups to cultivate shared identities and common interpretive frames across very different political and cultural contexts? Without presuming to be able to answer these questions here, we begin to examine them by looking at a TSMO that has mobilized a particularly diverse transnational constituency.

Evidence on Transnational Organizational Integration

EarthAction is a TSMO that was established in 1992 during the UN Conference on Environment and Development. It adopted a strategy modeled explicitly after that used by Amnesty International, namely, the use of transnational letter-writing and mass media campaigns focused on a single problem (or human rights victim). EarthAction has grown to become one of the most diverse TSMOs, with over one thousand five hundred organizational members (primarily organizations) from more than one hundred forty countries, and with more than two-thirds of its affiliates based in the global South.[8] The organization focuses largely on environmental and social justice (development) concerns, but it also works on disarmament and human rights issues.

We have selected EarthAction for this case study because it stands out among TSMOs in a number of ways. First, rather than focusing on a particular policy issue or campaign, it has adopted a broad, multi-issue agenda, and it concentrates on developing its transnational network of activists that can press many governments simultaneously to bring about policy change (Smith 1995a, 1997). In order to promote its goal of working with affiliates and developing a strong network of organizations, EarthAction's organizational headquarters is divided so that smaller regional offices are present in the United States, Britain, and Chile. While devoting much effort to the organization's political campaigns, EarthAction leaders also see their work as helping to foster communication among affiliates and to promote dialogue within the network of groups the organization comprises. It devotes an unusually large amount of energy and resources to fostering communication with its affiliates (Smith 1995a).[9] One consequence of this kind of organizing effort is that EarthAction is one of the most geographically dispersed transnational coalitions, with more than two-thirds of its affiliate organizations based in the global South. Table 10.1 summarizes the locations of EarthAction partners.

Compared with most other TSMOs, EarthAction has an extremely diverse membership base. The large number of countries from which its affiliates come should be expected to especially complicate the work of building common identities and action frames. The combination of the priority attached to network-building and the diversity of its affiliates makes EarthAction a particularly useful case for exploring the possibilities of building transnational solidarity.

As a result of its organizational mission, we should expect that transnational organizational integration would be strongest in a group like EarthAction—despite the presumed added difficulty of a membership base with more diverse national backgrounds than is found in most TSMOs. Should we find low levels of integration within this group, then the chances that other TSMOs—such as ones that concentrate more on their directly political action and less on their organizational integration and communicative and dialogue functions—overcome barriers to transnational solidarity-building are rather slim.

In order to assess the extent of organizational integration within transnational SMOs, we surveyed EarthAction affiliate organizations in 1998, asking questions about their organizations and their use of EarthAction materials. Survey questions sought to determine the factors that limited partners' participation in EarthAction campaigns.[10] Drawing from survey responses, we attempt to evaluate the extent to which we can claim that transnational associations like EarthAction help create shared experiences of global activism (which in turn foster a common identity as an EarthAction "Partner") and help reinforce a common interpretation of grievances within a global interpretive framework.

Participation in a transnational association should generate interactions that integrate participants into a common experience, at least by virtue of the fact that they are being asked to take action on an issue of joint concern, such as a campaign to ensure the legal protection of indigenous groups' land rights in Brazil. Background materials relate the local concerns of groups in Brazil to the global debates on human rights and on environmental protection (EarthAction 1993). With each "action kit," affiliates are reminded that they are a part of a global network spanning more than one hundred forty countries, with the implication that their action will be one of many more taken by groups around

TABLE 10.1
Geographic Distribution of EarthAction Affiliate Organizations

	All affiliate organizations	Survey Respondents
Africa	21.0	21.1
Asia	24.5	27.3
Europe	16.3	15.3
Latin America	19.3	21.1
North America	17.0	12.9
Pacific	2.0	2.4
Global South	69%	75%
N	1714	209

The sampled group over-represented groups in the global South in order to avoid possible nonresponse bias due to postal complications, language differences, etc.

the world on behalf of a given campaign. As one of the organization's promotional flyers reminds its potential affiliates: "[P]eople don't mind being pebbles, as long as they know they are part of an avalanche."

One indication that the idea of participating in global-change efforts resonates well among groups is the fact that, despite the frequent complaints of many that they have extremely limited financial resources and even more limited staff time, they seek more ways of generating contacts with groups from beyond their locales. There is strong evidence that EarthAction affiliates wish for even more interactive forms of participation, as responses suggest an interest in efforts to create an even stronger base of shared experience. For instance, a large number of partners have indicated in this survey and in other communications with EarthAction that they would like to have a conference of EarthAction affiliate organizations, or, at a minimum, a (second, updated) affiliate directory and summary of the activities of other partners.[11] These rather widespread affiliate interests in expanding the foundations of shared global experiences may be an outgrowth of the more limited interactions that transnational associations like EarthAction have fostered to date.

If participation in EarthAction helps to create shared experiences, then we should expect similar responses from groups in different parts of the world regarding the ways they respond to EarthAction campaigns. In particular, we would expect that differences between affiliates based in the global North and in the South would not mirror the prevailing structural inequalities found in the global system. If this were the case, we would expect that northern affiliates would make greater use of EarthAction materials and would otherwise find greater resonance with EarthAction campaigns, due to the fact that EarthAction's organizing template largely reflects a Western model and that the global institutions it seeks to influence were largely designed according to the institutional templates preferred by the core countries.

We compare the responses of EarthAction's northern and southern affiliate organizations to assess this expectation. Table 10.2 presents responses to other questions that assess the extent to which partners' participation in EarthAction affects their day-to-day operations.

The results in table 10.2 reinforce a robust pattern in these data of southern affiliates making greater use of EarthAction's materials. Nearly half of the southern groups reported that they have some standard way of using EarthAction's materials, whereas less than one-third of northern groups have routinized their participation in EarthAction campaigns. Further supporting this pattern, when asked about their participation in specific campaigns over the past year, southern groups claimed to have taken action on an average of 3.4 campaigns, compared with 2.8 campaigns for northern groups.[12] This is likely due to the fact that northern organizations typically have much greater access to other information resources, and thus EarthAction represents one among many sources of campaign ideas for them. In contrast, southern groups typically have fewer resources with which to work.

Table 10.2 shows that EarthAction's work has had an impact on most affiliates' day-to-day operations, and this is particularly true for southern groups. Whether it was regarding their outreach to the media or their work on international negotiations, for both northern and southern affiliates the average score of responses indicated that being part of EarthAction at least sometimes, and often closer to always, influenced some aspect of their work. The only statistically significant differences in the responses of northern and southern partners was that southern groups were substantially more likely to report that EarthAction has helped increase their work with nongovernmental organizations, the media, and their efforts to influence policymakers. Southern groups were also more likely to report that EarthAction has helped them increase the global focus of their work. But this has not meant that northern groups have not found EarthAction's work helpful to their organizational initiatives: on average, northern partners reported that they benefited from EarthAction's work at least sometimes. We can conclude from table 10.2 that EarthAction's work is helping many partners to engage in global political efforts, and that the organization is helping to reduce the inequalities in the informational resources available to citizens' groups in the global South.[13]

The local social and political contexts are likely to have strong impacts on the capacities of affiliates to engage in EarthAction campaigns and on the responses to local initiatives. Table 10.3 presents responses to survey questions on the extent to which affiliate organizations face obstacles in their efforts to engage in transnational political campaigns.

By far the strongest inhibitors to both northern and southern partners' participation in EarthAction campaigns are financial constraints. By contrast, language

TABLE 10.2

Effects of Participation in EarthAction on Routine Work of Affiliate Organizations

	Average response [a]		T-value [b]
	Southern partners	Northern partners	
EarthAction materials have improved our outreach to the media	3.48	2.63	3.56**
EarthAction materials aid our work with other NGOs	3.73	3.06	3.28**
EarthAction materials have increased our efforts to influence policymakers	3.72	3.24	2.30*
Being part of EarthAction has increased the global focus of our work	3.63	3.13	2.42*
Being part of EarthAction helps us link local issues to global negotiations	3.79	3.61	1.01
EarthAction helps us to work on issues we could not otherwise address	3.77	3.44	1.64
EarthAction materials help us better address the issues we normally cover	3.76	3.55	1.06
EarthAction makes us feel part of a global effort	3.85	3.75	0.59

Number of cases: approximately 209 (156 southern- and 53 northern-based organizations).

[a] 1 = «Never true»; 5 = «Always true»

[b] Test of difference of means

* p < .05; ** p < .01

differences and differences in national interests were far less important for explaining why some affiliates do not participate in EarthAction campaigns.[14] There were, however, two statistically significant differences between northern and southern groups in their abilities to participate in EarthAction campaigns. One not unexpected finding was that southern groups were more likely to report that local political conditions inhibited their ability to take action on some campaigns. Indeed, a few groups offered the comment that they appreciate being able to write letters to *other* governments, because either they cannot safely address their own government or because they believe that their efforts might be more effective if they target a more responsive, foreign government (Smith 1995a).[15] A second significant difference was that southern groups reported greater difficulties relating global issues to people's everyday concerns. We interpret this difference as a consequence of the greater access to global information sources enjoyed by societies in the North. The relative lack of access to mass media, computer, and other information resources in the global South appears to inhibit global organizing efforts by expanding the basic educational tasks required of social movement organizations. However, by providing information resources and organized background information to groups in less industrialized areas, transnational SMOs like EarthAction may be helping to narrow the global information gap.[16] Despite the vast diversity in the national political contexts of its affiliates, relatively few groups reported that they saw a conflict between the interests of people in their country and the global action proposals EarthAction promoted. And here no substantial differences were present between northern and southern affiliates, suggesting that affiliates share a view that their problems are interdependent and therefore must be addressed at a global level. Nevertheless, the fact that groups reported some difficulties in relating to the global issues of EarthAction campaigns and with relating global issues to people's everyday concerns suggests that EarthAction has not fully succeeded in generating a shared interpretation of problems in a global interdependence framework.[17]

Some support for our claim that transnational associations help generate common experiences in global political action and facilitate global interpretations of political problems and their solutions appear in many of the survey's written comments and in the communications that EarthAction receives from its affiliates. These suggest that the overwhelming value participants see in the organization is that it helps coordinate common actions across national contexts. Many groups emphasized how important it is for them to not "feel alone" in their efforts. For instance, leaders of Lakamali (Social & Environmental Concerns Institute) in Indonesia noted how participation in EarthAction helps them feel less isolated even though they work in a very rural area. Officials of National Adult Education in Uganda wrote of EarthAction: "your keeping in touch with us encourages us." Activists with Li Environmentica in India stated: "We are a part of global movement. EarthAction enables us to think globally." And the

TABLE 10.3

Obstacles to Participation in Transnational Campaigns

	Average response [a]		T-value [b]
	Southern partners	Northern partners	
Political conditions in our country make it difficult to take action on EarthAction campaigns	2.74	1.92	3.32**
We have difficulties relating global issues to people's everyday concerns	3.33	2.55	3.16**
We do not act on some EarthAction campaigns because we believe that our country's interests may be hurt by some of EarthAction's proposals	2.04	1.76	1.16
Financial limitations prevent us from taking action on EarthAction campaigns	3.64	3.37	1.29
Our organization finds it difficult to relate to the global issues in EarthAction's materials	2.84	2.77	0.25
It is difficult to participate in EarthAction campaigns because our organization works mainly on national or local issues	2.86	2.90	-.12
Language differences make it difficult for us to use EarthAction materials	1.96	1.82	0.65

Number of cases: approximately 209 (156 southern- and 53 northern-based organizations).

[a] 1 = «Never true»; 5 = «Always true»

[b] Test of difference of means

* p < .05; ** p < .01

extraordinary efforts of groups like one working in exile from the former Zaire (then in a state of renewed civil war) to return their survey (with apologies for the delay!), attest to the importance many affiliates attach to their connection with EarthAction.

As the world's political and economic institutions become increasingly integrated globally, shared activist frames are crucial for addressing the underlying injustices that are perpetuated or exacerbated by globalization processes. But this requires ideological work to overcome both inertia as well as the prevalence of what in some cases may be competing nationalist framing of global problems. We saw some evidence in table 10.3 above that TSMOs have provided opportunities for action by groups and individuals who wish to challenge their nation-state's positions on global issues. The fact that most partners did not view the suggestion that their "country's interests may be hurt by some of EarthAction's proposals" as a factor in their decisions to participate in campaigns supports the idea that EarthAction brings together activists that are working around a shared, *global* interpretation of problems and their solutions, and that this interpretation transcends localized interests. This global interpretive framework is also reflected in the fact that about one-quarter of northern partners and 45 percent of southern partners indicated that, since joining EarthAction, their organization has done more work related to the United Nations. Whether this is a consequence of changes in the global political system or of EarthAction's campaigns, we can argue that at the very least the organization's work has reinforced opportunities for globally-oriented collective action.

Table 10.4 presents responses to questions about partners' acceptance of the interpretive and action frames advanced by EarthAction. Given that EarthAction's main international offices are based in the North, and that the organization's international coordinators are from Western democracies, we might expect that the organization's frames would tend to reflect the ideological positions of northern partners more than those of southern ones. Indeed, this complaint appeared in a dozen or so of partners' written comments, but was not manifest in responses to survey questions summarized below.

The results shown in table 10.4 show no significant North-South differences, and that most affiliates believe that EarthAction's work corresponds with the interests of their organizations and of people in their regions. Average scores for all three measures indicated that the statements were, on average, true most of the time for respondents. If transnational solidarity did not exist, we would expect much greater disagreement with these statements, even among these self-selected groups which chose to affiliate with EarthAction and which we can presume are more predisposed than most to transantionalist frames. In the absence of effective solidarity-building, we would expect that southern affiliates would feel less affinity with EarthAction policy positions (perhaps interpreting them as imperialistic and reinforcing interests of global elites in the North) than would northern ones. However, southern affiliates were slightly more likely than

TABLE 10.4
Ideological Affinity with Global Campaigns

	Average response [a]		T-value [b]
	Southern partners	Northern partners	
The issues covered by EarthAction reflect the priorities of people in our region	3.88	3.63	1.26
Our organization agrees with the policy positions advocated by EarthAction	3.95	3.71	1.63
The issues covered by EarthAction reflect our organization's concerns	3.91	3.82	0.55

Number of cases: approximately 191 (156 southern- and 53 northern-based organizations).
[a] 1 = «Never true»; 5 = «Always true»
[b] Test of difference of means

northern ones to report that they tend to agree with EarthAction's policy positions and that EarthAction's issue agenda reflects their organization's concerns. They were also somewhat more likely to report that EarthAction campaigns reflect the priorities of people in their region.

This evidence suggests that the transnational frames promoted by this TSMO are widely shared and are not substantially influenced by national political contexts. While we cannot say whether the shared frames promoted by EarthAction are adopted by affiliates because of its campaigns or because of similar responses to globalization, we can say, based on the written comments of affiliates, that transnational solidarity frames are reinforced and supported by EarthAction's efforts.

Discussion

Responses to several different survey questions support our assertion that membership in EarthAction helps affiliate organizations to engage in global efforts by disseminating information and skills demanded for work within a global polity. The perceived benefits of affiliation with this TSMO were greater among southern organizations, which also reported higher levels of participation and use of EarthAction materials. This difference in levels of participation between northern and southern partners probably reflects the gap in availability of informational resources between these two groups. In that sense, umbrella organizations such as EarthAction serve an important function of reducing the resource gap and facilitating low-cost participation in global social movement efforts for a broader scope of organizations (cf. Staggenborg 1986). Despite these differences in levels of participation, northern and southern organizations equally acknowledge an important set of benefits from membership in EarthAction. They report that EarthAction helps them link local issues to global negotiations, better address issues of interest, and broaden the scope of issues they can address. Both southern and northern organizations indicated that EarthAction makes them feel part of a global effort.

Responses of affiliate organizations further revealed the importance of participation in a broad global organization. Interactions with other organizations and initiatives through EarthAction reduced feelings of isolation and promoted feelings of belonging to a broader global network. In their suggestions for changes in EarthAction activities they emphasize the need for more structured and regular interactions, suggesting meetings and conferences as means for promoting inter-group collaboration. These findings support our claim that transnational social movement activity like that of EarthAction contributes to an emerging transnational identity among participants.

There seems to be relatively a high correspondence between EarthAction's and its affiliates' approach to global campaigns. Regardless of the geographical positions, affiliate organizations agree with both the EarthAction's selection of issues to be addressed and with EarthAction's policy positions on these issues. Southern organizations faced more obstacles in the political environment when trying to participate in EarthAction campaigns, but there is no difference between North and South in terms of the perceived clash between EarthAction activities and national interests. Countering the expectation that there might be a northern bias in selection of campaigns, southern partners report more frequently that issues covered by EarthAction reflect the priorities of people in their region. EarthAction sponsors a globalist frame that is both accepted and apparently very much appreciated by its geographically and ideologically diverse constituency.

In summary, globalization has altered the social, political, and economic context in which social movements operate. Paralleling other forms of global integration, we have witnessed a tremendous growth in the numbers of transnationally organized social movement organizations. The presence of a transnational social movement sector means more than a simple extension of social movement activity to transnational institutions. It also means that activists from different national and cultural contexts are interacting around political campaigns. We have asked whether transnational social movement organizations signal the presence of a new transnationalism that is more reciprocal and more appreciative of global interdependence than were earlier forms of altruistic "Third World solidarity" activism. This evidence, while preliminary, suggests that such a transnationalism exists and that the transnational social movement sector provides an infrastructure for its advancement. The activities and action frames sponsored by transnationally organized social movements reinforce an emerging global polity that is increasingly institutionalized in places like the

United Nations and European Union. TSMOs may be seen as the connective tissues between the formal global political institutions and the people working at regional, national, and local levels whose lives are affected by decisions taken in these forums. The transnationalism they foster among participants results from the communications and other interactions manifest in these organizations. The global identities and agendas produced through the interactions within TSMOs are an important aspect of globalization, and they may help explain the variable impacts of transnational social movement activity.

Notes

1.   Our use of the global North-South distinction refers to economic rather than purely geographic distinctions, since countries in the southern hemisphere such as Australia are technically part of the "global North."

2.   Because the term "internationalism" implies the presence of states, we prefer the term "transnationalism" to describe the phenomena that Hunter identifies.

3.   Other analysts have also identified new cooperation among different movements. For instance, Keck and Sikkink (1998) describe the emergence of new forms of cooperation among environmental groups, women's groups, and human rights activists.

4.   For instance, the rise in transnational environmental organization began after the UN Conference on the Human Environment at Stockholm in 1972, and a sharp growth curve also followed the 1992 UN Conference on Environment and Development (see also Willetts 1996). Also see the *Yearbook of International Associations* on the formation of TSMOs (Smith 1995a).

5.   Even if an organization is founded upon altruistic motivations, the transnational interactions among individuals that are embedded within these organizations, coupled with the expectations arising from the experiences of and interactions with other transnational social movements, are likely to generate the more solidarity-based, globalist relationships we discuss here.

6.   Such legitimacy is increasingly important as the large number of nongovernmental organizations seeking access to the United Nations and other international institutions is forcing officials to restrict their access. A core criteria for selecting groups that will retain the most favored access is their representativeness of a broad international constituency.

7.   For instance, uncertainty over the effects of global warming have led some to predict that countries in the northern hemisphere would benefit from warming, while those in the South would suffer.

8.   This compares with an average of thirty-four membership countries for all other TSMOs, which tend to heavily over-represent European and North American memberships, and only 61 percent of which report *any* southern participation (Smith 1997, 49 [data are for 1994]).

9.   Interview with Lois Barber by J. Smith, 9 October 1998.

10.   The survey was supported by a grant from the Aspen Institute's Nonprofit Sector Research Fund. In June 1998, surveys were sent to a sample of 399 of the organization's more than 1,400 members, and by November 1998, 52 percent of the sampled groups

returned their surveys. No systematic nonresponse bias was detected in the geographic distribution of nonrespondents or in any other organizational characteristics for which we had data from both respondents and nonrespondents. For further methodological details, contact Smith (Department of Sociology, SUNY Stony Brook, Stony Brook, N.Y. 11794-4356. E-mail: jacsmith@notes.cc.sunysb.edu).

11.   In all cases, these comments were made to unstructured (open-ended) questions. The ideas for more interactive activities came not from EarthAction, but directly from the partners themselves. Moreover, these requests were by far the most common request from a wide range of partners—both in the South and in the North.

12.   The maximum number of campaigns was seven, and the difference between northern and southern responses was statistically significant (at the .05 level). This difference holds when we control for the scope of the organization's work (e.g., local, national, regional, or global).

13.   Our interpretation is supported by the fact that the differences between North and South were not in the direction anticipated by the null hypothesis, e.g., that transnational association does *not* effectively bridge national differences. In this scenario, EarthAction would be less relevant for southern than for northern groups, given that the language, cultural, and political differences are greatest between EarthAction's action repertoire and the southern affiliates.

14.   EarthAction materials are distributed in English, French, and Spanish.

15.   Written comments in 1998 EarthAction partner survey.

16.   This North-South difference remained when we controlled for organizational scope (e.g., local, national, regional, or global).

17.   Longitudinal or panel data on affiliate groups would help us better assess the longer-term impacts of transnational organizations on the views of their affiliates. Data that would contrast groups that lack transnational connections with those associated with EarthAction or another group would be most instructional, but quite difficult to assemble.

11

Solidarity Movement Organizations
Toward an Active Global Consciousness?

Simone Baglioni

We are here only as private individuals whose only right to speak out with a single voice is a certain shared difficulty in tolerating what is going on. . . . Who indeed has commissioned us? Nobody. And that very fact is what gives us the right
to speak out. . . . There is an "international citizenship" which implies its own
peculiar rights and duties, and which impels those who belong to it to rise in
protest against any abuse of power, whoever may be responsible for it, whoever
may be its victims. After all, we all number among the "governed," and as such
we are jointly responsible. . . . It is one of the duties of these international citizens always to set before the eyes and ears of governments the human plight for
which their governmental responsibility cannot be denied. Human woe must
never be a mute left-over from policy. Human woe gives rise to an absolute right
to stand up and speak out those who hold the reins of power. . . . Amnesty International, Terre des Hommes, Médecins du Monde, are initiatives that have affirmed and confirmed this new right: the right of private individuals to intervene
effectively in the field of international policies and strategies. The willingness,
the calm determination of individuals must be recognised as part and parcel of a
reality which governments have long sought to monopolise. Such a monopoly
must be worn down, little by little, day after day (Foucault 1995, 7).

It was 1981 when Michel Foucault gave this lecture in Geneva, announcing
the creation of an International Committee against Piracy, with the main goal
of helping "boat people" fleeing Vietnam. In his words we find a clear description of a solidarity movement and solidarity movement organizations
(SMOs),[1] such as Amnesty International, Terre des Hommes, and Médecins
du Monde. At the core of the analysis proposed in this essay are those organizations specialized on humanitarian action—entities that mobilize themselves

to defend the interests of other people, and "that are speaking for groups and individuals who do not believe that states are adequately representing their interests" (Otto 1996, 112).

When the French philosopher gave this speech in Geneva, the SMOs he mentioned had been active for years. Despite that, his words calling for a citizen's right to stand up and speak out could have appeared utopian in the eyes of the international community of states. Eighteen years later, one of the leading organizations of the solidarity movement, Médecins sans Frontières, received the Nobel Peace Prize as a tribute by the international community.

What has happened from 1981 to 1999 that changed not only the role of the organizations of the solidarity movement but also the perceptions that governments had of them? Which events occurred to generate a sharp increase in associations working for solidarity? How could small and unknown organizations become international networks with billion-dollar budgets, thousands of volunteers, and an increasing capability to intervene in man-made or natural disasters? Are we talking about organizations of social movement or are we witnessing their transformation into highly structured, formalized institutions, which have lost their independence? Finally, are those organizations working toward the creation of an active global consciousness?

In this chapter, I propose to answer those questions, hoping to underline the complex picture of the solidarity movement. First, I will briefly analyze the historical evolution of SMOs—from the experience of the solidarity movement during the world wars to the "French doctors"—which leads us to a better understanding of their role in the contemporary international system. I will than take into account the role played by several SMOs during the war in former Yugoslavia. This case study examines the essential question of political altruism. During this paradigmatic conflict, we must ask ourselves if we made a real effort to transform the principles of international solidarity into concrete action or to an instrumentalization of political altruism by the actors and the institutions of the realpolitik. In the conclusion, I will emphasize that solidarity movement organizations represent a real step forward toward the creation of an active global consciousness.

Historical Evolution
of Solidarity Movement Organizations

Solidarity movement organizations find their roots in Christian charity and in political liberalism; they are not a recent phenomenon. On the contrary, what is recent is their position in the international arena and their surprising transnational diffusion (Smith 1995b). In order to understand in full the role SMOs are playing today, we need to take a step back into their history. Taking into account the history of the twentieth century, we shall focus on the crucial stages of the recent evolution of SMOs.

The Red Cross: An Ambiguous Solidarity?

The first model of solidarity movement organizations in this century is the International Committee of the Red Cross (ICRC).[2] The history of the ICRC is paradigmatic for the whole constellation of solidarity movement organizations. In fact, its history represents both their potentialities and their ambiguities.

ICRC is relevant in our context for having definitively affirmed the principle of "permanence" (Rufin 1993) of the solidarity action. Wartime relief needs an organization able to act immediately in every corner of the globe, and it makes clear that solidarity is a technique which requires a permanent and specialized body. The foundation of ICRC fostered the flourishing of hundreds of thousand of associations dealing permanently with relief. But ICRC affirmed also the principle of neutrality of the solidarity actor, together with the observance of humanitarian law and the subjection of solidarity to state sovereignty. On one hand, these principles gave the Red Cross strong international legitimacy but, on the other hand, they bound the ICRC's activities to the states' permission. The ambiguity is clear: the original altruism of Henri Dunant, once it had taken the form of a structured and powerful organization, became a body unable to work if not accepted by the state. This ambiguity was experienced in World War II as well as during the conflicts in Biafra and Vietnam.

In opposition to the principles of neutrality and subjection to state sovereignty, a different generation of solidarity organizations were conceived. The new model of SMOs is based on the original concept of political altruism, acting, as pointed out by Jean Cristophe Rufin, "[j]ust in respect of victims and voluntarily infringing all the rules when they are utilized against human beings (1993, 34 [translated from French])."

Before looking at those "new" organizations it is important to take into consideration the events that caused this transformation in the solidarity movement. Solidarity movement organizations, from ICRC up to the most recent examples, have been created and developed in conjunction with wars and conflicts. World Wars I and II represent "key moments" in the development of the SMOs, especially in the United States, where they generated an important mobilization for, at first, halting the conflicts and, subsequently, planning moral and material reconstruction. If during World War I the International Committee of the Red Cross dominated the arena of international philanthropy, World War II witnessed an unexpected flourishing of solidarity organizations able to work in different scenarios: from relief to providing food and clothes.

But World War II is important not only for originating a large spectrum of organizations able to survive to the end of war emergencies and to enlarge and strengthen with the passage of time. In addition, World War II saw the rise of strong criticism against solidarity action as represented by the International Committee of the Red Cross. The failure of this organization during the world conflict was due to its respect for international law, and to its subjection to state sovereignty. Facing the choice between acting "out of law" but in the name of human rights, and immobility in the name of the state sovereignty, the Red Cross chose the latter, as demonstrated by its silence concerning the Nazi concentration camps (Rufin 1993, 43). The ambiguity of the solidarity movement was at its peak. It was not a question of cowardice but a conflict of fidelity. As pointed out by Rufin:

> The Red Cross was locked up in that respect of the law that the ICRC has set as a principle and which it refuses to derogate from; in its dependence on the state, whose sovereignty, power, and legitimacy of abusing that it acknowledges (1993, 44 [translated from French]).

The choice to keep to the only actions allowed by the Nazi regime led the Red Cross to paralysis and left the field open to new organizations.

Post-World War II

At the end of the war, the solidarity movement was characterized by highly structured and complex bodies with a growing influence in the international arena.[3] In those years, political altruism took the form of international organizations specializing in the management of reconstruction. However, once they accomplished their mandate, these organizations did not dissolve. A common will was arising to build a network to facilitate cooperation and to enforce their power vis-à-vis the states or other intergovernmental bodies. In the United States, where during the postwar period, the number of SMOs was steadily increasing, those networks were forming around different identities, primarily religious ones. Secular organizations played a secondary role: almost 80 percent of the SMOs had a religious origin (Curti 1963 [cited in Rufin 1993, 46]). One of the most important secular exceptions was CARE (Cooperative American Remittance to Europe), an organization born in 1945 and famous for its "ten in one" aid packages with ten rations of food (Ibid.).

After the war, once their rights were affirmed, the organizations of the solidarity movement had to re-think their roles in times of peace. Since emergencies were exceptions rather than the norm, SMOs had to reevaluate the context in which to conduct their work. The transition from the climate of a universal peace dreamed by Roosevelt to the bipolarism of U.S.-Soviet competition also marked the passage from SMO neutrality to their sharp politicization. The diffusion of communism in the world and the American opposition to it had a deep impact on the role played by solidarity movement organizations in the international arena. Due to their basis on independence and autonomy, it was dangerous for SMOs to operate in the midst of the Cold War: they risked criticism of their legitimacy and power of intervention. Being labeled as "partial" could have meant being excluded from operating in countries belonging to the "other side." However, in those years, the political role they played was not secondary. For example, CARE decided not to dismantle its structure and it changed the meaning of the "E" in its name (from Cooperative American Remittance to *Europe* to *Everywhere*). It also decided to accept the invitation of General Douglas MacArthur to work in Korea and Japan to help restrain the spread of Soviet power in East Asia.

Besides the SMOs that, like CARE, began to operate within the context of bipolar competition, other organizations chose to operate neither in Europe nor in the countries of the bipolar area, but within the so-called "developing countries." Several organizations tried to continue the jobs that they had done during the war, or during the immediate post-war period, but moved these same jobs into different scenarios. These organizations are best represented by the French Cimade (Comité Inter-Mouvements Auprès des Evacués). Founded in 1939 by the Protestant and Orthodox churches of France, it had the aim of helping prevent those people who were interned in concentration camps in the south of the country from being deported to Germany. Today, Cimade is one of the leading organizations dealing with issues of racism and development. The shift from its original mandate to an enlarged one took place in the period between the end of European reconstruction and the global strategic division between East and West.

During the 1950s it became clear that the center of solidarity action was shifting from Europe to other areas of the world. There were several reasons for this shift: an increasing consciousness by the developed world of the problems of underdevelopment, and the fear of diffusion of communism in developing countries. This phenomenon led to a change not only in the SMOs' operational structures, but also in their ideological foundations. Several SMOs, especially those created between the end of the 1950s and the beginning of the 1960s, started to disseminate ideas concerning the exploitation of the South by the richer North. The action of SMOs in that period focused on breaking the vicious circle bridling the potentialities of Southern economies. In this way, solidarity movement organizations gained more autonomy vis-à-vis the governmental bodies, and the ambiguity of altruism, typical of the bipolar system, was reduced. Several important organizations such as Terre des Hommes, Frères des Hommes, Oxfam, as well as the Comité Français contre la Faim et pour le Développement, demonstrate this change.

The New SMOs' Generation

The specialization of SMOs in the development field obscured their most typical action: humanitarian relief. Nonetheless, interest in humanitarian action revived in 1968. Key events were two wars: in Vietnam and in Biafra. The Vietnam War broke an important taboo: the respect for international humanitarian law and state sovereignty. Moreover, a new organizational

model of SMOs emerged (Rufin 1993). Indeed, the decision of North Vietnam to consider the war as a "criminal aggression" by the United States and
consequently to reject the Geneva Convention excluded the Red Cross from
intervening. The exclusion of the Red Cross opened the door to other organizations, which were ready to act without governments' permission and without respecting state sovereignty. Even more important from this perspective
was the Biafran conflict.[4] The Biafran War was an exceptional event due to
its manipulation by the world's mass media and for the indelible change it
provoked within the solidarity movement.

In the Biafran War, the Red Cross experienced another failure: it was
obliged to help government troops in order to obtain permission to help the
Ibos. In doing so, it transformed solidarity into a trade business, as asserted
by Rufin (1993, 60). In 1969, the ICRC was banned from working in Nige-
rian territory. French President Charles de Gaulle then decided to overcome
the diplomatic obstacle blocking him from aiding the Ibos, by sending in a
delegation from the French Red Cross. This organization was not equipped to
cope with an operation which involved war surgery and it applied for help
from a group of young volunteer doctors. This group spawned a new organizational model, known as the "French doctors," and it radically changed the
structure of the solidarity movement.

For the solidarity movement, the Biafran War represents a "new Solferino."
In Solferino, the idea of the Red Cross was born, just as Biafra presented the
occasion to discover humanitarian aid for the second time (Kouchner 1986).
To give a better understanding of the change in the SMOs structure, we can
look at the writings of one of the protagonists:

> In the horror of Biafra and in the improvisation of the relief, some of the lost
> members of the French Red Cross understood. They understood the essential role
> of public opinion, this new power created by the images of the children with their
> bloated bellies. They understood the importance of freedom and independence to
> oppose the tricks of a law that the states turn against their victims. They under-
> stood that the new wars, which are going to shake a just-born Third World, will
> be dirty and cruel wars, fought by dreadful people. [They understood] that the
> only ones able to act will be those who accept to be as dreadful, dirty, and bad,
> not respecting the laws, not accepting the governments' authority, and refusing
> the control and the hindrances, actually the free people (Rufin 1993, 61 [trans-
> lated from French]).

Those free men paved the way for the establishment of other SMOs such as
Médecins sans Frontières (Doctors without Borders, or MSF) or Médecins du
Monde (Doctors of the World, or MDM). MSF was created in 1971 unifying
the experiences of Biafra's volunteers and an appeal launched from the
French medical journal *Tonus* to help the population of East Pakistan (the
present Bangladesh) suffering from floods. MSF decided to establish an organization based on five elements: emergency medical aid; secular and independent action; the clandestine conduct in those contexts where its presence

was not formally allowed; witnessing and reporting; a voluntary base to contain costs (Caradec'h 1991).[5] In thirty years of activity, MSF refugee relief operations have been directed to Nicaragua, El Salvador, and countries in Africa and Asia.

As a concluding note about SMOs' history in this century, several elements should be underscored. There is an intimate connection between the evolution of such organizations and the political events characterizing the history of humanity. The solidarity movement organizations that we are analyzing in this chapter are actors working in the dust of dirty wars rather than in the clouds of philanthropy (Jean 1995). They were founded, indeed, during the world wars, with the aim of providing wartime relief.

Despite its success, the ICRC has proved to be ill-equipped vis-à-vis new conflicts that are based upon the violation of international humanitarian law, which constitutes the basis for the organization's actions. Therefore, new actors of the solidarity movement perceived the importance of establishing a new organizational model "without borders," sharply distinguished from governmental bodies, independent, and acting without the permission of state authorities. The model "sans frontiériste" was born.

MSF, MDM, and the other associations of this new generation were established on the basis of a severe censure of the preceding organizational models. They appeared sclerotic, managed by bureaucrats rather than experts and enthusiastic volunteers, and too often subject to the state's authority. The new SMOs are directed by expert volunteers (doctors, in the case of MDM and MSF); they bring solidarity action back to its starting point—amidst the wretches of the planet; they assure their own autonomy by relying on the force of public opinion; they act in the name of morality and in the exclusive interest of victims. They go where others do not go.[6]

The creation of the SMOs "sans frontières" correlates to political events of 1968 in Europe. After the initial enthusiasm, those who were committed to social change found the new forms of engagement and alternatives to political participation depreciated by the Soviet invasion of Prague. The creation of new organizations was a natural consequence of that atmosphere. For instance, France Terre d'Asile was established in 1971 by a network of activists who had mobilized in 1968 to defend foreign students prosecuted in France for their participation in the student movement (Baglioni 1997).

This trend continued, and during the last decades has taken an added dimension. Indeed, Lester Salamon wrote about a "global associational revolution" (1994, 109) to explain the choice by people to become activists in solidarity organizations. The crisis of ideologies and the disaffection for politics, played out mostly in the television arena, probably induced many citizens to pour their energies and their will to participate into new political arenas. The solidarity movement succeeded in guaranteeing that "normal" people have enough space—the possibility to count as individuals and to decide—and to experience significant interaction with others (Barbetta 1996).

The Role of Solidarity Movement Organizations
in a Paradigmatic Conflict

The solidarity movement organizations we are analyzing in this chapter have been established and have developed their structures in response to wars. Therefore, the weight that they carry in the contemporary international arena, as well as their capability to transform the principles of transnational solidarity into concrete actions, can be better understood if we study their involvement in a recent paradigmatic conflict: the war in former Yugoslavia.

We consider the war in former Yugoslavia paradigmatic, among other reasons, because it belongs to a wider category of complex humanitarian emergencies, that is, situations characterized by

> [t]he deterioration or complete collapse of central government authority; *ethnic or religious conflict and widespread human rights abuses*; episodic food insecurity, frequently deteriorating into mass starvation; macroeconomic collapse involving hyperinflation, massive unemployment and decreases in GNP; and *mass population movements of displaced people and refugees escaping conflict or searching for food* (Natsios 1995, 405 [emphasis mine]).

Such situations require the assistance of the SMOs specialized in relief because civil populations are directly involved in the conflicts. Indeed, forced migrations or "ethnic cleansing" become primary goals of contemporary wars (Shaw 1994). Consequently the tasks of the SMOs working in such fields become complex and difficult: from war surgery to providing food, from refugee protection to psychological assistance to rape victims.

In recent years, SMOs have become essential actors in humanitarian emergencies, also due to the weakness of governmental bodies such as the United Nations and its agencies. As solidarity movement organizations have often replaced the state in providing public services in the sectors of health or education in a national context, so have SMOs supplied effective answers to crises in the international system (Barbetta 1996; Donini 1995). The solidarity movement organizations have filled the gap of services provoked by the crisis of the nation-state. Especially when the crisis is caused by the revival of identity cleavages, SMOs offer virtually the only solutions that the international community is able to provide. This reveals a cynical abdication by international politics. Instead of acting directly, and settling political problems through politics, states prefer to delegate the task of stopping conflicts and answering every kind of emergency to the SMOs (Giugni and Passy 1998) and to their humanitarian skills. Humanitarian action, however, is still different from politics, as shown by Médecins sans Frontières in Ethiopia in 1985. There, MSF denounced the regime's attempt to control humanitarian aid with the acquiescence of Western powers. With these denunciations, MSF raised the fundamental issue of international solidarity as a substitute to politics. The organization brought to light the intent of developed countries to replace concrete policies for developing countries with a less-binding, but ambiguous, humanitarian assistance. The organization was expelled from the country, but it did succeed in stopping the forced displacement of much of the population.

Advocacy SMOs

We should distinguish two different groups of solidarity movement organizations intervening in a conflict, such as the Yugoslavian conflict: advocacy SMOs (for example, Amnesty International or Human Rights Watch) and operational SMOs (for example, Médecins sans Frontières, Médecins du Monde, CARE, Oxfam). The first are organizations dealing with legal or political protection or principles. Their action is not, or at least not primarily, carried out through material aid (food, medicines, blankets). The second are organizations that are specialized in humanitarian emergency aid, working directly in the field (Baglioni 1998).

Solidarity movement organizations playing advocacy or educational roles try, above all, to influence citizens or public opinion, as well as governmental policies. Their action takes place in third countries or inside international bodies such as the United Nations or the European Union. In the case of the war in former Yugoslavia, their activities for relocating Yugoslavian refugees in third countries (that is, in Europe) were particularly important. They established first-reception centers to provide refugees with food and clothes; organized language courses; and helped refugees gain legal refugee status. In France, for example, in 1994 one organization alone was able to give juridical assistance to 224 cases of asylum seekers (FTDA 1995, 44). In France, again, several SMOs were the first to collect rules of law and advice for everyday life to help refugees. This type of "guide" for asylum seekers has gained wide usage (FTDA et al. 1994).

More relevant for our study is an analysis of the SMOs' attitude toward the Western states' policies to limit the granting of the refugee status. Indeed, recent events demonstrate that the right of asylum is threatened by the Western countries' fear of invasion by asylum seekers from developing countries. Faced with the dynamics of migration flows, the reaction of the richest countries was swift. Concepts such as "safe country"[7] (Albert 1995) or "safe areas"[8] (UNHCR 1996) were conceived in order to reduce the number of asylum seekers. The fact that these concepts have a direct impact on policy is shown by data on applications for refugee status: in 1984 in France, 42 percent of the applications were accepted, but in 1995 this percentage was reduced to less than 10 percent (Jean 1996, 57). It is against such concepts and policies that the advocacy action of the SMOs has been strongest. Furthermore, it is interesting to note that those solidarity organizations whose budgets depend on public funds were able to speak out for the right of refugees, against their own governments' policies (Giugni and Passy 1998). Despite the fact that its budget is largely paid by public authorities, France Terre d'Asile, for instance, did not hesitate to protest against the authorities (FTDA 1996a). It also appealed to the president of the Republic and to the first minister asking them to renounce the new laws narrowing the right of asylum (FTDA 1996b).

The advocacy activities of SMOs involved in the Yugoslavian war also included the extremely important work of bearing witness to gross human rights violations. The reports of organizations such as Amnesty International and Human Rights Watch undergird the work done by the UN special agencies, in particular the UN Commission on Human Rights and its special rapporteur on war crimes (Baglioni 1998). The activities of bearing witness introduce us to the other group of SMOs: the operational organizations.

Operational SMOs

The intervention of solidarity movement organizations in internal conflicts increased after the end of the Cold War, when the international community began to tolerate, de facto, cross-border operations violating the respect of state sovereignty (Weiss 1996). During the Cold War, the United Nations was obliged, under the logic of bipolarism, to interpret its charter narrowly, preventing the United Nations from intervening in questions falling under domestic jurisdiction (UN Charter, art. 2.7). Since the end of the 1980s, the structural changes in international relations led to a revolutionary resolution approved by the UN General Assembly entitled "Humanitarian assistance to victims of natural disasters and similar emergency situations" (AG res. 43/131, 8 December 1988). This resolution ratified the principle of "free access to victims" (Bettati 1996, 108) and recognized the role SMOs could play in providing relief for civilian victims despite the confirming respect for state sovereignty. Later, the UN General Assembly approved another resolution introducing the concept of "humanitarian corridors" (AG res. 45/100, 14 December 1990) as neutral spaces through which victims would be provided with food, medicine and similar materials in emergency situations. These resolutions represent the first institutional steps toward the legalization of the *ingérence humanitaire* (humanitarian interference) whose aim is to stop the suffering of civilian populations during both internal and international armed conflicts (Mustafa 1996). We should note that the principles ratified by the UN resolutions were anticipated by the actions of the new generation of "sans frontières" SMOs.

With the institutionalization of the right to intervene, SMOs became critical actors in internal conflicts, in which governments, if not completely collapsed, are often in crisis, and unable to oppose the humanitarian intervention, even if they would like to (Weiss 1996). For this reason, recently SMOs have been accused of being increasingly the *longa manus* (long hand) of their national governments (Baglioni 1997; Boisgallais 1995; della Porta 1998).

The ambiguity underlying the intervention of those organizations in internal conflicts is not yet solved.

Usually, when SMOs intervene in a situation of war, their first aim is to save as many lives as possible. In this context, their action is purely technical and each organization has a specific contribution and an area of expertise. Medical SMOs will take care of problems concerning the wounded or sanitary precautions for refugees; other SMOs will provide transportation and distribute food or clothes.

However, the tasks of SMOs are not always sharply distinguished; indeed, several organizations specialized in medical assistance also play different roles. Médecins du Monde (MDM) intervened in former Yugoslavia using both its medical expertise—wartime surgery, vaccinations, doctors' and nurses' training—as well as witness bearing. Thanks to this organization, the public was informed of the massacre at Srebrenica in 1995 (Granjon 1995). MDM also denounced the disappearance of a whole generation of men in the enclaves of east Bosnia: fifteen thousand men aged between fifteen and fifty-five years were not found (Les nouvelles 39/1995, 4). Moreover, MDM collected one hundred twenty pieces of evidence of crimes committed during the conflict and sent them to the International Penal Tribunal at The Hague (Les nouvelles 34/1994, 10). Cooperation with the judges on the international penal tribunal is part of MDM's modus operandi. This organization strongly believes in the duty to witness (Les nouvelles 34/1994, 10). As pointed out by Claude Aiguesvives, the head of MDM's mission in former Yugoslavia, the task of witnessing is part of a clear strategy to put an end to the conflict: "It is essential that victims are listened to and torturers judged in order to achieve, one day, a complete reconciliation among Muslims, Serbs, Croats as it happened between France and Germany" (1994, 10).

The strategy of making the public aware of war atrocities has sharp political connotations. This is demonstrated by MDM's campaign *"Souvenez vous!"* ("Remember!") against Serb President Milosevic, in which he was compared to Hitler in many posters distributed in France (Bettati 1996, 87).

Another component of the action of solidarity organizations during conflicts is their role as diplomatic mediators or negotiators. In situations such as internal conflicts, SMOs have sometimes negotiated with rebels more successfully than have governmental representatives. The United Nations is able to deal with bureaucracies or with governments better than with rebels or armed factions. SMOs make up for this governmental deficiency. They have conducted important negotiations, as in the cases of the Italian community of Sant'Egidio in Mozambique or the Sudan Council of Churches in Sudan (Weiss 1996).

During the war in former Yugoslavia, SMOs played this "diplomatic" role. In 1991, Médecins sans Frontières succeeded in evacuating the wounded of Vukovar through a humanitarian corridor which had been opened through MSF pressure on the French government (Bettati 1996). A similar episode happened in 1993 in Karlovac when Médecins sans Frontières evacuated refugees to a safer place, as witnessed by the head of its Yugoslavian mission, Pierre Salignon: "The Parisian officials of MSF had to intervene repeatedly on UNHCR headquarters in Zagreb and in Geneva in order to obtain the evacuation" (Hertoghe 1993, 15).

The SMOs' power of influence on national and international governmental bodies has become relevant both in emergencies and in ordinary circumstances. The attention that the SMOs are able to get within their governments can be explained in different ways. From a realist perspective, we can attribute governmental permeability to its intention to control the organizations of solidarity and to use them to help pave the way for a governmental intervention into a critical situation. This was seen after World War II in the relation between the American government and few American SMOs. There is a risk that it will happen again, for instance, in France, where the international solidarity movement is a very powerful instrument at the disposal of the government (Rufin 1993). This strategy is facilitated by the presence inside the government of key people: those who act as liaison between the solidarity organizations and the state's interest. For instance, Bernard Kouchner, a well-known representative of the SMO community, has also served as minister in several French Left governments,[9] whereas conservative Alain Juppé gave one of the founders of Médecins sans Frontières, Xavier Emmanuelli, responsibility for "humanitarian affairs" (Baglioni 1997, 1998).

In order to complete the picture of the SMOs' activities during the conflict in former Yugoslavia we must look at "nonmaterial" aid. In 1994, for instance, Médecins sans Frontières started a program of psychological assistance. Through extensive field research, they discovered that 10 percent of the people interviewed had relatives in need of psychological assistance. People needed specific help in order to overcome post-traumatic stress. In response, MSF established projects on the reconstruction of individual psychologies and missions of "identity recovery" for those groups particularly affected by the war—such as Bosnians, women, children, elderly persons—in an attempt to find a remedy for the invisible lacerations of violence. This mission of identity "rebuilding" has been extremely important not only for the victims of that conflict but also for the mobilization of citizens of third countries.

In the territories of former Yugoslavia, the MSF works with refugee teenagers on an attempt to avoid any antisocial or deviational behavior. They worked as well with elderly persons with the aim of helping them regain their social position as witnesses of the past. Moreover, solidarity organizations were important supporters of social activities which created contacts among the different ethnic communities, as in Mostar between Catholics and Muslims (Baglioni 1998).

These activities of strengthening both individual and community identities went alongside a strong promotion of inter-community dialogue. We can argue that helping people find their roots and rediscover their dignity as human beings did not revive ethnic conflict because it was carried out by SMOs.

The very nature of these organizations, in particular their transnational character, their principles of solidarity and altruism, and their partisan disinterestedness, averted extremism.

In third countries, knowledge of and assistance to the sufferings of distant people contributed to an awareness of the dangers of ethnic claims. For example, Italians have supported many special education programs to promote peace and to provide education about ethnic difference to primary and secondary schools.

It is oversimplified to conclude that SMOs simply replace governments and international governmental bodies in emergency relief operations. Even if they may achieve the same objectives, the modus operandi of solidarity organizations is different. Due to the adoption of morality as the foundation for concrete action, the final output shows great commitment and a large contribution to resolving the root causes of the conflict. Moreover, the presence of this moral dimension does not allow us to consider solidarity organizations as pawns of governmental grandeur in the international political arena.

From a series of interviews with SMO representatives (Baglioni 1997, 1998), it became clear that they wished to outline their work not only in terms of "national or supranational interests" but also, and especially, in terms of values and ethical principles. Indeed, SMO recruitment processes pay attention to the motivation of applicants, as well as to their skills. Volunteers working in the field must be strongly committed, considering the risks, the inadequate salary, and an uncertain career prospect.

Concluding Considerations

The SMOs' intervention in conflict and in natural disasters is, by now, unavoidable and it is even solicited by the community of states. The United Nations High Commissioner for Refugees, Sadako Ogata, has praised the solidarity organizations as follows: "Your specific strengths and capacities make you the perfect foil to our own operations. Your presence in the field, knowledge of local conditions, and ability to mobilize quickly and effectively are key elements in emergency response" (Ogata 1994, 1).

The civil involvement in conflict attracted a strong mobilization of the solidarity organizations on a global scale, and leads to some analytical considerations. The action of the SMOs has contributed, on one hand, to the physical survival of the populations involved in the conflict, and, on the other hand, began a reconstruction of collective identities as an essential step toward a stable and durable peace. Moreover, we have seen that the duty to bear witness is a strong component of the solidarity organizations of the new generation. When SMOs denounced the atrocities of "ethnic cleansing" they opened a new, important chapter in their history. They let the international public know about events taking place in the territories of the former Yugoslavia. By acting as global informers they provoked a reaction from governments, but also from civil society which mobilized in small groups—religious communities, schools, ad hoc committees—as well as in more structured and complex organizations. In several countries, this mobilization took many forms of collective nonviolent action: sit-in, fund-raising, public petitions, voluntary service on the field. This demonstrated a change at the level of collective consciousness. From indifference to an active global consciousness, the citizens of the world seem to have decided to abdicate a passive role making concrete Foucault's far-sighted appeal: "We must refuse the way tasks are so often doled out, as if it were up to individuals to be indignant and to voice their indignation; and those in government to do the thinking and acting" (Foucault 1995, 7).

The solidarity organizations, with their moral commitment, their transnational linkages, their ability to intervene, have shown the possibility for civil society to overcome the "indignation phase." The SMOs' historical evolution has allowed civil society to act anywhere there is a need and to become a real actor in international relations. Indeed, today "the social action in a given time and place is increasingly conditioned in important respects by the consequences of social actions taking place in very distant places" (della Porta and Kriesi 1999, 1). It is legitimate for everybody to be concerned by the affairs of the whole of humanity. The capillary mobilization during the war in former Yugoslavia has demonstrated this, yet we have similar involvement in all the other post-modern conflicts such as those in Rwanda or the Caucasus. We can argue that in the contemporary era there will be no conflicts, wars, or emergencies that will be considered by citizens as "someone else's affairs." The presence of this global consciousness seems to permeate governmental organizations. For instance, during the World Trade Organization negotiations in Seattle in late 1999, even President Bill Clinton appealed to governmental representatives to give heed to the claims of the international civil groups.

In a slightly different perspective, it is important to mention how solidarity organizations contributed to the re-elaboration of group identity in a more inclusive sense. Faced with the inaction by traditional political groupings and the inflexibilities of realpolitik, several organized groups decided to act in others' territories, in the name of a common humanity. It is due to the presence of organized civil society, both in the field and in home countries, that the borders of the collectivity have been pushed beyond the limits of one's "own" territory or of one's "own" nationality to encompass a feeling of belonging to a global civil society. This new global civil society, through its organizations, represents a concrete challenge to a state-centered conception of democracy and to the mediation of social values. This challenge could bring about new forms of democracy and social mediation on a global scale. As pointed out by Scott Turner (1998, 32):

> [G]lobal civil society challenges the state's monopoly of authority by redefining the nature of legitimacy. As legitimacy is a function of public perception, the state's monopoly of authority is increasingly strained by a diverse and activated

global citizenry. Furthermore, this activated citizenry coordinates its activities and exercises its influence on global public opinion through information media and communication technologies that transcend the territorial boundaries of individual states.

Despite the risk of being co-opted by governments using humanitarian action as a new form of global politics, and the risk of increasingly bureaucratic specialization, SMOs could represent a powerful incentive toward a new perception of collectivities and communities. We are still at the stage of being an "incentive," but the activities of SMOs are not neutral in helping to make people become aware of belonging to an enlarged civil society, which overcomes national borders in the name of a new active global consciousness.

Notes

I am grateful to Devon Curtis, Veronica Federico, and Marco Giugni for their generous comments on previous drafts of this chapter.

1.   The acronym SMOs is used in the literature on social movements to indicate *social* movement organizations. By using this acronym here, I refer to *solidarity* movement organizations.

2.   After witnessing a battle at Solferino in 1859, the Swiss citizen Henri Dunant wrote a book—*Un souvenir de Solferino*—to inform the world about war crimes. Dunant's aim was to establish an organization working to relieve victims of conflicts, trying to "humanize" wars. His ideas succeeded in 1864 with the first Geneva Convention (Rufin 1994).

3.   This is the period marked by Franklin D. Roosevelt's policies of international philanthropy, by the creation of the United Nations, and by the 1949 Geneva Conference. During those years, the idea of a global peace based on people's self-government took root, and solidarity movement organizations were key to developing this environment.

4.   In 1967 an internal conflict broke out in Nigeria as a consequence of the secessionist claims of the Ibos, an ethnic group living in the Biafra region, one of the richest areas of the country. The fear of losing such a rich land and the threat of a "domino effect" in the rest of Africa led Nigeria to completely isolate the Ibos. In the end, exhausted by starvation and by the inhuman hygienic conditions provoked by the governmental blockade, the Ibos decided to capitulate.

5.   For the events leading to the birth of MSF, as well as for its activities, I refer, in addition to the existing literature, to the interviews I have conducted with its representatives in Paris in the spring of 1996.

6.   "Aller où les autres ne vont pas" was a famous MSF slogan.

7.   The notion of "safe country of origin" tends to bind the granting of refugee status to those applicants coming from countries considered not safe by the authorities giving the papers. Several authorities have compiled lists of "safe countries," and asylum seekers who have citizenship or resident status in one of these "safe" countries will not be recognized as refugees. The risk is that governments use this concept to refuse refugees access to their territories.

8.   The so-called "safe areas" are those areas that are internationally recognized as "safe" and protected by multinational (i.e., UN) forces despite the fact that they are placed in conflict. SMOs denounce the fact that states can limit their contribution to the resolution of the refugee problem by opening and recognizing safe areas instead of accepting refugees into their own territories. Moreover, on several occasions, safe areas were indeed not safe at all, as demonstrated by the Yugoslavian case. During the war, six safe areas were established (Sarajevo, Tuzla, Bihac, Srebrenica, Gorazde, and Zepa), but those areas witnessed cruel atrocities, such as the massacre of Muslims in Srebrenica (10-15 July 1995) perpetrated by Serbian troops.

9.   Kouchner is currently the official representative of the United Nations in Kosovo.

12

Concluding Remarks

Conceptual Distinctions for the Study of Political Altruism

Marco Giugni

This book opened with a number of research questions about the solidarity movement: Is this movement a genuine political expression of altruism? Being potentially distinct from other types of contentious collective action, does it follow its own specific logic of mobilization? And if yes, in what ways is it distinct from other movements whose members stand to benefit directly from the outcomes of their involvement? Some of these questions (as well as others) have been explicitly addressed in the previous chapters. Others have remained with more discretion in the background, but have nevertheless informed the discussion. My aim in this brief concluding chapter is not to make a synthesis of all that has been written in the preceding contributions. This would be both impractical and useless. Instead, I will try to bring to the fore a number of conceptual issues that underlie those analyses. It seems to me that five such issues are worth discussing here in the form of conceptual distinctions: charitable/political, national/transnational, structure/action, private/public, and self-interested/altruistic. Each of them covers aspects regarding the definition as well as the explanation of our subject matter. As will soon become clear, some of them partly overlap. Yet I think it is helpful to keep them separate from an analytical point of view. The first two distinctions are more "substantial" and refer mostly to the solidarity movement as a collective political actor; the last three tackle more "theoretical" issues about political altruism.

Charitable/Political

In her introductory chapter, Florence Passy has defined the actions carried out by participants in the solidarity movement as collective, altruistic, and political. Although this operational definition is helpful as a starting point, it must not prevent us from seeing that the solidarity movement is the outcome of the interplay between individual involvement based on charitable motivations and collective interactions in the political realm. People who are engaged in the solidarity movement often do so not on the basis of political motives, but rather guided by the goal of bringing relief to those who suffer from some kind of injustice. This is particularly true for the so-called voluntary sector, which is an area of participation largely alien from political forms of civic involvement. Here the willingness to engage in what Wuthnow (1991) has called "acts of compassion" rather than political fervor is what brings people to become involved.

This distinction between charitable and political aims is reflected in the movement's organizational basis. The two objectives are not mutually exclusive and are often carried by the same organization. Yet the most politicized areas of solidarity are to be found in those organizations that emerged starting from the late 1960s and which have contributed to the renewal of civic participation in the new social movements. On the other hand, the older organizations often remain tied to a more traditional type of direct and "neutral" intervention. Thus, there is a sort of "division of tasks" within the contemporary solidarity movement between organizations that focus on the provision of services and those that target the authorities and public opinion in an attempt to influence government policies and to bring about a collective awareness of issues such as human rights, development aid, immigration, and antiracism. This distinction holds at both the national and the international level, for both routine interventions and emergency situations such as civil wars. Here the distinction proposed by Simone Baglioni between advocacy and operational organizations is particularly relevant. The former act on behalf of unprivileged or endangered populations in the political realm, whereas the latter specialize in humanitarian aid and hence intervene directly in the field. By combining these two kinds of activity, the solidarity movement is able to provide immediate relief in situations of crisis while at the same time to help reestablish collective identities and put the needs of those populations higher in the political and public agendas.

The charitable/political distinction evokes the difference between religious and secular tendencies within the solidarity movement, which has emerged in some of the chapters in this volume, most notably in Costanzo Ranci's discussion of the Italian voluntary sector. As he points out, religious beliefs and values are one of the principal causes of participation in nonprofit organizations and activities. In Italy—but not only there—for example, there is a dense network of ties linking voluntary organizations to the Catholic world. Many of the people involved in nonprofit organizations and activities have a religious background. More generally, many of the members of organizations active in the field of solidarity are recruited among those who have deep religious beliefs. The Christian emphasis on helping the other person and giving assistance to suffering people provides a powerful "cultural tool kit" (Swidler 1986) from which to draw the resources to be invested in the movement. Of course, it is not the only one, but one that has often played a crucial role in recruiting new members and participants. As pointed out by Passy, the solidarity movement draws from three cultural traditions: the Christian cosmology, the humanist component of the Enlightenment, and the socialist tradition. Each provides the movement and the organizations active in it with crucial cultural and symbolic resources, but also with social, material, and human ones.

National/Transnational

The contributions in this book reflect the multilevel action scope of the solidarity movement. We have specifically focused on the national and transnational levels. The five chapters in part II examine the activities of the movement as well as its interactions with other social and political actors within the national state. The relationship between the movement and the state itself is particularly important. As various studies of social movements have shown during the past three decades or so (for example, Kitschelt 1986; Kriesi et al. 1995; McAdam 1982; McAdam et al. 1996a; Tarrow 1998; Tilly 1978), state institutions both set constraints and provide opportunities for collective action, hence also for altruistic collective action. This can be most explicitly seen in Paul Statham's contribution to the volume. He turns our attention away from individual motivations and incentives to focus on the sets of political opportunities for the solidarity movement in a political issue field in which much altruistic mobilization arises: immigration and ethnic relations. Yet he makes us aware that opportunities are not only institutional. They also have a cultural and discursive side, which include access to legitimating discourses, to alliance networks, and to public support in the information media and more generally in the public space. In this sense, the selective incentives for mobilization pointed out by Olson (1965) and by much work in social movements after him are not given as such, but depend on the political opportunities provided by the state's policy stance toward the beneficiary group. I will deal more in detail below with Olson's theory of collective action and its relevance for the issues addressed in this book.

In spite of the continuing saliency of the national level, clearly the solidarity movement is among those which put the greater emphasis on the international and the transnational levels. The five chapters that form part III of the book focus on these levels, each highlighting a specific aspect that contributes to making this movement an important actor on a world scale. The issues raised by the solidarity movement lend themselves to a transnationalization of activism. Supporting or fighting a given political regime in the so-called Third World, providing relief to populations who are victims of civil wars, raising funds to help people in danger of starvation due to famine in particularly underdeveloped zones of the planet, acting in favor of political and war refugees, and so forth are all activities that presuppose an action scope that goes well beyond the national borders. But it is not only because of the nature of the issues it addresses that the solidarity movement becomes a transnational social movement, to use the formulation of Ivana Eterovic and Jackie Smith. As their and Baglioni's chapters in particular illustrate, we are witnessing the emergence of a new dimension of solidarity, one we may call global to the extent that it begins and ends on a world scale. While traditional international activism, like that described by Sarah Soule, starts at the national or even at the local level, the new transnationalism largely transcends that scope. The rock-for-a-cause events described by Christian Lahusen seem to me a clear example of this. To be sure, the traditional internationalist pattern still prevails. Yet the unprecedented compression of time and space, which Giddens (1990) points to as a core feature of the process of globalization, indicates that global solidary action will gain importance and centrality in the future.

Local and national activities, however, will not disappear. Quite the contrary, globalization is also likely to bring up new problems, or make old ones more salient, which must be dealt with nationally or even locally. While the solidarity movement takes on a transnational character, this does not necessarily means that its activities are going to become global in the sense of being conducted on a world scale. Its mobilization can also be transnational— that is, go beyond the borders of national states—in that it refers to the increasing importance of regions, much the same as the process of European integration has brought to the fore regional cooperation and exchanges. Immigration is an example. Thus, the contemporary (and most likely the future) solidarity movement is characterized by a multilevel action scope in which local, national, and transnational (at both the world and the regional level) activities are all part of this type of civic participation.

Structure/Action

Involvement in the solidarity movement, as any other type of collective action, can be studied from different points of view. In her introductory chapter, Passy distinguishes among rationalist, culturalist, and structuralist accounts of political altruism, stressing both the strengths and weaknesses of each. It would be useless to go back to them at this stage. What is worth recalling, however, is that the study of political altruism must take into account several levels of analysis. The various chapters in this volume reflect this multilevel character of the study of the solidarity movement and political altruism. The distinction among micro-, meso-, and macro-levels of analysis (Gerhards and Rucht 1992) can be applied to this area of research as well. First of all, as Olivier Fillieule argues in his methodological reflections based on the French case, it is important to start with a micro-sociological analysis that focuses on individual reasons and motivations, and hence depart from a substantialist definition of groups as undivided units. People come to be engaged in altruistic actions from different personal trajectories and with different social and cultural backgrounds. Therefore, to look at these individual characteristics provides us with a key to understand why people act altruistically. At the same time, however, he points to the need to anchor individual histories in the social and associative contexts in which they are located. On the one hand, it is important to study the work of solidarity movement organizations, at both the national and the transnational level. What kinds of claims they make in the public space, how they recruit their staff and members, what relationships they entertain among them, as well as with other types of associations—these and related questions must capture our attention, and they did so in this book. On the other hand, participation in the solidarity movement is facilitated by preexisting social networks. Finally, we must not forget that movement organizations are embedded in a larger institutional, cultural, and discursive context which sets the opportunities and constraints for altruistic collective action. As I mentioned earlier, the concept of opportunity structure, as it was developed in social movement research, proves all its value here. The chapter by Statham, in particular, is there to remind us of the importance of looking at the solidarity movement in its interactions with social and political institutions which can either stimulate or discourage its mobilization.

When it comes to theories and explanations, these three levels of analysis, in a way, translate into the classical dualism of structure and action. Although some scholars have replaced the notion of dualism with that of duality to signal that structure and action presuppose one another (Giddens 1984), the sources and origins of human agency have long been the object of a relentless controversy between objectivists and subjectivists, between methodological individualists and institutionalists or cultural analysts, between structural theorists and action theorists. Political altruism does not escape this theoretical challenge.

Although trade-offs between perspectives that focus on structure and perspectives that focus on action are inevitable, solutions to this tension in the field of contentious politics exist and have indeed been proposed (Lichbach 1998). A possible way out of the dead end of rationalist voluntarism and of both cultural and structural determinism consists in examining the interactions between individual and groups which lead one to display an altruistic behavior. The chapters that form this volume have shown that political altruism is largely the product of social relations. The relational nature of the solidarity movement is most clearly visible in Charles Tilly's contribution. He rightly points out that an *ex ante* definition of a behavior as altruistic presupposes that people anticipate individual costs and benefits, and that to explain altruistic collective action we should turn away from *ex ante* decisions toward relational processes that promote self-sacrifice. Fillieule makes a similar point when he suggests that we would be better to avoid taking notions such as solidarity as relevant categories for the analysis. Finally, Passy and Marco Giugni have attempted to show empirically that political altruism, as any other form of contentious politics, is a product of social relations. But, although perhaps less explicitly, the other chapters as well have pointed to the need of looking at social relations and interactive dynamics if we are to understand how altruistic collective action emerges and is sustained over time.

Private/Public

Any analysis of social movements entails, explicitly or implicitly, a discussion of the relation between the private and the public. Of course, when it comes to collective action, the mother of all discussions in this respect is that spurred by Mancur Olson's *Logic of Collective Action*. Not surprisingly, many of the chapters in this volume refer to Olson's seminal book or take his work as a point of departure. At the same time, they stress the limits of an analysis of altruistic behaviors simply in terms of individual motivations and selective incentives. According to Olson, collective action for the production of common—that is, public—goods is very unlikely in the absence of selective incentives that yield certain private gains. For the marginal gain of participants is very small and, moreover, they will benefit from these goods even if they do not act, thanks to the action of others. In such a situation, the strategy of "free riding" prevails. Hence the need of selective incentives for action. This is the essence of the theory, at least as it was applied to the mobilization by social movements.

As Passy points out in the introduction, the important point for our present purpose is that this dilemma of collective action is all the more salient in the case of the solidarity movement, which in its pure definition is aimed at producing a public good from which only those who do not participate can benefit. Ruud Koopmans speaks quite aptly of a double dilemma of collective action. Mobilization, for the reasons I just recalled, is unlikely and hindered among people who benefit from the public good thus produced. Yet it should be all the more difficult when participants will not benefit from that good even if they act. In such a situation, selective incentives—or, as Koopmans suggests, selective frames—must not only induce people to act for a public good from which they will enjoy benefits, but also to act for an altruistic common aim. In the end, however, it might well be possible that this theory of collective action is simply not applicable, as such, to groups that mobilize with altruistic and philanthropic aims, or at least, as Olson himself was inclined to believe, is insufficient to explain these cases. But it may be inapplicable not for the reasons he evokes, namely, because "mass movements" are characterized by a "low degree of rationality" or because the relationship between the interests of members and those of the organization are particularly "rich and obscure." Rather, the theory is perhaps incomplete to account for these situations because acting collectively to defend the interests, rights, and identities of other individuals and groups introduces an element that changes the logic of collective action aimed at producing public goods.

To go back more directly to the contributions in this volume, I see three principal ways in which the private/public dialectic has surfaced. The first way is the one I just discussed, that is, the relationship between private interests and public goods. The main line of inquiry here concerns the question of how private aims and concerns can be overstepped in order for people to be able to engage in collective actions for the production of common goods. The second way, mentioned, for example, by Tilly, involves the concept of identity. As he points out, contentious politics imply the public representation of identity. When people make public claims in the name of their identities, an interactive process occurs in which we observe not only the politicization of those identities, but also their "publicization" in the interpenetration of the private and the public. Finally, Ranci's contribution points to a third way of articulating this conceptual distinction. The area of voluntary organizations and practices is often indicated as the "third sector" between—or rather beyond—the state and the market. Against the classical view that tends to set in opposition the private (economic, market-oriented) sector and the public (political, government-oriented) sector, the past few decades have witnessed the rise of an area of civic participation and political action that has a private nature but a public aim. This area of civic participation is part of that sphere of social interaction between the economy and the state which forms the civil society (Cohen and Arato 1992) and which includes the solidarity movement as a crucial component of it.

Self-Interested/Altruistic

From the point of view of individual participation in collective action, the distinction between the private sphere and the public sphere is partly reflected in that between self-interest and altruism, which in the final analysis is the *fil rouge* of this book. Speaking of Olson and the challenges that the preceding chapters have addressed to his well-known thesis, we still can raise some other aspects of the apparent contradiction of rational and self-interested people engaging themselves on behalf of others without taking any (material) advantage from it.

One point that arises from the various chapters in this book is that human action for collective purposes does not merely respond to an exigency of fulfilling one's own self-interest. People do act to defend the interests, rights, and identities of others, even if they will not stand to benefit from their actions. As Tilly states, genuine cases of altruism do exist. On the one hand, this shows that, as Soule maintains, activism can be guided by moral, rather than selfish, concerns. She reminds us in this regard of Hannah Arendt's (1961) idea that political action is motivated by principles and not only by individuals' self-interest. On the other hand, however, Koopmans' discussion of selective framing suggests that the interactive dynamics that produce political altruism do not necessarily refer to feelings of empathy or beliefs of generosity, but can involve interests as well. This shows all the complexity of the relationship between the concept of interest and that of altruism.

In a way, this raises the issue of whether what we define as political altruism after the fact is real altruism or some other kind of behavior disguised. Far from resolving this issue, I would like briefly to go back to it, as it is in a way at the core of the whole project of this volume. As said in the preface, the book's main title deliberately ends with a question mark. This was intended to avoid determining *ex ante* something that must be assessed after careful examination of facts and explanations. In other words, in order to avoid determining at the outset whether the types of behaviors and collective actions described in the chapters to follow were instances of political altruism and thus to fall into the trap of tautology, we preferred to leave the question open. So, what can we say at this point?

To answer this question it is helpful to go back to the definition of the solidarity movement, which, after all, represents the main object of study of this book. Social movements have been defined as sustained challenges to power holders on behalf of an unprivileged population (Tarrow 1996; Tilly 1994), usually through noninstitutional means of action (della Porta and Diani 1999). Following this definition, social movements are a particular form of social relation, "historically specific clusters of political performances" (Tilly 1994) in which a group of challengers engage in public claim-making addressed to the authorities with the aim of influencing their decisions and behaviors. This characteristic sets social movements apart from other forms of contentious politics, such as revolutions, riots, insurrections, civil wars, and so forth, a broader category that can be defined as "collective activity on the part of claimants—or those who claim to represent them—relying at least in part on noninstitutionalized forms of interaction with elites, opponents, or the state"

(Tarrow 1996, 874). Most of the chapters in this volume deal with the solidarity movement as defined in these terms. This, at least, was our point of departure. Indeed, the brief overview of the movement's mobilization which Passy provides in her introductory chapter sticks mostly with it. There is an important qualification to be made, though. As she argues, the solidarity movement is distinguished from other movements insofar as people involved in it defend the interests, rights, and identities of other individuals and groups. In brief, participants in this movement act altruistically, which means in Tilly's terms that they produce benefits for other actors while enduring net losses themselves, regardless of possible benefits or losses for third parties.

However, as Koopmans and Statham (1999a) have aptly pointed out, the boundaries of a social movement can be expanded or retrenched depending on what we consider as being part of the movement. As they maintain, "far from a neat separation between 'members' and 'challengers,' democratic polities are characterized by cross-cutting alliances between polity members and challengers, and a mutual interpenetration of institutional and non-institutional politics" (208). These two authors' respective contributions in this book clearly indicate that this rule applies to the solidarity movement as well. They show that political altruism is a field of contention that goes well beyond the area of social movements, strictly defined, and within which altruistic and solidary attitudes and behaviors arise from social relations. This is perhaps the most important lesson of this book: We do not behave altruistically because we are fundamentally "good," nor because in our society we are taught to do something for others. Both are, in a way, true. Yet, if we are to understand why we act altruistically in certain situations and egoistically in others, we had better abandon both a totally voluntaristic and a completely deterministic view to embrace a perspective acknowledging that (what at least appears as) altruistic behavior is the product of situations and circumstances, that is, of social relations.

In addition, as Passy and Giugni maintain, just as the definition of the public good has changed in the course of history, the appraisal of altruistic acts depends on the philosophical view of the human being one endorses. It therefore seems more reasonable to avoid engaging in sterile discussions of the "true" nature of collective action in favor of others and move to the search for explanations of this type of behavior. As Tilly points out in his contribution, the task is, then, to identify the causal mechanisms involved in such relations rather than to wonder whether the observed behavior is genuinely altruistic or guided by other motives. Thus social relations rather than individual motivations should be the ground on which we judge the altruistic nature of the actions of the solidarity movement. We should avoid letting our explanations of political altruism rest on a normative point of view about the nature of the humans and allow for an assessment separate from individual aims and desires.

To conclude, let me reiterate that these very sketchy remarks are not intended as a summary of the content of the previous chapters, nor a synthesis of the main arguments and themes developed in this book. All I have tried to do is to underscore, without going into the details, a certain number of concepts which I think lie at the heart of any analysis of the solidarity movement and, more generally, of political altruism. Yet the five conceptual distinctions stressed in this conclusion permeate all the chapters that compose this volume, and therefore in a way they summarize, if not its substantial content, at least its conceptual skeleton. I think I can speak on behalf of all the authors who have contributed to the book if I maintain that charitable/political, national/transnational, structure/action, private/public, and self-interested/altruistic are all conceptual distinctions that should be kept in mind when studying this subject matter in all its multifaceted aspects.

References

Agrikoliansky, Eric. 1997. "La Ligue des Droits de l'Homme (1947-1990): Perennisation et transformation d'une entreprise de défense des causes civiques." Ph.D. diss., Institut d'Etudes Politiques, Paris.

Aguirre, Adalberto, and Jonathan H. Turner. 1998. *American Ethnicity*. 2d ed. Boston: McGraw-Hill.

Aiguesvives, Claude. 1994. "Testimony." *Les nouvelles* 34: 10.

Alber, Jens. 1982. *Vom Armenhaus zim Wohlfahrtsstaat*. Frankfurt: Campus.

Albert, Sophie. 1995. *Les réfugiés bosniaques en Europe*. Paris: Montchrestien.

Alexander, Jeffrey C., and Bernhard Giesen. 1987. "From Reduction to Linkage: The Long View of the Micro-Macro Debate." In *The Micro-Macro Link*, edited by Jeffrey C. Alexander, Bernhard Giesen, Richard Münch, and Neil J. Smelser, 1-42. Berkeley and Los Angeles: University of California Press.

Archambault, Edith, Edith Bon, and Marc Le Vaillant. 1991. *Les dons et le bénévolat en France*. Paris: Laboratoire d'économie sociale/Fondation de France/Institut de sondage Lavialle.

Archambault. Edith, and Judith Boumendil. 1994. *Le secteur sans but lucratif en France*. Paris: Laboratoire d'économie sociale.

Archer, Margaret S. 1995. *Realist Theory: The Morphogenetic Approach*. Cambridge: Cambridge University Press.

Arendt, Hannah. 1961. *Between Past and Future*. New York: World Publishing.

Ascoli, Ugo, ed. 1987. *Azione volontaria e welfare state*. Bologna: il Mulino.

Babcock, Barbara A. 1984. "Arrange Me into Disorder: Fragments and Reflections on Ritual Clowning." In *Rite, Drama, Festival, Spectacle: Rehearsals Toward a Theory of Cultural Performance*, edited by John J. MacAloon, 241-80. Philadelphia: Institute for the Study of Human Issues.

Baglioni, Simone. 1997. "Organizzazioni non governative tra identità e globalizzazione: Un case study sul ruolo delle NGOs francesi nella guerra in ex Jugoslavia." Tesi di laurea, Faculty of Political Science, University of Florence.

———. 1998. *Organizzazioni non governative e conflittualità postmoderne: Il caso delle ONG francesi nella guerra in ex-Jugoslavia*. Florence: Forum on the problems of peace and war.

Bandura, Albert. 1977. *Social Learning Theory*. Englewood Cliffs, N.J.: Prentice-Hall.

Bandura, Albert, and Richard H. Walters. 1963. *Social Learning and Personality Development*. New York: Holt, Rinehart and Winston.

Barber, Benjamin. 1984. *Strong Democracy*. Berkeley and Los Angeles: University of California Press.

Barbetta, Gian Paolo, ed. 1996. *Senza scopo di lucro: Dimensioni economiche, legislazione e politiche del settore nonprofit in Italia*. Bologna: il Mulino.

Barbetta, Paolo, ed. 1997. *The Nonprofit Sector in Italy*. Manchester: Manchester University Press.

Barfield, Thomas J. 1989. *The Perilous Frontier: Nomadic Empires and China*. New York: Blackwell.

Baringhorst, Sigrid. 1998. *Politik als Kampagne: Zur medialen Erzeugung von Solidarität*. Opladen: Westdeutscher Verlag.

Bar-Tal, Daniel. 1976. *Prosocial Behavior*. Washington, D.C.: Hemisphere Publishing.

———. 1985-86."Altruistic Motivation to Help: Definition, Utility, and Operationalization." *Humbolt Journal on Social Relations* 13: 3-4.

Barthélémy, Martine. 1994. *Les associations dans la société française: Un état des lieux*. Paris: Cahiers du CEVIPOF.

Bartolini, Stefano, and Peter Mair. 1990. *Identity, Competition and Electoral Availability: The Stabilization of European Electorates 1885-1985*. Cambridge: Cambridge University Press.

Baston, C. Daniel, and Laura L. Shaw. 1991. "Evidence for Altruism: Toward a Pluralism of Prosocial Motives." *Psychological Inquiry* 2: 107-22.

Baugnet, Lucy. 1996. "Participation associative et rapport au politique: L'engagement social des jeunes." In *Des jeunes et des associations*, edited by Bertrand Roudet, 37-52. Paris: L'Harmattan.

Bearman, Peter S. 1991. "Desertion as Localism: Army Unit Solidarity and Group Norms in the U.S. Civil War." *Social Forces* 70: 321-42.

Beck, Ulrich. 1986. *Risk Society: Towards a New Modernity*. London: Sage.

Bell, Daniel. 1973. *The Coming of Post-Industrial Society*. New York: Basic Books.

Berger, Peter, and Thomas Luckmann. 1966. *The Social Construction of Reality*. Garden City, N.J.: Doubleday.

Berkowitz, Leonard. 1972. "Social Norms, Feelings, and Other Factors Affecting Helping and Altruism." *Advances in Experimental Social Psychology* 6: 63-108.

Bettati, Mario. 1996. *Le droit d'ingérence*. Paris: Odile Jacob.

Beveridge, Lord W. 1948. *Voluntary Action: A Report on Methods of Social Action*. London: Allen and Unwin.

Bikhchandani, Sushil, David Hirshleifer, and Ivo Welch. 1998. "Learning from the Behavior of Others: Conformity, Fads, and Informational Cascades." *Journal of Economic Perspectives* 12: 151-70.

Billis, David. 1993. *Organising Public and Voluntary Agencies*. London: Routledge.

Blake, Robert R., Jane S. Mouton, and Jack D. Hain. 1956. "Social Forces in Petition Signing." *Southwestern Social Science Quarterly* 36: 385-90.

Blake, Robert R., Milton Rosenbaum, and Richard A. Duryea. 1955. "Gift-Giving as a Function of Group Standards." *Human Relations* 8: 61-73.

Boisgallais, Antoine S. 1995. "ONG entre doute et colère." *Croissance* 383 (June).

Booth, Gregory D., and Terry Lee Kuhn. 1990. "Economic and Transmission Factors as Essential Elements in the Definition of Folk, Art, and Pop Music." *The Musical Quarterly* 74: 411-38.

Borzaga, Carlo, ed. 1991. *Il terzo sistema: Una dimensione della complessità economica e sociale*. Padova: Fondazione Zancan.

Bottomore, Thomas, ed. 1983. *A Dictionary of Marxist Thought*. Cambridge, Mass.: Harvard University Press.

Bourdieu, Pierre. 1972. *Esquisse d'une théorie de la pratique, précédé de trois études d'ethnologie Kabyle*. Geneva: Droz.

———. 1977. *Outline of a Theory of Practice*. Cambridge: Cambridge University Press.

———. 1984. "La grève et l'action politique." In *Questions de sociologie*. Paris: Les éditions de Minuit.

———. 1994. "Un acte désintéressé est-il possible?" In *Raisons Pratiques: Sur la théorie de l'action*, 149-67. Paris: Seuil.

Bowles, Samuel, and Herbert Gintis. 1998. "The Evolution of Strong Reciprocity." Working Paper 98-08-073, Santa Fe Institute Economics Research Program.

Brace, Tim, and Paul Friedlander. 1992. "Rock and Roll on the New Long March: Popular Music, Cultural Identity, and Political Opposition in the People's Republic of China." In *Rockin' the Boat: Mass Music and Mass Movements*, edited by Reebee Garofalo, 115-27. Boston: South End Press.

Brand, Karl-Werner. 1982. *Neue soziale Bewegungen: Entstehung, Funktion und Perspektive neuer Protestpotentiale*. Opladen: Westdeutscher Verlag.

Brass, Paul R. 1994. *The Politics of India Since Independence*. The New Cambridge History of India, IV-1. 2d ed. Cambridge: Cambridge University Press.

———. 1996, ed., *Riots and Pogroms*. New York: New York University Press.

———. 1997. *Theft of an Idol: Text and Context in the Representation of Collective Violence*. Princeton; N.J.: Princeton University Press.

Brehm, Jack W. 1966. *A Theory of Psychological Reactance*. New York: Academy Press.

Brint, Steven. 1984. "'New Class' and Cumulative Trend Explanations of the Liberal Political Attitudes of Professionals." *American Journal of Sociology* 90: 30-71.

Brunner, Matthias. 1999. "Générations et changements de valeurs." *Travaux et Communications* 1, Department of Political Science, University of Geneva.

Bryan, James H., and Mary Ann Test. 1967. "Models and Helping: Naturalistic Studies in Aiding Behavior." *Journal of Personality and Social Psychology* 6: 400-407.

Brysk, Alison. 1993. "From Above and Below: Social Movements, the International System, and Human Rights in Argentina." *Comparative Political Studies* 26: 259-85.

———. 1996. "Turning Weakness into Strength: The Internationalization of Indian Rights." *Latin American Perspectives* 89: 38-57.

Bütschi, Danielle. 1997. "Information et opinions." Ph.D. diss., University of Geneva.

Caillé, Alain. 1981. "La sociologie de l'intérêt est-elle intéressante? A propos de l'utilisation du paradigme économique en sociologie." *Sociologie du travail* 3: 257-74.

———. 1994. *Don, intérêt et désintéressement: Bourdieu, Mauss, Platon et quelques autres*. Paris: La Découverte/MAUSS.

Caradec'h, Jean Michel. 1991. "Les French Doctors ont 20 ans: Entretiens avec Rony Brauman et Xavier Emanuelli." *L'Express* (26 December).

Castel, Robert. 1995. *Les métamorphoses de la question sociale: Une chronique du salariat*. Paris: Fayard.

Cerulo, Karen A. 1997. "Identity Construction: New Issues, New Directions," *Annual Review of Sociology* 23: 385-409.

Charng, Hon-Wen, Jane A. Piliavin, and Peter L. Callero. 1988. "Role Identity and Reasoned Action in the Prediction of Repeated Behavior." *Social Psychology Quarterly* 51: 303-17.

Chaves, Mark. 1998. "The Religious Ethic and the Spirit of Nonprofit Entrepreneurship." In *Private Action and the Public Good*, edited by Walter W. Powell and Elisabeth S. Clemens, 47-65. New Haven, Conn.: Yale University Press.

Chazel, François. 1986. "Individualisme, mobilisation et action collective." In *Sur l'individualisme*, edited by Pierre Birnbaum and Jean Leca, 213-38. Paris: Presses de la Fondation nationale des sciences politiques.

Chong, Dennis. 1991. *Collective Action and the Civil Rights Movement*. Chicago: University of Chicago Press.

Cialdini, Robert B., Betty Lee Darby, and Joyce E. Vincent. 1973. "Transgression and Altruism: A Case for Hedonism." *Journal of Experimental Social Psychology* 9: 502-16.

Clemens, Elisabeth S. 1997. *The People's Lobby: Organizational Innovation and the Rise of Interest Group Politics in the United States, 1890-1925*. Chicago: University of Chicago Press.

Cloonan, Martin, and John Street. 1997. "Politics and Popular Music: From Policing to Packaging." *Parliamentary Affairs* 50: 223-34.

Clutton-Brock, T. H., M. J. O'Riain, P. N. M. Brotherton, D. Gaynor, R. Kansky, A. S. Griffin, and M. Manser. 1999. "Selfish Sentinels in Cooperative Mammals." *Science* 284: 1640-44.

CNVA (Conseil National de la Vie Associative). 1993. *Les associations à l'épreuve de la décentralisation: Bilan de la vie associative, 1991-1992*. Paris: La Documentation française.

———. 1996. *Bilan de la vie associative en 1994-1995*. Paris: La Documentation française.

Cohen, Jean L. 1985. "'Strategy or Identity': New Theoretical Paradigms and Contemporary Social Movements." *Social Research* 59: 663-717.

Cohen, Jean L., and A. Arato. 1992. *Civil Society and Political Theory*. Cambridge, Mass.: MIT Press.

Coleman, James S. 1990. *Foundations of Social Theory*. Cambridge, Mass.: The Belknap Press of Harvard University Press.

Collins, Randall. 1992. "The Romanticism of Agency/Structure versus the Analysis of Micro/Macro." *Current Sociology* 40: 77-97.

Colozzi, Ivo, and Giovanna Rossi. 1985. "I gruppi di volontariato in Italia: Elementi per una classificazione." In *Volontariato ed enti locali*, edited by Luciano Tavazza, 13-51. Bologna: Dehoniane.

Cooper, Lee. 1988. "Social Concerns, Political Protest, and Popular Music." *The Social Studies* 79: 53-60.

Copland, Ian. 1998. "The Further Shores of Partition: Ethnic Cleansing in Rajasthan 1947." *Past and Present* 160: 203-39.

Cotgrove, Stephen, and Adrew Duff. 1980. "Environmentalism, Middle Class Radicalism and Politics." *Sociological Review* 28: 333-51.

———. 1981. "Environmentalism, Values and Social Change." *British Journal of Sociology* 32: 92-110.

Dalton, Russel J., and Manfred Kuechler, eds. 1990. *Challenging the Political Order*. Cambridge: Polity Press.

d'Anjou, Leo. 1996. *Social Movements and Cultural Change: The First Abolition Campaign Revisited.* New York: de Gruyter.

Dekker, Paul, and Andries van den Brock. 1998. "Civil Society in Comparative Perspective: Involvement in Voluntary Associations in North America and Western Europe." *Voluntas: International Journal of Voluntary and Nonprofit Organizations* 9: 11-38.

della Porta, Donatella. 1988. "Recruitment Processes in Clandestine Political Organizations: Italian Left-Wing Terrorism." In *From Structure to Action*, edited by Bert Klandermans, Hanspeter Kriesi, and Sidney Tarrow, 155-72. Greenwich, Conn.: JAI Press.

———. 1998. "Globalization, Social Movement and Citizenship Rights." Paper prepared for the conference on "Citizenship Claims: Social Movements and Globalization," Harvard University, 23-24 October.

———. 1996. *Movimenti collettivi e sistema politico in Italia: 1960-1995.* Bari: Laterza.

della Porta, Donatella, and Mario Diani. 1999. *Social Movements: An Introduction.* Oxford: Blackwell.

della Porta, Donatella, and Hanspeter Kriesi. 1999. "Social Movements in a Globalizing World: An Introduction." In *Social Movements in a Globalizing World*, edited by Donatella della Porta, Hanspeter Kriesi, and Dieter Rucht, 3-22. London: Macmillan.

Diani, Mario. 1996. "Linking Mobilization Frames and Political Opportunities: Insights from Regional Populism in Italy." *American Sociological Review* 61: 1053-69.

DiMaggio, Paul J., and Walter P. Powell. 1983 "The Iron Cage Revisited: Institutional Isomorphism and Collective Rationality in Organizational Fields." *American Sociological Review* 48: 147-60.

Dobry, Michel. 1986. *Sociologie des crises politiques.* Paris: Presses de la Fondation nationale des sciences politiques.

Donati, Pierpaolo. 1993. *La cittadinanza societaria.* Bari: Laterza.

Donini, Antonio. 1995. "The Bureaucracy and the Free Spirits: Stagnation and Innovation in the Relationship between the UN and NGOs." *Third World Quarterly* 16: 421-40.

Downs, Anthony. 1957. *An Economic Theory of Democracy.* New York: Harper.

Drescher, Seymour. 1986. *Capitalism and Antislavery: British Mobilization in Comparative Perspective.* London: Macmillan.

———. 1994. "Whose Abolition? Popular Pressure and the Ending of the British Slave Trade." *Past and Present* 143: 136-66.

Duneier, Mitchell, and Harvey Molotch. 1999. "Talking City Trouble: Interactional Vandalism, Social Inequality, and the 'Urban Interaction Problem.'" *American Journal of Sociology* 104: 1263-95.

Durkheim, Emile. 1964. *The Division of Labor in Society.* New York: Free Press.

Duyvendak, Jan Willem. 1995. *The Power of Politics: New Social Movements in France.* Boulder, Colo.: Westview Press.

EarthAction. 1993. *Protect Indian Lands in Brazil.* Action Kit. Amherst, Mass.: EarthAction.

Eder, Klaus. 1993. *The New Politics of Class.* London: Sage.

———. 1996. *The Social Construction of Nature.* London: Sage.

Eisel, Stephan. 1990. *Politik und Musik: Musik zwischen Zensur und politischem Mißbrauch.* München: Bonn Aktuell.

Elias Norbert. 1985. *La société de cour.* Paris: Flammarion-Champs.

Elster, Jon. 1990. "Selfishness and Altruism." In *Beyond Self-Interest*, edited by Jane Mansbridge, 44-52. Chicago: University of Chicago Press.

Emirbayer, Mustafa. 1997. "Manifesto for a Relational Sociology." *American Journal of Sociology* 103: 281-317.

Emirbayer, Mustafa, and Jeff Goodwin. 1994. "Network Analysis, Culture, and the Problem of Agency." *American Journal of Sociology* 99: 1411-54.

Emirbayer, Mustafa, and Ann Mische. 1998. "What Is Agency?" *American Journal of Sociology* 103: 962-1023.

Etzioni, Amitai. 1993. *The Spirit of Community: Rights, Responsibility, and the Communitarian Agenda.* New York: Crown.

Evers, Adalbert. 1995. "Part of the Welfare Mix: The Third Sector as an Intermediate Area between Market Economy, State and Community." *Voluntas: International Journal of Voluntary and Nonprofit Organizations* 6: 159-82.

Eyerman, Ron, and Andrew Jamison. 1995. "Social Movements and Cultural Transformation: Popular Music in the 1960s." *Media, Culture & Society* 17: 449-68.

Fernandez, Roberto, and Doug McAdam. 1988. "Social Networks and Social Movements: Multiorganizational Fields and Recruitment to Mississippi Freedom Summer." *Sociological Forum* 3: 357-82.

Ferrand-Bechmann, Dan. 1992. *Bénévolat et solidarité.* Paris: Syros.

Fillieule, Olivier. 1997. *Stratégies de la rue: Les manifestations en France.* Paris: Presses de la Fondation nationale des sciences politiques.

Fillieule, Olivier, and Christophe Broqua. Forthcoming. "Raisons d'agir dans l'économie de l'engagement à AIDES, 1984-1998." In *Ce qui nous relie*, edited by André Micoud and Michel Peroni. Paris: Editions de l'Aube.

Fillieule, Olivier, and Jan Willem Duyvendak. 1999. "Gay and Lesbian Activism in France: Between Integration and Community-Oriented Movements." In *The Global Emergence of Gay and Lesbian Politics: National Imprints of a Worldwide Movement*, edited by Barry D. Adam, Jan Willem Duyvendak, and André Krouwel. Philadephia: Temple University Press.

Fireman, Bruce, and William Gamson. 1979. "Utilitarian Logic in the Resource Mobilization Perspective." In *The Dynamics of Social Movements*, edited by Mayer N. Zald and John D. McCarthy, 8-45. Cambridge, Mass.: Winthrop Publishers.

Fivol (Fondazione Italiana per il Volontariato). 1996. *Il volontariato sociale in Italia.* Roma: Fivol.

Foucault, Michel. 1995. "Foreword." In *Preventive Diplomacy and Humanitarian Action*, edited by Médecins du Monde and the French Platform of the CLONG-D Europe. Paris: MDM and CLONG-D Europe.

FTDA (France Terre d'Asile). 1995. *Rapport Annuel 1994.* Paris: FTDA.

———. 1996a. *Communiqué de presse.* 15 March. Paris: FTDA.

———. 1996b. *Communiqué de presse.* 7 March. Paris: FTDA.

FTDA (France Terre d'Asile) et al. 1994. *Accueil des exilés de l'ex Yougoslavie en France.* Paris: FTDA.

Fredrickson, George M. 1997. *The Comparative Imagination: On the History of Racism, Nationalism, and Social Movements.* Berkeley and Los Angeles: University of California Press.

Frisanco, Renato, Costanzo Ranci, eds. 1999. *Le dimensioni della solidarietà: Secondo rapporto sul volontariato sociale italiano*. Roma: Fondazione Italiana per il Volontariato.

Frith, Simon. 1987. "The Industrialization of Popular Music." In *Popular Music and Communication*, edited by James Lull, 53-77. London: Sage.

Frith, Simon, and John Street. 1992. "Rock Against Racism and Red Wedge: From Music to Politics, from Politics to Music." In *Rockin' the Boat: Mass Music and Mass Movements*, edited by Reebee Garofalo, 67-80. Boston: South End Press.

Gabriel, Christina, and Laura Macdonald. 1994. "NAFTA, Women and Organizing in Canada and Mexico: Forging a 'Feminist Internationality.'" *Millenium* 23: 535-62.

Gamson, William A. 1975. *The Strategy of Social Protest*. Homewood, Ill.: Dorsey Press.

———. 1988. "Political Discourse and Collective Action." In *From Structure to Action: Comparing Social Movement Research Across Cultures*, edited by Bert Klandermans, Hanspeter Kriesi, and Sidney Tarrow, 219-44. Greenwich, Conn.: JAI.

———. 1990. *The Strategy of Social Protest*. 2d ed. Belmont, Calif.: Wadsworth.

———. 1992. *Talking Politics*. Cambridge: Cambridge University Press.

Gamson, William A., Bruce Fireman, and Steven Rytina. 1982. *Encounters with Unjust Authority*. Homewood, Ill.: Dorsey Press.

Gamson, William A., and David S. Meyer. 1996. "Framing Political Opportunity.' In *Comparative Perspectives on Social Movements*, edited by Doug McAdam, John D. McCarthy, and Mayer N. Zald, 275-90. Cambridge: Cambridge University Press.

Gamson, William, and Andre Modigliani. 1989. "Media Discourse and Public Opinion on Nuclear Power: A Constructionist Approach." *American Journal of Sociology* 95: 1-38.

Garofalo, Reebee. 1992a. "Popular Music and the Civil Rights Movement." In *Rockin' the Boat: Mass Music and Mass Movements*, edited by Reebee Garofalo, 231-40. Boston: South End Press.

———. 1992b. "Understanding Mega-Events: If We Are the World, Then How Do We Change It?" In *Rockin' the Boat: Mass Music and Mass Movements*, edited by Reebee Garofalo, 15-35. Boston: South End Press.

———. 1992c. "Introduction." In *Rockin' the Boat: Mass Music and Mass Movements*, edited by Reebee Garofalo, 1-13. Boston: South End Press.

Gaskin, Katharine, and Justin Davis Smith. 1995. *A New Civic Europe?* London: The Volunteer Centre.

Gerhards, Jürgen, and Dieter Rucht. 1992. "Mesomobilization: Organizing and Framing in Two Protest Campaigns in West Germany." *American Journal of Sociology* 98: 555-95.

Giddens, Anthony. 1984. *The Constitution of Society*. Cambridge: Polity Press.

———. 1990. *The Consequences of Modernity*. Cambridge: Polity Press.

Gitlin, Todd. 1985. "Divestment Stirs a New Generation." *The Nation* (18 May): 585-87.

Giugni, Marco, and Florence Passy. 1993. "Etats et nouveaux sociaux, comparaison de deux cas contrasté: La France et la Suisse." *Revue Suisse de Sociologie* 19: 545-70.

———. 1998. "Contentious Politics in Complex Society. New Social Movements between Conflict and Cooperation." In *From Contention to Democracy*, edited by

Marco Giugni, Doug McAdam, and Charles Tilly, 81-108. Lanham, Md.: Rowman & Littlefield.

Godelier, Maurice. 1996. *L'énigme du don.* Paris: Arthème Fayard.

Goldstone, Jack A. 1994. "Is Revolution Individually Rational? Groups and Individuals in Revolutionary Collective Action." *Rationality and Society* 6: 139-66.

Goodwin, Jeff, James Jasper, Charles Tilly, Francesca Polletta, Sidney Tarrow, David Meyer, and Ruud Koopmans (1999): "Mini-Symposium on Social Movements." *Mobilization* 14: 27-136.

Gore, Georgiana. 1997. "The Beat Goes On: Trance, Dance and Tribalism in Rave Culture." In *Dance in the City*, edited by Helen Thomas, 50-67. London: Macmillan.

Gould, Roger V. 1991. "Multiple Networks and Mobilization in the Paris Commune, 1871." *American Sociological Review* 56: 716-29.

———. 1993. "Collective Action and Network Structure." *American Sociological Review* 58: 182-96.

———. 1999. "Collective Violence and Group Solidarity: Evidence from a Feuding Society." *American Sociological Review* 64: 356-80.

Granjon, Bernard. 1995. "Testimony." *Les nouvelles* 39: 3.

Greif, Avner. 1994. "Cultural Beliefs and the Organization of Society: A Historical and Theoretical Reflection on Collectivist and Individualist Societies." *Journal of Political Economy* 102: 912-50.

Green, Donald P., and Ian Shapiro. 1994. *Pathologies of Rational Choice Theory: A Critique of Applications in Political Science.* New Haven, Conn.: Yale University Press.

Greven, M.T., and U. Willems. 1994. "Moral Demands and Rational Moralists in a World of Special Interests." Paper for the XVI World Congress of the International Political Science Association, Berlin, 21-25 August.

Habermas, Jürgen. 1984. *The Theory of Communicative Action.* Boston: Beacon Press.

Hamidi. Camille. 1997. "La spécificité des comportements politiques des jeunes de la deuxième génération d'origine algérienne." Mémoire pour le DEA d'Etudes politiques de l'Institut d'Etudes Politiques, Paris.

Handelman, Don. 1990. *Models and Mirrors: Towards an Anthropology of Public Events.* Cambridge: Cambridge University Press.

Hansmann, Henry. 1980. "The Role of Nonprofit Enterprise." *Yale Law Journal* 89: 835-98.

Hardin, Russell. 1982. *Collective Action.* Baltimore, Md.: Johns Hopkins University Press.

———. 1995. *One for All: The Logic of Group Conflict.* Princeton, N.J.: Princeton University Press.

Harrington, Michael. 1968. *Toward a Democratic Left: A Radical Program for a New Majority.* New York: Macmillan.

Hartup, Willard W., and Brian Coates. 1967. "Imitation of a Peer as a Function of Reinforcement from the Peer Group and Rewardingness of the Model." *Child Development* 58: 1003-1116.

Hechter, Michael. 1987. *Principles of Group Solidarity.* Berkeley and Los Angeles: University of California Press.

Helson, Harry, Robert Blake, and Jane Srygley Mouton. 1958. "Petition-Signing as Adjustment to Situational and Personal Factors." *Journal of Social Psychology* 48: 3-10.

Hertoghe, Alain. 1993. "Des réfugiés bosniaques abandonnés sous les bombes." *La Croix* (15 September): 15.

Hirsch, Eric L. 1986. "The Creation of Political Solidarity in Social Movement Organizations." *Sociological Quarterly* 27: 373-87.

———. 1990. "Sacrifice for the Cause: Group Processes, Recruitment, and Commitment in a Student Social Movement." *American Sociological Review* 55: 243-54.

Horch, H. 1994. "On the Socio-Economics of Voluntary Organizations." *Voluntas: International Journal of Voluntary and Nonprofit Organizations* 5: 219-30.

Hornstein, Harvey A. 1970. "The Influences of Social Models on Helping." In *Altruism and Helping Behavior*, edited by Jacqueline MacCauley and Leonard Berkowitz, 29-41. New York: Academic Press.

Hunter, Allen. 1995. "Globalization from Below? Promises and Perils from the New Internationalism." *Social Policy* 25: 6-13.

IDAF (International Defence Aid Fund for Southern African). 1983. *Apartheid: The Facts.* London: IDAF (in cooperation with the United Nations Centre Against Apartheid).

Imig, Doug, and Sidney Tarrow. 1999 "The Europeanization of Movements? A New Approach to Transnational Contention." In *Social Movement in a Globalizing World*, edited by Donatella della Porta, Hanspeter Kriesi, and Dieter Rucht, 112-33. London: Macmillan.

Inglehart, Ronald. 1977. *The Silent Revolution: Changing Values and Political Styles Among Western Publics.* Princeton, N.J.: Princeton University Press.

———. 1990. "Values, Ideology, and Cognitive Mobilization in New Social Movements." In *Challenging the Political Order*, edited by Russel J. Dalton and Manfred Kuechler, 43-66. Cambridge: Polity Press.

International Fellowship of Reconciliation. 1999. "Women Lead the Way to Peace." Conference Panel on Transnational Organizing in Chiapas and the Former Yugoslavia. Hague Appeal for Peace Conference, The Hague, 14 May.

Ion, Jacques, and Bertrand Ravon. 1998. "Causes publiques, affranchissement des appartenances et engagement personnel." *Lien Social et Politiques—Revue Internationale d'Action Communautaire* 39: 59-69.

IREF (Istituto di Ricerche Educative e Formative). 1998. *La società civile in Italia.* Roma: Edizioni Lavoro.

Isen, A.M., and A. Noonberg. 1979. "The Effect of Photographs of the Handicapped on Donations to Charity: When a Thousand Words May Be Too Much." *Journal of Applied Social Psychology* 9: 426-31.

Jackson, John L. 1992. "The Symbolic Politics of Divestment: Protest Effectiveness on U.S. College and University Campuses." Paper presented at the NEH Seminar Symposium, Cornell University, Ithaca, NY, August.

James, Estelle, ed. 1989. *The Nonprofit Sector in International Perspective: Studies in Comparative Culture and Policy.* New York: Oxford University Press.

Jasso, Guillermina. 1999. "How Much Injustice Is There in the World? Two New Justice Indexes." *American Sociological Review* 1999: 133-68.

Jean, François. 1995. "Nourrir la guerre." *Courrier de la Planète* 27: 16-17.

———. 1996. "Profughi fardello del mondo." In *Popolazioni in pericolo 1996*, edited by Julia Groenewold, 45-59. Rome: Edizioni Periodici Culturali-Limes.

Jegstrup, Elsebet. 1985-86. "Spontaneous Action: The Rescue of the Danish Jews from Hannah Arendt's Perspective." *Humbolt Journal of Social Relations* 85-86: 260-84.

Jencks, Christopher. 1990. "Varieties of Altruism." In *Beyond Self-Interest*, edited by Jane Mansbridge, 53-67. Chicago: University of Chicago Press.

Jenkins, J. Craig, and Charles Perrow. 1977. "Insurgency of the Powerless: Farm Worker Movements." *American Sociological Review* 42: 249-68.

Jenson, Jane. 1998. "Social Movement Naming Practices and the Political Opportunity Structure." Working Paper 1998/114, Instituto Juan March de Estudios e Investigaciones, Madrid.

Johnston, Alastair Iain. 1995. *Cultural Realism: Strategic Culture and Grand Strategy in Chinese History*. Princeton, N.J.: Princeton University Press.

Juhem, Philippe. 1999. "SOS-racisme: Histoire d'une entreprise de mobilisation a-politique. Contribution à l'analyse des transformations des représentations politiques après 1981." Ph.D. diss., University of Nanterre.

Keck, Margaret, and Katherine Sikkink. 1998. *Activists Beyond Borders: Advocacy Networks in International Politics*. Ithaca, N.Y.: Cornell University Press.

Khawaja, Marwan. 1993. "Repression and Popular Collective Action: Evidence from the West Bank." *Sociological Forum* 8: 47-71.

Kidder, Thalia, and Mary McGinn. 1995. "In the Wake of NAFTA: Transnational Workers Networks." *Social Policy* 25: 14-21.

Kitschelt, Herbert. 1986. "Political Opportunity Structures and Political Protest: Anti-Nuclear Movements in Four Democracies." *British Journal of Political Science* 16: 57-85.

Klandermans, Bert. 1988 "The Formation and Mobilization of Consensus.". In *From Structure to Action*, edited by Bert Klandermans, Hanspeter Kriesi, and Sidney Tarrow, 173-97. Greenwich, Conn.: JAI Press.

———. 1984. "Mobilization and Participation: Social-Psychological Expansions of Resource Mobilization Theory." *American Sociological Review* 49: 583-600.

———. 1997. *The Social Psychology of Protest*. Oxford: Blackwell.

Kliment, Tibor. 1998. "Durch Dramatisierung zum Protest? Theoretische Grundlegung end empirischer Ertrag des Framing-Konzepts."In *Paradigmen der Bewegungsforschung: Entstehung und Entwicklung von Neuen sozialen Bewegungen und Rechtsextremismus*, edited by Kai-Uwe Hellmann and Ruud Koopmans, 69-89. Opladen: Westdeutscher Verlag.

Knoke, David. 1988. "Incentives in Collective Action Organizations." *American Sociological Review* 53: 311-29.

———. 1990. *Organizing for Collective Action*. New York: de Gruyter.

Konecni, Vladimir J. 1972. "Some Effects of Guilt on Compliance: A Field Replication." *Journal of Personality and Social Psychology* 23: 30-32.

Koopmans, Ruud. 1996. "Asyl: Die Karriere eines politischen Konfliktes." In *Kommunikation und Entscheidung: Politische Funktionen öffentlicher Meinungsbildung und diskursiver Verfahren*, edited by Wolfgang van den Daele and Friedhelm Neidhardt, 167-192. Berlin: Sigma.

Koopmans, Ruud, and Jan Willem Duyvendak. 1995. "The Political Construction of the Nuclear Energy Issue and Its Impact on the Mobilization of Anti-Nuclear Movements in Western Europe." *Social Problems* 42: 235-51.

Koopmans, Ruud, and Paul Statham. 1999a. "Political Claims Analysis: Integrating Protest Event and Political Discourse Approaches." *Mobilization* 4: 203-21.

———. 1999b. "Ethnic and Civic Conceptions of Nationhood and the Differential Success of the Extreme Right in Germany and Italy." In *How Social Movements Matter*, edited by Marco Giugni, Doug McAdam, and Charles Tilly, 225-51. Minneapolis: University of Minnesota Press.

———. 2000. "Political Claims-Making against Racism and Discrimination in Britain and Germany." In *Comparative Perspectives on Racism*, edited by Jessika ter Wal and Maykel Verkuyten, 139-70. Aldershot: Ashgate.

Kouchner, Bernard. 1986. *Charité business*. Paris: Le Pré-aux-Clercs.

Kramer, Ralph M. 1981. *Voluntary Agencies in the Welfare State*. Berkeley and Los Angeles: University of California Press

Kramer, Ralph M., Hakon Lorentzen, Willem B. Melief, and Sergio Pasquinelli. 1993. *Privatization in Four European Countries: Comparative Studies in Government-Third Sector Relationships*. New York: Sharpe.

Kramnick, Rebecca. 1985. "Encampment Kicks Off Day of Apartheid Protest." *Harvard Crimson* (11 October): 1.

Krebs, Dennis L. 1970. "Altruism—An Examination of the Concept and a Review of Literature." *Psychological Bulletin* 73: 258-302.

Kriesberg, Louis. 1997. "Social Movements and Global Transformation." In *Transnational Social Movements and Global Politics: Solidarity Beyond the State*, edited by Jackie Smith, Charles Chatfield, and Ron Pagnucco, 3-18. Syracuse, N.Y.: Syracuse University Press.

Kriesi, Hanspeter. 1989. "New Social Movements and the New Class in the Netherlands." *American Journal of Sociology* 94: 1078-1116.

———. 1993. *Political Mobilization and Social Change*. Aldershot: Avebury.

Kriesi, Hanspeter, and Philip van Praag. 1987. "Old and New Politics: The Dutch Peace Movement and the Traditional Political Organizations." *European Journal of Political Research* 15: 319-46.

Kriesi, Hanspeter, Ruud Koopmans, Jan Willem Duyvendak, and Marco G. Giugni. 1995. *New Social Movements in Western Europe: A Comparative Analysis*. Minneapolis: University of Minnesota Press.

Lacey, Marc. 1985. *Cornell Daily Sun* (9 May): 1.

Lagrange, Hugues. 1989. "Strikes and the War." In *Strikes, Wars, and Revolutions in an International Perspective*, edited by Leopold Haimson and Charles Tilly. Cambridge: Cambridge University Press.

Lagroye, Jacques et al. 1996. "La production de la solidarité." Rapport du groupe de travail sur la solidarité du Centre de recherches politiques de la Sorbonne, Paris, MIRE.

Lahusen, Christian. 1991. *"Unsere Stimme erwacht": Populäre Musikkultur und nationale Frage im heutigen Spanien*. Saarbrücken: Breitenbach.

———. 1996. *The Rhetoric of Moral Protest: Public Campaigns, Celebrity Endorsement and Political Mobilization*. Berlin/New York: de Gruyter.

Laitin, David. 1999. "The Cultural Elements of Ethnically Mixed States: Nationality Reformation in the Soviet Successor States." In *State/Culture: State Formation after the Cultural Turn*, edited by George Steinmetz. Ithaca, N.Y.: Cornell University Press.

Lake, David A., and Donald Rothchild. 1998. "Spreading Fear: The Genesis of Transnational Ethnic Conflict." In *The International Spread of Ethnic Conflict: Fear, Diffusion, and Escalation*, edited by David A. Lake and Donald Rothchild. Princeton, N.J.: Princeton University Press.

Landau, Camille L. 1987. "About 300 Protest South African's Speech." *Harvard Crimson* (25 March): 4.

Laville, Jean-Louis. 1994. *L'Economie solidaire*. Paris: Desclée de Brouwer.

Laville, Jean-Louis, and Renaud Sainsaulieu, eds. 1997. *Sociologie de l'association: Des organisations à l'épreuve du changement social*. Paris: Desclée de Brouwer.

Layton-Henry, Zig. 1994. "Britain: The Would-Be Zero-Immigration Country." In *Controlling Immigration: A Global Perspective*, edited by Wayne A. Cornelius, Philip L. Martin, and James F. Hollifield, 273-96. Stanford, Calif.: Stanford University Press.

Lester, Anthony. 1998. "From Legislation to Integration: Twenty Years of the Race Relations Act." *Race Relations in Britain: A Developing Agenda*, edited by Tessa Blackstone, Bhiku Parekh, and Peter Saunders, 22-35. London: Routledge.

Levi, Margaret. 1997. *Consent, Dissent, and Patriotism*. Cambridge: Cambridge University Press.

Lichbach, Mark Irving. 1987. "Deterrence or Escalation? The Puzzle of Aggregate Studies of Repression and Dissent." *Journal of Conflict Resolution* 31: 266-97.

———. 1997. "Social Theory and Comparative Politics." In *Comparative Politics*, edited by Mark Irving Lichbach and Alan S. Zuckerman, 239-76. Cambridge: Cambridge University Press.

———. 1998. "Contending Theories of Contentious Politics and the Structure-Action Problem of Social Order." *Annual Review of Political Science* 1: 401-24.

Lipset, Seymour M., and Stein Rokkan, 1967. "Cleavage Structures, Party Systems, and Voter Alignments. An Introduction." In *Party Systems and Voter Alignments: Cross-National Perspectives*, edited by Seymour M. Lipset and Stein Rokkan, 1-67. New York: Free Press.

Lipsitz, George. 1992. "Chicano Rock: Cruising around the Historical Bloc." In *Rockin' the Boat: Mass Music and Mass Movements*, edited by Reebee Garofalo, 267-79. Boston: South End Press.

Lipsky, Michael. 1968. "Protest as a Political Resource." *American Political Science Review* 62: 1144-58.

Loeb, Paul Rogat. 1994. *Generation at the Crossroads: Apathy and Action on the American Campus*. New Brunswick, N.J.: Rutgers University Press.

Long, Theodore E., and Jeffrey K. Hadden. 1983. "Religious Conversion and the Concept of Socialization: Integrating the Brainwashing and Drift Models." *Journal for the Scientific Study of Religion* 1: 1-14.

Lopes, Paul D. 1992. "Innovation and Diversity in the Popular Music Industry, 1969 to 1990." *American Sociological Review* 57: 56-71.

Loveman, Mara. 1998. "High-Risk Collective Action: Defending Human Rights in Chile, Uruguay, and Argentina." *American Journal of Sociology* 104: 477-525.

Luhmann, Niklas. 1982. *The Differentiation of Society*. New York: Columbia University Press.

MacCauley, Jacqueline, and Leonard Berkowitz, eds. 1970. *Altruism and Helping Behavior*. New York: Academic Press.

Macdonald, Laura. 1995. "A Mixed Blessing: The NGO Boom in Latin America." *NACLA Report on the Americas* 28: 30-35.

Mactaggart, Fiona, and Trevor Phillips. 1995. "Anti-Racism: New Alliances, New Agendas." *Renewal* 3: 63-71.

Macy, Michael. 1991. "Chains of Cooperation: Threshold Effects of Collective Action." *American Sociological Review* 56: 730-47.

Madelin, Anne. 1998. "Carrières militantes à la Ligue des Droits de l'homme: Sections des XVIII° et XX° arrondissements de Paris." Mémoire pour le DEA d'Etudes politiques de l'Institut d'Etudes Politiques, Paris.

Mansbridge, Jane. 1990. *Beyond Self-Interest.* Chicago: University of Chicago Press.

———. 1998. "On the Contested Nature of the Public Good." In *Private Action and the Public Good,* edited by Walter W. Powell and Elisabeth S. Clemens, 3-19. New Haven, Conn.: Yale University Press.

Marks, Gary, and Doug McAdam. 1996. "Social Movements and the Changing Structure of Political Opportunity in the European Union." *West European Politics* 19: 249-78.

Marullo, Sam, Ron Pagnucco, and Jackie Smith. 1996. "Frame Changes and Social Movement Contraction: U.S. Peace Movement Framing After the Cold War." *Sociological Inquiry* 66: 1-28.

Marwell, Gerald, and Pamela Oliver. 1993. *The Critical Mass in Collective Action: A Micro-Social Theory.* Cambridge: Cambridge University Press.

Marx Ferree, Myra. 1992. "The Political Context of Rationality: Rational Choice Theory and Resource Mobilization." In *Frontiers in Social Movement Theory,* edited by Aldon D. Morris and Carol McClurg Mueller, 29-52. New Haven, Conn.: Yale University Press.

Marx, Anthony W. 1998. *Making Race and Nation: A Comparison of the United States, South Africa, and Brazil.* Cambridge: Cambridge University Press.

Mason, David. 1995. *Race and Ethnicity in Modern Britain.* Oxford: Oxford University Press.

Mauss, Marcel. 1950. *Essai sur le don.* Paris: PUF.

MAUSS (Mouvement Anti-Uilitariste dans les Sciences Sociales). 1998. *Une seule solution, l'association?* Paris: Revue du MAUSS.

Mayer, Nonna. 1997. "Action collective et nouveaux mouvements sociaux: L'exemple du mouvement anti-Front National." In *Produire les solidarités: La part des associations,* edited by MIRE Rencontres et recherches, 314-24. Paris: MIRE/Fondation de France.

McAdam, Doug. 1982. *Political Process and the Development of Black Insurgency, 1930-1970.* Chicago: University of Chicago Press.

———. 1986. "Recruitment to High Risk Activism: The Case of Freedom Summer." *American Journal of Sociology* 92: 64-90.

———. 1988. *Freedom Summer.* New York: Oxford University Press.

McAdam, Doug, John D. McCarthy, and Mayer N. Zald, eds. 1996a. *Comparative Perspectives on Social Movements.* Cambridge: Cambridge University Press.

McAdam, Doug, John D. McCarthy, and Mayer N. Zald. 1996b. "Introduction: Opportunities, Mobilizing Structures, and Framing Processes—Toward a Synthetic, Comparative Perspective on Social Movements." In *Comparative Perspectives on Social Movements,* edited by Doug McAdam, John D. McCarthy, and Mayer N. Zald, 1-22. Cambridge: Cambridge University Press.

McAdam, Doug, and Ronnelle Paulsen. 1993. "Specifying the Relationship between Social Ties and Activism." *American Journal of Sociology* 99: 640-67.

McAdam, Doug, and Dieter Rucht. 1993. "The Cross-National Diffusion of Movement Ideas." *The Annals of the American Academy of Political and Social Science* 528: 56-74.

McCarthy, John D., and Mayer N. Zald. 1977. "Resource Mobilization and Social Movements: A Partial Theory." *American Journal of Sociology* 82: 1212-41.

———. 1987. "Resource Mobilization and Social Movements: A Partial Theory." In *Social Movements in an Organizational Society*, edited by Mayer N. Zald and John D. McCarthy, 15-42. New Brunswick, N.J.: Transaction Books.

McPherson, J. Miller, and Thomas Rotolo. 1996. "Testing a Dynamic Model of Social Composition: Diversity and Change in Voluntary Groups." *American Sociological Review* 61: 179-202.

Melucci, Alberto. 1980. "The New Social Movements: A Theoretical Approach." *Social Science Information* 19: 199-226.

———. 1985. "The Symbolic Challenge of Contemporary Movements." *Social Research* 52: 789-815.

———. 1989. *Nomads of the Present: Social Movements and Individual Needs in Contemporary Society*. Philadelphia: Temple University Press.

———. 1996. *Challenging Codes: Collective Action in the Information Age*. Cambridge: Cambridge University Press.

Meyer, John W., John Boli, George M. Thomas, and Francisco O. Ramirez. 1997. "World Society and the Nation-State." *American Journal of Sociology* 103: 144-81.

Modood, Tariq, Richard Berthoud et al. 1997. *Ethnic Minorities in Britain: Diversity and Disadvantage*. London: Policy Studies Institute.

Moe, Terry M. 1980. *The Organization of Interests*. Chicago: University of Chicago Press.

Moore, Barrington, Jr. 1979. *Injustice: The Social Bases of Obedience and Revolt*. White Plains, N.Y.: M. E. Sharpe.

Mustafa, Jasim Tawfik. 1996. *L'ingerenza umanitaria: Il caso dei Kurdi. Profilo storico-giuridico*. Pisa: Biblioteca Franco Serantini Editore.

Muxel, Anne. 1996. *Les jeunes et la politique*. Paris: Hachette.

Natsios, Andrew S. 1995. "NGOs and the UN System in Complex Humanitarian Emergencies: Conflict or Cooperation?" *Third World Quarterly* 16: 405-20.

Negus, Keith. 1993. "Global Harmonies and Local Discords: Transnational Policies and Practices in the European Recording Industry." *European Journal of Communication* 8: 295-316.

Nesse, Randolph M. 1999. "The Evolution of Hope and Despair." *Social Research* 66: 429-70.

Obasanjo, Olusegun. 1977. "Notes and Documents from the World Conference for Action Against Apartheid." United Nations Centre Against Apartheid, Department of Political and Security Council Affairs, Lagos, Nigeria (no. 1, part II, August): 7.

Oberschall, Anthony. 1973. *Social Movements and Social Conflicts*. Englewood Cliffs, N.J.: Prentice-Hall.

———. 1980. "Loosely Structured Collective Conflict: A Theory and an Application." *Research in Social Movements, Conflict and Change* 3: 45-68. Greenwich, Conn.: JAI Press.

———. 1993. *Social Movements*. New Brunswick, N.J.: Transaction Books.

Ogata, Sadako. 1994. "Keynote Address by Mrs. Sadako Ogata, United Nations High Commissioner for Refugees, at the Opening Ceremony of the Parinac Global Conference." Oslo: UNHCR.

Oliner, Samuel P., and Pearl M. Oliner. 1988. *The Altruistic Personality*. New York: Free Press.

Olivier, Johan. 1991. "State Repression and Collective Action in South Africa, 1970-84." *South African Journal of Sociology* 22: 109-17.

Olson, Mancur. 1965. *The Logic of Collective Action: Public Goods and the Theory of Groups*. Cambridge, Mass.: Harvard University Press.

———. 1968. *The Logic of Collective Action: Public Goods and the Theory of Groups*. Cambridge, Mass.: Harvard University Press.

———. 1971. *The Logic of Collective Action: Public Goods and the Theory of Groups*. Cambridge, Mass.: Harvard University Press.

Opp, Karl-Dieter. 1985. "Soft Incentives and Collective Action: Participation in the Anti-Nuclear Movement." *British Journal of Political Science* 16: 87-112.

———. 1989. *The Rationality of Political Protest*. Boulder, Colo.: Westview Press.

Opp, Karl-Dieter, and Wolfgang Roehl. 1990. "Repression, Micromobilization, and Political Protest." *Social Forces* 69: 521-47.

Orman, John. 1984. *The Politics of Rock Music*. London: Nelson Hall.

Ostrom, Elinor. 1998. "A Behavioral Approach to the Rational Choice Theory of Collective Action." *American Political Science Review* 92: 1-22.

Otto, Dianne. 1996. "Nongovernmental Organizations in the United Nations System: The Emerging Role of International Civil Society." *Human Rights Quarterly* 18: 107-41.

Paci, Massimo. 1987. "Long Waves in the Development of Welfare Systems." In *Changing Boundaries of the Political: Essays on the Evolving Balance between the State and Society, Public and Private in Europe*, edited by Charles S. Meier, 179-97. Cambridge: Cambridge University Press.

Passy, Florence. 1998. *L'Action altruiste: Contraintes et opportunités de l'engagement dans les mouvements sociaux*. Geneva: Droz.

Passy, Florence. 1999. "Supranational Political Opportunities as a Channel of Globalization of Politics Conflicts: The Case of the Rights of the Indigenous Peoples." In *Social Movements in a Globalizing World*, edited by Donatella della Porta, Hanspeter Kriesi, and Dieter Rucht, 148-69. London: Macmillan.

Paton, Alan. [1948] 1986. *Cry the Beloved Country*. Charles Scribner's Sons.

Patton, Cindy. 1989. "The AIDS Industry: Construction of 'Victims', 'Volunteers and 'experts'." In *Taking Liberties: AIDS and Cultural Politics*, edited by Erica Carter and Simon Watney, 113-26. London: Serpent Tail.

Paugam, Serge. 1997. "La dynamique de l'engagement humanitaire." In *Produire les solidarités: La part des associations*, edited by in MIRE Rencontres et recherches, 246-68. Paris: MIRE/Fondation de France.

Payne, Charles M. 1995. *I've Got the Light of Freedom: The Organizing Tradition and the Mississippi Freedom Struggle*. Berkeley and Los Angeles: University of California Press.

Pearce, Jone L. 1993. *Volunteers*. London: Routledge.

Piliavin, Jane A., and Hong-Wen Charng. 1990. "Altruism: A Review of Recent Theory and Research." *Annual Review of Sociology*: 27-65.

Piven, Frances Fox, and Richard A. Cloward. 1979. *Poor People's Movements*. New York: Vintage Books.

Polletta, Francesca. 1998a. "'It Was Like A Fever . . .' Narrative and Identity in Social Protest." *Social Problems* 45: 137-59.

———. 1998b. "Contending Stories: Narrative in Social Movements." *Qualitative Sociology* 21: 419-46.

Postal, Leslie. 1985. *Cornell Daily Sun* (10 May): 1.

Powell, Walter W., and Elisabeth S. Clemens, eds. 1998. *Private Action and the Public Good*. New Haven, Conn.: Yale University Press.

Powell, W. W., and R. Friedkin. 1987. "Organizational Change in Nonprofit Organizations." In *The Nonprofit Sector: A Research Handbook*, edited by W. W. Powell, 180-94. New Haven, Conn.: Yale University Press.

Pratt, Ray. 1990. *Rhythm and Resistance*. London: Praeger.

Przeworski, Adam. 1997. "The State in a Market Economy." In *Transforming Post-Communist Political Economies*, edited by Joan M. Nelson, Charles Tilly, and Lee Walker. Washington, D.C.: National Academy Press.

Przeworski, Adam, and Henry Teune. 1970. *The Logic of Comparative Social Inquiry*. New York: Wiley-Interscience.

Putnam, Robert D. 1993. *Making Democracy Work*. Princeton, N.J.: Princeton University Press.

Ranci, Costanzo. 1985. *Volontariato bisogni servizi*. Milano: Angeli.

————. 1992. "La mobilitazione dell'altruismo: Condizioni e processi di diffusione dell'azione volontaria in Italia." *Polis* 6: 467-505.

Ranci, Costanzo, Ugo De Ambrogio, and Sergio Pasquinelli. 1991. *Identità e servizio: Il volontariato nella crisi del welfare*. Bologna: il Mulino.

Raschke, Joachim. 1985. *Soziale Bewegungen: Ein historisch-systematischer Grundriss*. Frankfurt: Campus.

Ravon Bertrand, and Roland Raymond. 1997. "Engagement bénévole et expérience de soi: L'exemple des restos du cœur." In *Engagement public et exposition de la personne*, edited by Jacques Ion and Michel Peroni, 99-110. Paris: Editions de l'Aube.

Rawlings, Edna. 1968. "Witnessing Harm to Other: A Reassessment of the Role of Guilt in Altruistic Behavior." *Journal of Personality and Social Psychology* 10: 377-80.

————. 1970. "Reactive Guilt and Anticipating Guilt in Altruistic Behavior." In *Altruism and Helping Behavior*, edited by Jacqueline MacCauley and Leonard Berkowitz, 163-77. New York: Academic Press.

Raynaud, Emmanuelle. 1980. "Le militantisme moral." In *La sagesse et le désordre*, edited by Henri Mendras, 271-86. Paris: Gallimard.

Rebelle, Bruno, and Fabienne Swiatly. 1999. *Libres Associations*. Paris: Desclée de Brouwer.

Regan, Dennis T. 1971. "Effects of a Favor and Liking on Compliance." *Journal of Experimental Social Psychology* 7: 627-39.

Rietveld, Hillegonda C. 1998. *This is Our House: House Music, Cultural Spaces and Technologies*. Aldershot: Ashgate Arena.

Robertson, Roland. 1992. *Globalization: Social Theory and Global Culture*. London: Sage.

Rochon, Thomas R. 1998. *Culture Moves: Ideas, Activism, and Changing Values*. Princeton, N.J.: Princeton University Press.

Roemer, John. 1982. *A General Theory of Exploitation and Class*. Cambridge, Mass.: Harvard University Press.

Rokkan, Stein. 1970. *Citizens, Elections, Parties*. Olso: Universitetsforlaget.

Rorty, Richard. 1989. *Contingency, Irony and Solidarity*. Cambridge: Cambridge University Press.

Rosenbaum, Milton E. 1956. "The Effect of Stimulus and Background Factors on the Volunteering Response." *Journal of Abnormal and Social Psychology* 53: 118-21.

Rosenbaum, Milton, and Robert R. Blake. 1955. "Volunteering as a Function of Field Structure." *Journal of Abnormal and Social Psychology* 50: 193-96.

Rosenhan, David. 1970. "The Natural Socialization of Altruistic Autonomy." In *Altruism and Helping Behavior*, edited by Jacqueline MacCauley and Leonard Berkowitz, 251-68. New York: Academic Press.

Rosenhan, David, and Glenn White. 1967. "Observation and Rehearsal as Determinants of Prosocial Behavior." *Journal of Personality and Social Psychology* 5: 424-31.

Rucht, Dieter. 1995. "Mobilizing for 'Distant Issues': German Solidarity Groups in Non-Domestic Issues Areas." Paper presented at the annual meeting of the American Sociological Association, Washington, D.C., 19-23 August.

————. 1996. "The Impact of National Contexts on Social Movement Structures: A Cross-Movement and Cross-National Comparison." In *Comparative Perspectives on Social Movements*, edited by Doug McAdam, John D. McCarthy, and Mayer N. Zald, 185-204. Cambridge: Cambridge University Press.

————. 1997. "Limits to Mobilization: Environmental Policy for the European Union." In *Transnational Social Movements and Global Politics: Solidarity Beyond the State*, edited by Jackie Smith, Charles Chatfield, and Ron Pagnucco, 195-213. Syracuse, N.Y.: Syracuse University Press.

————. Forthcoming. "Distant Issue Movements in Germany: Empirical Description and Theoretical Reflections." In *Globalizations and Social Movements: Culture, Power and the Transnational Public Sphere*, edited by John A. Guidry, Michael D. Kennedy, and Mayer N. Zald. Ann Arbor: University of Michigan Press.

Rucht, Dieter, Ruud Koopmans, and Friedhelm Neidhardt, eds. 1998. *Acts of Dissent: New Developments in the Study of Protest*. Berlin: Sigma.

Rufin, Jean-Christophe. 1993. *La piège humanitaire*. 2d ed. Paris: Hachette Pluriel.

————. 1994. *L'aventure humanitaire*. Paris: Gallimard.

Rushton, J. Phillipe. 1980. *Altruism, Socialization, and Society*. Englewood Cliffs, N.J.: Prentice-Hall.

Sahlins, D. Marshall. 1965. "On the Sociology of Primitive Exchange." In *The Relevance of Models for Social Anthropology*, edited by Michael Banton, 139-236. London: Tavistock.

Salamon, Lester M. 1994. "The Rise of Nonprofit Sector." *Foreign Affairs* 73: 109-22.

Salamon, Lester M., and Helmut K. Anheier. 1996. *The Emerging Nonprofit Sector: An Overview*. Manchester: Manchester University Press.

————. 1998. "Social Origins of Civil Society: Explaining Nonprofit Sector Cross-Nationally." *Voluntas: International Journal of Voluntary and Nonprofit Organizations* 9: 213-48.

Sandell, Rickard. 1998. *Social Movements and Social Networks*. Stockholm Series on Social Mechanisms, no. 1, Department of Sociology, Stockholm University.

Sandler, Todd. 1992. *Collective Action*. Ann Arbor: University of Michigan Press.

Sassen, Saskia. 1997. *Globalization and Its Discontents*. New York: New Press.

Schulze, Gerhard. 1994. "Jenseits der Erlebnisgesellschaft. Zur Neudefinition von Solidarität." *Gewerschaftliche Monatshefte* 6: 337-43.

Schumpeter, Joseph A. 1947. *Capitalism, Socialism, and Democracy*. 2d ed. New York: Harper & Brothers.

Schwarz, Samuel. 1977. "Normative Influences on Altruism." In *Advances in Experimental Social Psychology*, edited by Leonard Berkowitz, 221-79. New York: Academic Press.

Scott, James C. 1985. *Weapons of the Weak: Everyday Forms of Peasant Resistance.* New Haven, Conn.: Yale University Press.

———. 1998. *Seeing Like a State: How Certain Schemes to Improve the Human Condition Have Failed.* New Haven, Conn.: Yale University Press.

Seibel, Wolfgang. 1989. "The Function of Mellow Weakness. Nonprofit Organizations as Nonsolvers in Germany." In *The Nonprofit Sector in International Perspective: Studies in Comparative Culture and Policy*, edited by Estelle James, 177-92. New York: Oxford University Press.

Seidman, Gay W. 1993. "'No Freedom without the Women': Mobilization and Gender in South Africa, 1970-1992." *Signs* 18: 291-320.

———. 1999. "Gendered Citizenship: South Africa's Democratic Transition and the Construction of a Gendered State." *Gender & Society* 13: 287-307.

Seligman, Adam B. 1991. *The Idea of Civil Society.* New York: Free Press.

Shaw, Martin. 1994. *Global Society and International Relations.* Cambridge: Polity Press.

Shklar, Judith N. 1990. *The Faces of Injustice.* New Haven, Conn.: Yale University Press.

Shubik, Martin. 1993. "Models of Strategic Behavior and Nuclear Deterrence." In *Behavior, Society, and International Conflict*, volume 3, edited by Philip E. Tetlock et al. New York: Oxford University Press.

Shukra, Kalbir. 1998. *The Changing Pattern of Black Politics in Britain.* London: Pluto Press.

Sikkink, Kathryn, and Jackie Smith. Forthcoming. "Infrastructures for Change: Transnational Organizations, 1953-1993." In *Restructuring World Politics: The Power of Transnational Agency and Norms*, edited by Sanjeev Khagram, James Riker, and Kathryn Sikkink.

Sills, David L. 1957. *The Volunteers: Means and Ends in a National Organization.* New York: Free Press.

Siméant, Johanna. 1998. *La cause des sans-papiers.* Paris: Presses de la Fondation nationale des sciences politiques.

Simmel, Georg. 1971. *On Individuality and Social Forms.* Chicago: University of Chicago Press.

Smelser, Neil J. 1962. *Theory of Collective Behavior.* New York: Free Press.

Smith, Christian. 1996. *Resisting Reagan.* Chicago: University of Chicago Press.

Smith, Jackie. 1995a. "Organizing Global Action: Transnational Social Movements and World Politics." Ph.D. diss., University of Notre Dame.

———. 1995b, "Transnational Political Processes and the Human Rights Movement. In *Research in Social Movements, Conflict and Change* 18: 187-221.

———. 1997. "Characteristics of the Modern Transnational Social Movement Sector." In *Transnational Social Movements and Global Politics: Solidarity Beyond the State*, edited by Jackie Smith, Charles Chatfield, and Ron Pagnucco, 42-58. Syracuse, N.Y.: Syracuse University Press.

———. 1998. "Global Civil-Society? Transnational Social-Movement Organizations and Social Capital." *American Behavioral Scientist* 42: 93-107.

———. 1999. "Global Politics and Transnational Social Movement Strategies: The Transnational Campaign Against Trade in Toxic Wastes." In *Social Movements in a*

Globalizing World, edited by Hanspeter Kriesi, Donatella della Porta, and Dieter Rucht, 170-88. London: Macmillan.

Smith, Jackie, Charles Chatfield, and Ron Pagnucco, eds. 1997. *Transnational Social Movements and Global Politics: Solidarity Beyond the State*. Syracuse, N.Y.: Syracuse University Press.

Smith, Jackie, Ron Pagnucco, and Charles Chatfield. 1997. "Transnational Social Movements and Global Politics: A Theoretical Framework." In *Transnational Social Movements and Global Politics: Solidarity Beyond the State*, edited by Jackie Smith, Charles Chatfield, and Ron Pagnucco, 59-77. Syracuse, N.Y.: Syracuse University Press.

Smith, Jackie, Ron Pagnucco, and George A. Lopez. 1998. "Globalizing Human-Rights: Report on a Survey of Transnational Human-Rights NGOs." *Human Rights Quarterly* 20: 379-412.

Snow, David A., and Robert D. Benford. 1988. "Ideology, Frame Resonance, and Participant Mobilization." In *From Structure to Action*, edited by Bert Klandermans, Hanspeter Kriesi, and Sidney Tarrow, 197-217. Greenwich, Conn.: JAI Press.

Snow, David, and Robert D. Benford 1992. "Master Frames and Cycles of Protest." In *Frontiers in Social Movement Theory*, edited by Aldon Morris and Carol McClurg Mueller, 133-55. New Haven, Conn.: Yale University Press.

Snow, David A., E. Burke Rochford, Steven K. Worden, and Robert Benford. 1986. "Frame Alignment Processes, Micromobilization, and Movement Participation." *American Sociological Review* 51: 464-81.

Somers, Margaret R. 1992. "Narrativity, Narrative Identity, and Social Action: Rethinking English Working-Class Formation." *Social Science History* 16: 591-630.

———. 1994. "The Narrative Constitution of Identity: A Relational and Network Approach." *Theory and Society* 23: 605-50.

Soule, Sarah A. 1995. "The Student Anti-Apartheid Movement in the United States: Diffusion of Protest Tactics and Policy Reform." Ph.D. diss., Cornell University.

———. 1997. "The Student Divestment Movement in the United States and the Shantytown: Diffusion of a Protest Tactic." *Social Forces* 75: 855-83.

———. Forthcoming. "Divestment by Colleges and Universities in the United States: Institutional Pressures Toward Isomorphism. In *Institutional Analysis: Expansions and Refinements*, edited by Walter W. Powell and Dan Jones. Proceedings of the Workshop in Institutional Analysis, 29-30 March 1996, Department of Sociology, University of Arizona.

Soysal, Yasmin Nuhoglu. 1994. *Limits of Citizenship: Migrants and Postnational Membership in Europe*. Chicago: University of Chicago Press.

Staggenborg, Suzanne. 1986. "Coalition Work in the Pro-Choice Movement: Organizational and Environmental Opportunities and Obstacles." *Social Problems* 33: 374-89.

Stanley, William. 1996. *The Protection Racket State: Elite Politics, Military Extortion, and Civil War in El Salvador*. Philadelphia: Temple University Press.

Statham, Paul. 1998. "The Political Construction of Immigration Politics in Italy: Opportunities, Mobilisation and Outcomes." FS III-102, Berlin, WZB.

———. 1999. "Political Mobilisation by Minorities in Britain: A Negative Feedback of 'Race Relations'?" *Journal of Ethnic and Migration Studies* 25: 565-73.

Stinchcombe, Arthur L. 1995. *Sugar Island Slavery in the Age of Enlightenment: The Political Economy of the Caribbean World*. Princeton, N.J.: Princeton University Press.

Strang, David, and Sarah A. Soule. 1998. "Diffusion in Organizations and Social Movements: From Hybrid Corn to Poison Pills." *Annual Review of Sociology* 24: 265-90.

Street, John. 1986. *Rebel Rock*. Oxford: Basil Blackwell.

Swedberg, Richard. 1999. "Civil Courage (*Zivilcourage*). The Case of Knut Wicksell." *Theory and Society* 28: 501-28.

Swidler, Ann. 1986. "Culture in Action: Symbols and Strategies." *American Sociological Review* 51: 273-86.

Szemere, Anna. 1992. "The Politics of Marginality: A Rock Musical Subculture in Socialist Hungary in the Early 1980s." In *Rockin' the Boat: Mass Music and Mass Movements*, edited by Reebee Garofalo, 93-114. Boston: South End Press.

Tambiah, Stanley J. 1996. *Leveling Crowds: Ethnonationalist Conflicts and Collective Violence in South Asia*. Berkeley and Los Angeles: University of California Press.

———. 1997. "Friends, Neighbors, Enemies, Strangers: Aggressor and Victim in Civilian Ethnic Riots." *Social Science and Medicine* 45: 1177-88.

Tarrow, Sidney. 1989. *Democracy and Disorder: Protest and Politics in Italy*. Oxford: Oxford University Press.

———. 1995. "The Europeanisation of Conflict: Reflections from a Social Movement Perspective." *West European Politics* 18: 223-51.

———. 1996. "Social Movements in Contentious Politics: A Review Article." *American Political Science Review* 90: 874-83.

———. 1998. *Power in Movement: Social Movements and Contentious Politics*. 2d ed. New York: Cambridge University Press.

te Brake, Wayne. 1998. *Shaping History: Ordinary People in European Politics, 1500-1700*. Berkeley and Los Angeles: University of California Press.

Teske, Nathan. 1997. *Political Activists in America*. Cambridge: Cambridge University Press.

Thorton, Bill, Gayle Kirchneer, and Jacqueline Jacobs. 1991. "Influence of a Photograph on a Charitable Appeal: A Picture May Be Worth a Thousand Words When It Has to Speak for Itself." *Journal of Applied Social Psychology* 21: 433-45.

Tilly, Charles. 1978. *From Mobilization to Revolution*. Reading, Mass.: Addison-Wesley.

———. 1986a. *The Contentious French*. Cambridge, Mass.: Harvard University Press.

———. 1986b. "Action collective et mobilisation individuelle." In *Sur l'individualisme*, edited by Pierre Birnbaum and Jean Leca, 213-43. Paris: Presses de la Fondation nationale des sciences politiques.

———. 1992. "Conclusions." In *Strikes, Social Conflict and the First World War: An International Perspective*, edited by Leopold Haimson and Giulio Sapelli. Milan: Feltrinelli, Fondazione Giangiacomo Feltrinelli, *Annali* 1990/1991.

———. 1993. *European Revolutions, 1492-1992*. Oxford: Blackwell.

———. 1994. "Social Movements as Historically Specific Clusters of Political Performances." *Berkeley Journal of Sociology* 38: 1-30.

———. 1995a. *Popular Contention in Great Britain, 1758-1834*. Cambridge, Mass.: Harvard University Press.

————. 1995b. "The Emergence of Citizenship in France and Elsewhere." In *Citizenship, Identity and Social History*, edited by Charles Tilly. Cambridge: Cambridge University Press.

————. 1996. "Invisible Elbow." *Sociological Forum* 11: 589-601.

————. 1998a. *Durable Inequality*. Berkeley and Los Angeles: University of California Press.

————. 1998b. "Contentious Conversation." *Social Research* 65: 491-510.

————. 1998c. "Political Identities." In *Challenging Authority: The Historical Study of Contentious Politics*, edited by Michael P. Hanagan, Leslie Page Moch, and Wayne te Brake. Minneapolis: University of Minnesota Press.

————. 1999a. "Power—Top Down and Bottom Up." *Journal of Political Philosophy* 7: 306-28.

————. 1999b. "The Trouble with Stories." In *The Social Worlds of Higher Education: Handbook for Teaching in a New Century*, edited by Ronald Aminzade and Bernice Pescosolido. Thousand Oaks, Calif.: Pine Forge Press.

Tilly, Charles, Louise Tilly, and Richard Tilly. 1975. *The Rebellious Century, 1830-1930*. Cambridge, Mass.: Harvard University Press.

Titmuss, Richard M. 1971. *The Gift Relationship: From Human Blood to Social Policy*. New York: Vintage Books.

Tocqueville, Alexis de. [1835] 1956. *Democracy in America*. New York: Vintage Books.

Tolbert, Pamela, and Lynne Zucker. 1983. "Institutional Sources of Change in Formal Structure of Organizations: The Diffusion of Civil Service Reform, 1880-1935." *Administrative Science Quarterly* 28: 22-39.

Tomkins, Silvan S. 1965. "The Psychology of Commitment: The Constructive Role of Violence and Suffering for the Individual and for His Society." In *Affect, Cognition, and Personality*, edited by Silvan Solomon Tomkins and Carroll E. Izard, 148-71. New York: Springer.

Touraine, Alain. 1973. *Production de la société*. Paris: Seuil.

————. 1978. *La voix et le regard*. Paris: Seuil.

————. 1984. *Le retour de l'acteur*. Paris: Seuil.

Turner, Ralph H., and Lewis M. Killian. 1957. *Collective Behavior*. Englewood Cliffs, N.J.: Prentice-Hall.

Turner, Scott. 1998. "Global Civil Society, Anarchy and Governance: Assessing an Emerging Paradigm." *Journal of Peace Research* 1: 27-42.

Turner, Victor. 1982. *From Ritual to Theatre: The Human Seriousness of Play*. New York: Performing Arts Journal Publications.

UNHCR (United Nations High Commissioner for Refugees). 1996. *In Search of Solutions: The State of World Refugees 1995*. New York: Oxford University Press.

Ullestad, Neal. 1992. "Diverse Rock Rebellions Subvert Mass Media Hegemony." In *Rockin' the Boat: Mass Music and Mass Movements*, edited by Reebee Garofalo, 37-53. Boston: South End Press.

Vellela, Tony. 1988. *New Voices: Student Activism in the '80s and '90s*. Boston: South End Press.

Vermunt, Riël, and Herman Steensma, eds. 1991. *Social Justice in Human Relations*. 2 vols. New York: Plenum.

Vila, Pablo. 1992. "ROCK NACIONAL and Dictatorship in Argentina." In *Rockin' the Boat: Mass Music and Mass Movements*, edited by Reebee Garofalo, 209-29. Boston: South End Press.

Wallis, Roger. 1990. "Internationalisation, Localisation and Integration: The Changing Structure of the Music Industry and its Relevance for Smaller Countries and
Cultures." Ph.D. diss., Gothenburg University.

Walzer, Michael. 1995. "The Idea of Civil Society." *Dissent* (spring): 293-304.

Weiner, Jon. 1986. "Students, Stocks, and Shanties: Colleges Divest from South
Africa." *The Nation* (11 October): 337-40.

Weisbrod, Burton A. 1977. *The Voluntary Nonprofit Sector: An Economic Analysis.*
Lexington, Mass.: Lexington Books.

Weiss, Thomas G. 1996, "Nongovernmental Organizations and Internal Conflict." In
The International Dimensions of Internal Conflict, edited by Michael E. Brown,
435-59. Cambridge, Mass.: MIT Press.

White, Louise G. 1976. "Rational Theories of Participation." *Journal of Conflict
Resolution* 20: 255-78.

Willems, Helmut, Roland Eckert, Stefanie Würtz, and Linda Steinmetz. 1993. *Frem-
denfeindliche Gewalt: Einstellungen Täter Konflikteskalation.* Opladen: Leske und
Budrich.

Willetts, Peter. 1996. *The Conscience of the World: The Influence of NGOs in the
United Nations System.* London: C. Hurst.

Williams, Dennis, George Raine, Susan Katz, Elisa Williams, and Susan Hutchinson.
1985. "A New Breed of Activism." *Newsweek* (13 May): 61-62.

Williams, Lena. 1986. "Pressure Rises on Colleges to Withdraw South Africa Interests." *New York Times* (2 February, sec. 1, part 1): 14.

Williams-Slope, Mark. 1971. "A Letter to the Workers of America." United Nations
Unit on Apartheid, Department of Political and Security Council Affairs, Notes and
Documents 21 (no. 71, May).

Wilson, John, and Marc A. Musick. 1999. "Attachment to Volunteering." *Sociological
Forum* 14: 243-72.

Wiltfang, Gregory L., and Doug McAdam. 1991. "A Study of Sanctuary Movement
Activism." *Social Forces* 69: 987-1010.

Wisler, Dominique, and Marco G. Giugni. 1996. "Social Movements and Institutional
Selectivity." *Sociological Perspectives* 39: 85-109.

Wolf, Eric R. 1999. *Envisioning Power: Ideologies of Dominance and Crisis.* Berkeley
and Los Angeles: University of California Press.

Wolfe, Alan. 1998. "What is Altruism?" In *Private Action and the Public Good*,
edited by Walter W. Powell and Elisabeth S. Clemens, 36-46. New Haven, Conn.:
Yale University Press.

Wuthnow, Robert. 1991. *Acts of Compassion: Caring for Others and Helping Ourselves.*
Princeton, N.J.: Princeton University Press.

———, ed. 1995. *Learning to Care.* New York: Oxford University Press.

Young, Dennis R. 1991. "The Structural Imperatives of International Advocacy Associations." *Human Relations* 44: 921-41.

Young, Iris Marion. 1990. *Justice and the Politics of Difference.* Princeton, N.J.:
Princeton University Press.

Ysmal, Colette. 1995. "Transformations du militantisme et déclin des partis." In
L'engagement politique, edited by Pascal Perrineau. Paris: Presses de la Fondation
nationale des sciences politiques.

Zablocki, Benjamin. 1980. *Alienation and Charisma: A Study of Contemporary American
Communes.* New York: Free Press.

Zhou, Xueguang. 1993. "Occupational Power, State Capacities, and the Diffusion of Licensing in the American States: 1890-1950." *American Sociological Review* 58: 536-52.

Zook, Kristal Brent. 1992. "Reconstructions of Nationalist Thought in Black Music and Culture." In *Rockin' the Boat: Mass Music and Mass Movements*, edited by Reebee Garofalo, 255-66. Boston: South End Press.

Zukerman, M., and H. Y. Reiss. 1978. "Comparison of Three Models for Predicting Altruistic Behavior." *Journal of Personality and Social Psychology* 36: 468-510.

Index

269

About the Contributors

Simone Baglioni graduated in political science from the University of Florence (Italy) with a thesis on the role of French solidarity movement organizations during the war in former Yugoslavia. He has been visiting scholar at the Institut d'Etudes Politiques (Paris), at the Lester B. Pearson Peacekeeping Training Center in Nova Scotia (Canada), and at the University of Geneva. He is currently a Ph.D. student at the department of political science, University of Geneva, where he works on citizenship and citizen involvement in Switzerland.

Ivana Eterovic received her undergraduate training at the department of sociology, University of Zagreb, Croatia. She is currently a doctoral candidate at the department of sociology, State University of New York at Stony Brook. Her interests include social movements and political culture in Eastern Europe.

Olivier Fillieule is a researcher at the Centre national de la recherche scientifique (Centre de Recherche et d'Etudes Sociologiques Appliquées de la Loire) and teaches political science at the Institute of Political Science in Paris. His main fields of research include social movements, gay politics, and public order and the police. He has published three books, among them *Stratégies de la rue* (1997). Currently he is engaged in a European Commission-funded comparative research project on the transformation of environmental activism.

Marco Giugni is a researcher at the department of political science, University of Geneva, Switzerland. He has authored or co-authored various books and articles on social movements. His current research focuses on political claims-making in the fields of immigration, unemployment, and social exclusion.

Ruud Koopmans is a senior researcher at the department of The Public Sphere and Social Movements of the Wissenschaftszentrum Berlin für Sozialforschung. He has published widely on comparative European and German politics, and on social movements and political participation. His current

282 *About the Contributors*

research focuses on the politics of immigration and citizenship, and the claims-making of xenophobic, antiracist, and ethnic minority groups in several Western European countries.

Christian Lahusen is a member of the department of sociology at Otto-Friedrich-University of Bamberg. He studied in Düsseldorf and Madrid, and received his Ph.D. at the European University Institute in Florence. He has published articles and books in German and English on social movements, popular culture, and public campaigns—among them "The Aesthetic of Radicalism: The Relationship between Punk and the Patriotic Nationalist Movement of the Basque Country," in *Popular Music* (1993) and *The Rhetoric of Moral Protest* (1996). He is currently studying international campaigns and interest representation in the European Union.

Florence Passy teaches at the Institute of Political and International Studies, University of Lausanne, Switzerland. She has written extensively on social movements and political participation. She is the author of *L'action altruiste* (1998) and co-author of *Histoires de mobilisation politique en Suisse* (1997). Her current research focuses on mobilization over ethnic relations, citizenship and immigration in a cross-national perspective.

Costanzo Ranci is a researcher at the department of urban studies at the Polytechnic of Milan, Italy. His research interests include transformation and changes in social policy, and the role of voluntary organizations and social movements in policy making. He has published numerous articles and books on social policy, the third sector, and social participation, including "The Third Sector in Welfare Policies in Italy: The Contradictions of a Protected Market," in *Voluntas: International Journal of Voluntary and Nonprofit Organizations* (1994), and "Government Policy and Future Issues," in *The Nonprofit Sector in Italy* (1997).

Jackie Smith is an assistant professor of sociology at the State University of New York at Stony Brook. She is co-editor of *Transnational Social Movements and World Politics* (1997), and author or co-author of numerous articles on transnational social movements and globalization. Her current research focuses on mobilizations against global trade liberalization and the World Trade Organization.

Sarah A. Soule is an assistant professor of sociology at the University of Arizona. Her current research interests include the diffusion of collective action and the diffusion of outcomes of collective action. Some recent publications include "The Diffusion of an Unsuccessful Innovation: The Case of the Shantytown Protest Tactic," in *The Annals of the American Academy of Political and Social Science* (1999), "Protest Events: Cause or Consequence of State Action? The U.S. Women's Movement and Federal Congressional Activities, 1956-1979," in *Mobilization* (1999), and "Black Church Arson in the United States, 1989-1996," in *Ethnic and Racial Studies* (1999).

Paul Statham is senior research fellow at the Institute of Communications Studies, University of Leeds, England. He runs a European Political Communications Center conducting social movements research. His recent work has focused on comparative approaches to mobilization by migrants and ethnic minorities. He recently co-edited and contributed to a special volume of the *Journal of Ethnic and Migrations Studies*, and published articles in the *American Journal of Sociology* and *Mobilization*. He is co-editor and contributor to a new volume entitled *Challenging Immigration and Ethnic Relations Politics* (2000).

Charles Tilly teaches social sciences at Columbia University. His most recently published books are *Roads from Past to Future* (1997), *Work under Capitalism* (with Chris Tilly, 1998), and *Durable Inequality* (1998). With Doug McAdam and Sidney Tarrow, he has recently completed *Dynamics of Contention*, forthcoming.

QM LIBRARY
(MILE END)